DAKOTA
TERRITORY

THE A...
OLD ...
OF THE 1880S

od

NEBRASKA

IOWA

Abilene

Kansas City

MISSOURI

KANSAS

Dodge City

Wichita

Coffeyville

PUBLIC LAND

Fort Gibson

INDIAN

Fort Smith

TERRITORY

ARKANSAS

Fort Worth

TEXAS

GUNFIGHTERS

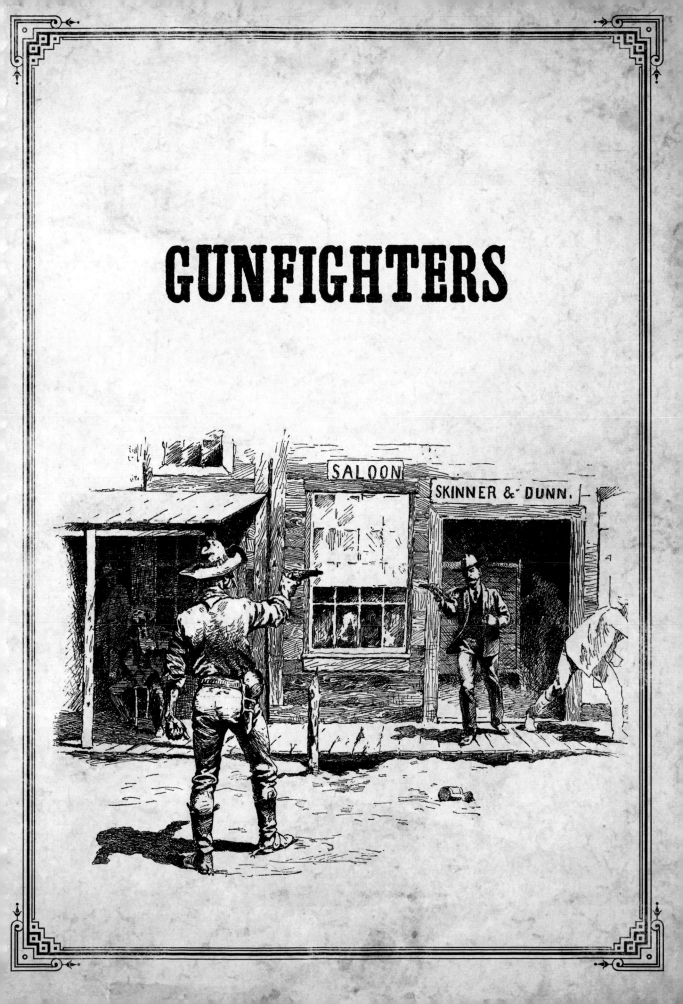

GUNFIGHTERS

A CHRONICLE OF DANGEROUS MEN AND VIOLENT DEATH

AL CIMINO

CHARTWELL
BOOKS

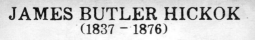

JAMES BUTLER HICKOK
(1837 – 1876)

Better known as "Wild Bill," James Butler
Hickok was a legendary figure in the West.

CONTENTS

INTRODUCTION

After the end of the Civil War, the United States continued its relentless march west. The railroads opened up the plains. There were gold rushes and land grabs. Cattle were herded up from Texas to the Kansas cow towns for shipment onward to feed the growing population of the east. At the end of the trail, cowboys wanted whiskey, gambling, and saloon girls. As a result there were gunfights.

Then there were the rustlers, the claim-jumpers, the bank robbers, the road agents, the stagecoach stick-up men, the railroad hold-up men, gangsters, and gunmen who put little value on human life—including their

own. They would shoot first and ask questions ... well, never.

Until the beginning of the twentieth century, the West was a lawless place. The deputies, sheriffs, and even the U.S. marshals were often former outlaws, or went on to have a career on the other side of the law, or indeed switched sides whenever it suited them. The ability to use a gun was a prerequisite, whichever side of the line you were on.

Although many of the gunfighters were happy—even eager—to die young, a surprising number survived to live a more settled and constructive life in their later years,

I'M CALLING THE HAND THAT'S IN YOUR HAT

Wild Bill Hickok at Cards by N.C. Wyeth is an illustration from Colonel William F. Cody's 1916 autobiography. Cody retold how Hickok challenged a gambling cheat by shoving a pistol in the man's face saying: "I'm calling the hand that's in your hat."

A DASH FOR THE TIMBER
BY FREDERIC S. REMINGTON (1899)

The most successful western illustrator of the late nineteenth century, Remington's style highlighted the people and animals of the West. One of the riders in the picture is already wounded but remains on his horse.

or found fame in dime novels or Wild West shows. Nor were they the ill-educated saddle-tramps often portrayed, a good number went on to write their memoirs and worked on the movies that their adventures had spawned.

While there were many really bad men, several outlaws of the Old West sought to portray themselves as Robin Hood. Indeed, the first book about Robin Hood, *The Merry Adventures of Robin Hood of Great Renown in Nottinghamshire* by American writer and illustrator Howard Pyle that pieced together scraps of old English ballads, was published by Scribner's in New York in 1883. Robin Hood was in vogue and soon took to the stage in that city.

The history of the United States is littered with great intellects—Benjamin Franklin, Thomas Jefferson, Robert Oppenheimer; and men of towering moral stature—Paul Revere, Franklin D. Roosevelt, Martin Luther King; but there is still room in the heart of all Americans for Jesse James, Wyatt Earp, Butch Cassidy, Kid Curry, and Johnny Ringo. Perhaps because of the movies—that most American of mediums—what happened on the dusty streets of towns in Kansas, Missouri, Texas, Arizona, Montana, Arkansas, Oklahoma, and New Mexico over a hundred years ago, in the brief window between 1865 and 1900, has formed a myth that inhabits the nation's soul.

The reader should also remember that the events depicted in this book happened in an era before modern sensibilities. They happened directly after the Civil War when there was little love lost between the races, especially among those from the South. There was a deep antipathy between Native Americans and newcomers. And gunmen were just that—gunmen. There were, of course, some women who also wielded a gun, but most female outlaws in the West worked, some of the time at least, as prostitutes. Regrettable though all that may be, we can't change history. We must simply learn to understand it.

You've got to know when to hold 'em
Know when to fold 'em
Know when to walk away
And know when to run.
You never count your money
When you're sitting at the table,
There'll be time enough for counting
When the dealing is done.

Lyrics from The Gambler *by Don Schlitz (1978)*

PART ONE

GAMBLERS AND GUNSLINGERS

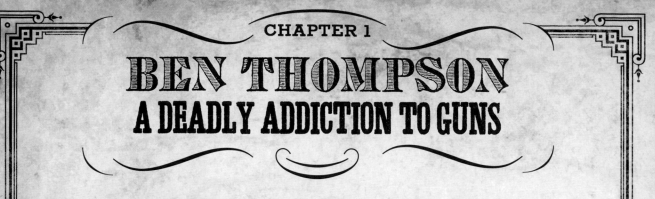

CHAPTER 1

BEN THOMPSON
A DEADLY ADDICTION TO GUNS

"HIS AIM WAS AS TRUE AS HIS NERVES WERE STRONG AND STEADY."

Bat Masterson about Ben Thompson

Few men alive on the western frontier crowded more violent drama into a forty-year lifespan than Ben Thompson—Confederate cavalry officer, mercenary in Maximilian's army, saloon owner, hired gun, gambler and gunfighter in almost every town in the West, and a cold-blooded and ruthless killer.

"It is doubtful, whether in his time there was another man living who could equal him with a pistol in a life and death struggle," wrote Bat Masterson, sheriff of Dodge City during its wildest years.

Although addicted to gunplay from an early age, Ben Thompson came from a most unexpected background for a gunfighter in the Old West. He was born in England, at Knottingley in the West Riding of Yorkshire, in 1843. His father served as an officer in the British Royal Navy. When Ben was nine, his parents emigrated to the United States and settled in Austin, Texas, a town whose population then was around a thousand. By the time he was twelve, he and his younger brother were fighting the bullies who tormented their father, who was now a serious drunk. As a youth, Ben was known to be bright and handsome, but also to possess an "explosive temper."

At thirteen he blasted another youngster with birdshot in a dispute over his marksmanship. A frontier paper said that Ben "through some means got clear of punishment." He was also thought to have fought a duel with shotguns over some geese. In 1858, he was fined $100 and jailed for six days for wounding an African-American youth.

However, through his brush with the law he caught the eye of Colonel John A. Green, a prominent Austin attorney who sent him to school, where he earned honors in every class. Then Green found young Ben a job as an apprentice printer on Austin's *Southern Intelligencer*, before he moved to the *New Orleans Picayune*.

DUEL IN THE DARK

The story is told that, one day, Thompson got into a fight with a young Frenchman named Emile de Tours who was "forcing his unwelcome attentions on a young woman." When Thompson intervened, Tours challenged him to a duel. As a result, Thompson was to pick weapons. He said that they should fight to the death with knives, blindfold in a darkened room.

The bout had only been in progress a few minutes when there was a knock on the door. The seconds rushed to open it. Thompson emerged still blindfold. Inside was the lifeless body of Tours, slashed to pieces.

Returning to Austin, Thompson learned how to use a six-shooter. In a gunfight, he killed a gambler who accused him of cheating at cards. Then when five young girls were taken by Indians, Ben joined the posse. Thanks to his marksmanship, the girls were rescued and only one of the raiding party escaped alive.

The following year, he shot a thief and was arrested, though, at trial, he was acquitted.

A KILLER'S EDUCATION

As with so many other western gunslingers, Thompson's real education as a killer came from fighting in wars. In June 1861, he joined the Second Texas Mounted Rifles. During his time in the army, he was thought to have killed one John Coombes in a private quarrel, though the records are incomplete. It is also said that he killed and seriously wounded two fellow cavalry men, though he was absent without leave at the time. When he re-enlisted he was demoted.

One night, he and his brother Billy were playing a three-card monte game with some Mexican soldiers. By 2:00 a.m., possibly cheating, Thompson had won $1,800 and tried to close the game. Lieutenant Martino Gonzales objected, saying that Thompson must at least return the guns he had won off them the day before—they were government property. When Ben refused, Gonzales went for his gun. Another of the players, Sergeant Miguel Zertuche, jammed a gun against Thompson's chest and pulled the trigger. The gun misfired. Ben shot him in the head and put a bullet in Gonzales' chest.

After the war, he married Catherine Moore of Travis County, who gave him two children. However, in Austin, he got into a fight with some of the Union occupation troops. Two or three soldiers were killed and Thompson was jailed. He bribed the guards and slipped across the Rio Grande to join the army of the doomed Emperor Maximilian who was recruiting former Confederate soldiers for his army.

A combination of intelligence and gun skills got Thompson the job of protecting Maximilian's treasure train that was attacked by two Republican army brigades. He later told the tale to his biographer, William M. Walton, an Austin judge, who had known him as a child.

Ben Thompson while acting as city marshal of Austin, Texas, 1881.

THE DEVIL JUMPED OUT OF HIS EYES

Accompanying General Tomás Mejía, Ben Thompson went to the rescue of Emperor Maximilian who had withdrawn with what was left of his army to Querétaro. On the way, Thompson stopped at a fandango hall where he danced with "the handsomest and most graceful senorita I ever saw." When the dance was over, he was approached by a man who asked him to step outside.

"The devil was already jumping out of him through his eyes," said Thompson.

The man had his hand on his knife, but he hesitated for a moment—just long enough for Thompson to draw his pistol and crack him over the head with it. He then put four bullets in him. The man was dead before he hit the floor.

Thompson fled to the quarters of General Mejía, who gave him two rolls of gold—some $2,000. They moved on to Querétaro where Thompson met Emperor Maximilian. The city was surrounded. Maximilian and Mejía were captured and executed, while Thompson escaped back over the border.

HUNTSVILLE STATE PENITENTIARY

Though Thompson insisted that he behaved himself when he got back to the U.S., he went to the defense of Judge Julius Schuetze who was being attacked by five men. They drew knives. Thompson drew his pistol and drove them off. Meanwhile his brother, Billy Thompson, had shot Private William Burk, the U.S. Adjutant General's chief clerk, in an Austin bordello. Ben organized Billy's getaway to the Indian Territory.

Then, in 1868, during a family dispute, Ben shot and wounded his wife's brother, Jim Moore, whom he had heard was physically abusing her. Already a fugitive, 25-year-old Thompson was charged with murder and sentenced to ten years hard labor in Huntsville State Penitentiary, but was pardoned in 1870 when civilian rule was restored in Texas.

WILD BILL NEEDS KILLIN'

By 1870, Texas longhorn cattle were making their way up the Chisholm Trail to the railheads of Kansas. Thompson heard from the drovers that the boomtown of Abilene, Kansas, was wide-open for gambling of all sorts. He arrived there, in 1870, with only enough to pay for a night's lodgings and breakfast. So he pawned his six-shooter and, within a few hours, had won $2,583 at poker.

Phil Coe, who had served on the Rio Grande with Thompson, arrived at about the same time. He had a few thousand dollars and together they bought The Bull's Head Saloon, in 1871. Thompson hated Yankees and Wild Bill Hickok, Abilene's new city marshal and a native of Illinois, hated Texans.

Coe and Thompson outraged the townspeople by painting a bull, complete with an erect penis, on the outside wall of their establishment as a form of "advertisement." Hickok threatened to burn the saloon to the ground if the offending animal was not painted over. Instead, he hired some men to paint over the bull, and stood guard with a shotgun. Coe and Thompson were furious and the three men became enemies.

Back at the Bull's Head, Thompson and Coe had made the acquaintance of wanted gunslinger John Wesley Hardin, and actively recruited him in an attempt to rid the town of the marshal. Hardin, then living under the assumed name of "Wesley Clemmons" (but better known to the townspeople by the alias "Little Arkansaw") replied, "If Wild Bill needs killin', why don't you kill him yourself?" A few nights later Hardin killed another man in a fight and left for Texas.

In Kansas, Thompson grew lonely and telegraphed his wife to join him. Kate and their six-year-old son arrived at Kansas City. But just outside town their carriage overturned. Kate's arm was crushed and had to be amputated. Their son's foot was broken, and Ben's leg was fractured. After recuperating in Kansas City, the family traveled back to Austin. On the way, Thompson heard that Coe had been gunned down by Hickok in a fatal shoot-out.

SHOOT-OUT IN ELLSWORTH

In 1872, Thompson traveled to Ellsworth, Kansas, to join his brother Billy as a professional gambler at the Grand Central Hotel. Thompson had heard that Ellsworth, was as wide-open for gambling as Abilene, and he and Billy hoped to win big money.

In fact, it was tame by comparison. Sheriff Chauncey B. Whitney, a veteran of the Indian

THE EMPEROR MAXIMILIAN

The Archduke Maximilian of Austria was installed as emperor of Mexico by the French emperor Napoleon III in 1864, supported by the French army. However, with the end of the Civil War, the U.S. demanded withdrawal of French troops for a violation of the Monroe Doctrine, which forbade European powers retaking their former colonies in the Americas.

When French troops withdrew in March 1867, Maximilian refused to abdicate. His small band of followers were defeated by the Mexican army under the former president Benito Juarez. Refused clemency, Maximilian was executed by firing squad outside Querétaro on June 19, 1867.

Wars, allowed the cowhands fresh from the trail to let off steam, riding around town, shooting at signs and shattering windows—provided they paid damages.

Thompson often helped Whitney disarm drunken, would-be gunfighters and the two became firm friends.

In Joe Brennan's saloon, Thompson was running a game of three-card monte and had lined up some side bets with a gambler named John Sterling, who agreed to split his winnings. Drunk, Sterling left without doing so. Thompson found him drinking in another saloon with Deputy Sheriff "Happy Jack" Morco. Words were exchanged. Sterling hit the unarmed Thompson in his face. Morco then pulled a gun and forced Ben to back off.

When Thompson returned to Brennan's, Morco and Sterling turned up, shouting: "Get your gun, you damn Texas son-of-a-bitch."

Ben headed to the hotel to collect his Winchester and a six-shooter. On the way,

he met his brother Billy, staggering drunk and wielding a shotgun. Ben warned him to be careful, but Billy pulled one of the triggers, narrowly missing two innocent bystanders.

Whitney turned up. In an attempt to cool things down, he invited them for a drink in Brennan's. Just as they were entering, some bystanders shouted: "Look out, Ben."

He turned to see Morco and Sterling coming down the street with guns in their hands. Ben raised his rifle. Morco ducked into a doorway and the bullet smashed the woodwork.

Ben heard a roar and turned to see Whitney reeling—he had been accidentally shot by Billy. The sheriff died three days later. Meanwhile Ben bundled his brother out of town and returned to the hotel to await his fate.

None of the local police force dared approach him. Finally, Mayor James Miller asked Ben to hand over his guns. When he refused, Miller fired the entire police force.

GOVERNOR'S PROCLAMATION.

WHEREAS, C. B. Whitney, Sheriff of Ellsworth County, Kansas, was murdered in the said county of Ellsworth, on the 15th day of August, 1873, by one William Thompson, said Thompson being described as about six feet in height, 26 years of age, dark complexion, brown hair, gray eyes and erect form; and Whereas, the said William Thompson is now at large and a fugitive from justice;

NOW THEREFORE, know ye, that I, Thomas A. Osborn, Governor of the State of Kansas, in pursuance of law, do hereby offer a reward of FIVE HUNDRED DOLLARS for the arrest and conviction of the said William Thompson, for the crime above named.

 L. S.

IN TESTIMONY WHEREOF, I have hereunto subscribed my name, and caused to be affixed the Great Seal of the State. Done at Topeka, this 22d day of August, 1873.

THOMAS A. OSBORN.

By the Governor:
W. H. SMALLWOOD, Secretary of State.

This governor's proclamation was issued in 1873 for Billy Thompson's arrest.

Eventually, Deputy Sheriff Ed Hogue persuaded Morco to disarm. Then Thompson did the same and was taken into custody.

Next day in court, Morco did not turn up and Ben was released. He left for Kansas City. Soon after, popular Texan drover Cad Pierce was killed in a gunfight and Texans threatened to burn Ellsworth down. A band of vigilantes then threw the undesirables out of town.

MURDER AT CHRISTMAS

Back in Austin in 1876, Thompson was celebrating Christmas when he heard that James Burdett, one of his friends, had been thrown out of the Capital Variety Theater. Ben rallied to his support.

The owner Mark Wilson, anticipating trouble from Thompson, had stacked a small arsenal behind the bar. When a confrontation ensued, Wilson ducked behind the bar and came out with a shotgun. As the revelers scattered, someone nudged Wilson's arm. The shotgun went off. The buckshot flew over his head, but Thompson had already drawn his gun and fired three shots into Wilson, killing him instantly.

The bartender Charles Matthews then pulled a rifle and squeezed off a shot, grazing Thompson's hip. Ben shot him in the mouth, knocking out several teeth. The bullet lodged in his throat, but he survived.

Thompson surrendered and was charged with murder, but was acquitted the following May.

MYTH OF THE GUNFIGHTER

During the 1870s, Ben Thompson had the reputation of being one of the most dangerous gunfighters on the frontier. Legend credited him with killing twenty-one men, but more realistic newspaper reports and his many court appearances total his victims at about eight.

Bat Masterson, who probably was a witness to more gunfights and killings during his lawman's career in Dodge City than any man in the West, recalled Thompson's skill with a six-shooter:

> *Thompson in the first place possessed a much higher order of intelligence than the average gunfighter or man killer of his time. He was absolutely without fear and his nerves were those of the finest steel. He shot at an adversary with the same precision and deliberation that he shot at a target. A past master in the use of a pistol, his aim was as true as his nerves were strong and steady.*

Ben Thompson's brother Billy was a wanted man.

BEN THOMPSON'S GUIDE TO SUCCESSFUL GUNFIGHTING

I always make it a rule to let the other fellow fire first. If a man wants to fight, I argue the question with him and try to show him how foolish it would be. If he can't be dissuaded, why, then the fun begins but I always let him have first crack. Then when I fire, you see, I have the verdict of self-defense on my side. I know that he is pretty certain, in his hurry, to miss. I never do.

THE HIRED GUN

Thompson's reputation led to a new opportunity in 1875, when Masterson was recruiting an army of gunmen for the Atchison, Topeka & Santa Fe Railroad (AT&SF), who wanted to prevent the Denver & Rio Grande Western Railroad (D&RGW) getting first access to Royal Gorge, where the Arkansas River cuts through the Colorado Mountains.

Thompson commanded a band of Texans, guarding a large roundhouse south of Pueblo. When the courts finally ordered the AT&SF to relinquish its property to the D&RGW, a Pueblo sheriff and a hundred deputies surrounded it. But Thompson refused to surrender, arguing that he had been hired by the Santa Fe Railroad and would only leave if ordered to do so by them. The sheriff replied that he had come to "disperse a mob." Thompson replied that there was no mob there, "only construction workers."

The following day, Thompson went outside on the pretext of holding a parley with the sheriff and was arrested. The rest of his band of Texans quickly gave up. The sheriff accompanied him back to the depot and Thompson returned to Austin richer by $2,300 and a number of diamonds. He had been paid by the Denver & Rio Grande Western Railroad to go quietly.

Now in funds, Thompson became something of a dandy. Some drunken visitors from San Saba County took him for an Easterner and one of them knocked his new hat off.

"I am Ben Thompson and equal to a dozen white-livered fiends like you," said Thompson.

The man ducked behind an awning post and fired at him. Ben returned fire, nicking the man's ear. He fled. Thomson was arrested, but cleared of a charge of assault.

TURNING LAWMAN

Eventually, realizing that he could make money legally, Thompson ran for city marshal in Austin but was defeated. However, the winner did not serve a full term. Ben took over in December 1880. Though he never spent a sober day in office, he was re-elected the following year.

It was said that he was an excellent police officer. Black, white, or Mexican prisoners or complainants were treated alike. The crime rate fell and, according to the town's records, there was not a murder or burglary within the city limits during his term of office.

However, he had not totally given up his bad ways and developed a long-running feud with Jack Harris, one of the owners of the notorious Vaudeville Variety Theater and Gambling Saloon in San Antonio. Thompson was barred, but insisted on going in anyway.

Asked to leave, Thompson complied. Jack Harris taunted him, brandishing a shotgun and saying: "Come on, I'm ready for you."

As Harris raised his weapon, Ben pulled his gun and fired through the Venetian blinds, hitting Harris in the right lung. He died that night.

Thompson resigned as marshal of Austin, but was acquitted of the murder charge as the killing was ruled as self-defense. When he returned to Austin, he was greeted by crowds of well-wishers with a band, and a spontaneous parade to the state capitol.

AMBUSH AT THE VAUDEVILLE THEATER

On March 11, 1884, Ben visited San Antonio with John King Fisher, a gunman and deputy sheriff from Uvalde County. After drinking heavily, they made an unwelcome return to see a show at the Vaudeville Variety Theater, the scene of the Jack Harris shooting. Taking their place in a box upstairs, they were joined by Harris's erstwhile partners Billy Simms and Joe Foster, along with the bouncer Jacob Coy.

The men all had a drink together, but when the conversation turned to the Harris killing, Fisher got up and tried to persuade Thompson to leave. Harsh words were exchanged between Foster and Thompson. Coy stepped in, warning Ben not to make trouble. Thompson then slapped Foster, pulled his six-gun, and stuck it in Foster's mouth. Coy grabbed the cylinder of the gun.

In the resulting scuffle, Thompson pulled the trigger. The bullet hit Foster in the leg. It was the only shot he or Fisher had a chance to fire. In anticipation of trouble from Thompson, the saloon bosses had stationed vaudeville performer Harry Tremaine, gambler Canada Bill Jones, and a bartender named McLaughlin in the next booth, and they jumped out with rifles and shotguns blazing. In the ensuing barrage of bullets Thompson and Fisher didn't stand a chance.

Thompson lay dead with nine bullets in him, Fisher thirteen. The shots were fired from such close range that there were powder burns on their faces. Joe Foster had his leg amputated, but died anyway. The shooting, seen as revenge for Ben Thompson's killing of Jack Harris two years earlier, became known as the Vaudeville Theater Ambush.

At age forty, Ben Thompson was a product of the violent times he lived in, and he died the death of most Western gunfighters—bloody and inevitable. He is buried at Oakwood Cemetery, Austin, Texas.

Jack Harris's Vaudeville Variety Theater, San Antonio, Texas in 1885. Jack Harris, Ben Thompson and John King Fisher were killed here.

CHAPTER 2

DOC HOLLIDAY
THE DEVIL'S RIGHT HAND

"THE NERVIEST, SPEEDIEST, DEADLIEST MAN WITH A SIX-GUN THAT I EVER KNEW."

Wyatt Earp about Doc Holliday

John Henry "Doc" Holliday was a man whose background did not really pick him out to be a gunfighter. A son of the antebellum South, he was born in 1851 in Griffin, Georgia, to a prosperous, land-owning family. His father was a druggist. Legend has it that, when young, Holliday suffered from a cleft palate and spent much of his childhood in intensive speech therapy even though his uncle, who was a doctor, had performed an operation on his condition.

The family moved to Valdosta, Lowndes County, Georgia, where Holliday's father was elected mayor in 1863. When he was fifteen, Holliday's mother died of tuberculosis and seems to have passed the disease to her son.

His father then married a twenty-three-year-old war widow, causing a rift between father and son.

John Holliday went to live with his mother's relatives in Philadelphia, enrolling in the Pennsylvania College of Dental Surgery in September 1870, and graduating in March 1872, after writing a thesis entitled "Diseases of the Teeth."

GOING WEST

It is generally thought that Holliday moved out to the West, seeking a drier climate for his TB. However, he told Bat Masterson that one Sunday he had fired a shotgun at black boys swimming in a pond used by white boys, "killing two outright and wounding several others." Holliday justified this, on the grounds that former slaves had to be "disciplined, and he knew of no more effective way of doing it. His family, however, thought it would be best for him to go away for a while and allow the thing to die out," said Masterson.

John Henry Holliday, age 20, in 1872.

First he headed to Lamar, Missouri, where he inquired after his father's friend Nicholas Porter Earp, Wyatt Earp's father. Moving on to Dallas, Texas, he set up a dental surgery in 1875, earning himself the nickname "Doc." However, he spent more time drinking and gambling than performing dentistry.

INTENT TO MURDER

On New Year's Day 1875, Holliday and saloon owner Charles W. Austin fired a few rounds at each other. No one was injured, but Holliday was charged with assault with intent to murder. A jury acquitted him, but plainly it was time to move on.

After living briefly in Denison, Texas, Holliday traveled to Fort Griffin, which had a reputation as being one of the wildest places in all of the West. Holliday became a faro dealer in the notorious gambling saloons of Hidetown, a particularly lawless area just outside the fort. At its height, Fort Griffin had a permanent population of about 1,000 and an estimated transient population of nearly twice that. In addition to the honest pioneers who settled in the area for legitimate reasons of ranching, agriculture, and commerce, Fort Griffin was bustling with buffalo hunters, cowboys, gunfighters, outlaws, gamblers and "painted ladies." Holliday met outlaw gang leader Hurricane Bill Martin, John H. Selman (the man who killed John Wesley Hardin), and Lottie Deno, the West's most celebrated woman gambler, who ran a brothel at Fort Griffin. He also met "Big Nose Kate" Elder—a.k.a. Fisher—a saloon girl who became Holliday's common-law wife.

In June 1875, Doc Holliday and a gambler named Mike Lynch were indicted for playing "a game with cards in a house in which spirituous liquors were sold." They were bailed, but to stop Holliday absconding, Sheriff John C. Jacobs chained him to an eye-bolt in the floor of his hotel room. Big Nose Kate caused a diversion by setting fire to a haystack at the back of the hotel, cut Holliday's chains, and they escaped after knifing a guard.

DOC HOLLIDAY IN DALLAS, 1875

Gambling was not only the principal and best-paying industry of the town at the time, but it was also reckoned among its most respectable and, as the hectic Georgian had always shown a fondness for all things in which the elements of chance played an important part, his new environment furnished him with no cause for complaint. In a short time those who wished to consult professionally with the doctor, had to do so over a card table in some nearby gambling establishment, or not at all. While Holliday never boasted about the killing down in Georgia, he was nevertheless regarded by his new-made Texas acquaintances who knew about the occurrence, as a man with a record; and a man with a record of having killed someone in those days was looked upon as something more than the ordinary mortal; wherefore the doctor on that account was given instant recognition by the higher circles of society in Dallas.

From *Famous Gunfighters of the Western Frontier* by Bat Masterson

THE DEVIL'S RIGHT HAND

Doc Holliday traveled widely in the West and was never far from trouble. In 1876, he was thought to have stabbed a card player named Bud Ryan in Denver. There were reports of him in Fort Concho, Texas, and in Jacksboro, Texas, where he was said to have killed a soldier from the U.S. Eleventh Infantry during a card game. He was a volatile man, and always close to the edge of pulling a pistol. His dangerous devil's right-hand draw gave few men a second chance.

Returning to Fort Griffin in 1877, legend has it that Doc Holliday first met Wyatt Earp at Shaunissy's Saloon, though Earp is thought to have known Big Nose Kate— an occasional prostitute—earlier. She even allegedly used the alias "Kate Earp" when she was once arrested and fined in Wichita.

Holliday briefly set up another dentistry practice in Dodge City, Kansas. While there, Wyatt Earp said that Holliday "came to my rescue and saved my life when I was surrounded by desperadoes." He was also thought to have ridden with Bat Masterson and Ben Thompson in their efforts to secure the right of way through the Royal Gorge for the Santa Fe Railroad.

Often traveling under the alias Tom Mackey, Tom Mckey, or Tom McKee, Holliday was reported to have wounded a gambler named Kid Colton. Then he went to work in a saloon in Las Vegas which attracted some of the more infamous cutthroats and hard cases in the West. These included David Rudabaugh, an accomplice of Billy the Kid,

Mysterious Dave Mather who was a con man, lawman, and killer, and Heinrich "Dutch Henry" Borne, the most disreputable horse thief in the West.

In Las Vegas, Holliday is thought to have exchanged fire with bartender and part-time gambler Charles White, his bullet just nicking White's spine. Then ex-Army scout and gambler Mike Gordon fell for a bargirl in the saloon Holliday ran with an ex-Dodge City peace officer, John Joshua Webb. When she refused to quit her job, Gordon fired a shot into the saloon. When he fired again, Holliday stepped out and killed him.

GOING TO TOMBSTONE

In 1880, Holliday and Big Nose Kate moved on to Tombstone, Arizona, where Wyatt Earp and his brothers had already established themselves. Doc worked as a dealer in the Oriental Saloon before moving on to the Alhambra Saloon, where he bought a percentage of the gambling interest.

On March 15, 1881, at 10:00 p.m., three cowboys attempted to rob the Benson stagecoach carrying $26,000 in silver bullion. The popular driver Eli "Budd" Philpot and passenger Peter Roerig were killed. Cowboy Bill Leonard, a former watchmaker from New York and a good friend of Holliday, was one of three men implicated in the robbery. When Kate and Holliday had a fight, County Sheriff Johnny Behan and Milt Joyce, owner of the Oriental Saloon, decided to frame Holliday and collect the reward.

Behan and Joyce plied Kate with alcohol and got her to testify that Holliday had done the shooting. Holliday was arrested, but the district attorney threw out the charges, labeling them "ridiculous" after Wyatt Earp found witnesses to provide Doc with an alibi. He was released and Kate quickly left town. Milt Joyce was in the Oriental when Holliday found him, and opened fire. He hit Joyce in the hand and one of the bartenders in the foot. But when Joyce tried to get revenge six months later, Sheriff Behan arrested him for carrying firearms within the city limits.

Mysterious Dave Mather, gunman, lawman and killer, during his term as assistant marshal of Dodge City, June 1, 1883 – April 10, 1884.

BAT MASTERSON ON DOC HOLLIDAY

While he never did anything to entitle him to a statue in the Hall of Fame, Doc Holliday was nevertheless a most picturesque character on the western border in those days when the pistol instead of law courts determined issues. Holliday was a product of the state of Georgia, and the scion of a most respectable and prominent family. He graduated as a dentist from one of the medical colleges of his native state before he left it, but did not follow his profession very long after receiving his diploma. It was perhaps too respectable a calling for him. Holliday had a mean disposition and an ungovernable temper, and under the influence of liquor was a most dangerous man. In this respect he was very much like the big Missourian who had put in the day at a cross-road groggery, and after getting pretty well filled up with the bug juice of the Moonshine brand, concluded that it was about time for him to say something that would make an impression on his hearers; so he straightened up, threw out his chest and declared in a loud tone of voice, that he was "a bad man when he was drinking, and managed to keep pretty full all the time." So it was with Holliday.

Physically, Doc Holliday was a weakling who could not have whipped a healthy fifteen-year old boy in a go-as-you-please fist fight, and no one knew this better than himself, and the knowledge of this fact was perhaps why he was so ready to resort to a weapon of some kind whenever he got himself into difficulty. He was hot-headed and impetuous and very much given to both drinking and quarrelling, and, among men who did not fear him, was very much disliked.

He possessed none of the qualities of leadership such as those that distinguished such men as H.P. Myton, Wyatt Earp, Billy Tilghman and other famous western characters. Holliday seemed to be absolutely unable to keep out of trouble for any great length of time. He would no sooner be out of one scrape before he was in another, and the strange part of it is he was more often in the right than in the wrong, which has rarely ever been the case with a man who is continually getting himself into trouble.

From *Famous Gunfighters of the Western Frontier* by Bat Masterson

Bat Masterson, 1879, age 26.

ON THE RUN WITH WYATT EARP

Holliday stood beside Wyatt Earp in the gunfight at the O.K. Corral. Soon after, Wyatt Earp stopped a gunfight between Holliday and Johnny Ringo. They were fined $30 each for violating the city's firearms ordinance. After the gunfight at the O.K. Corral, Holliday again joined the Earps in the killing of Frank Stilwell and Indian Charlie Cruz. He then fled with them to Colorado. Sheriff Robert H. Paul—who had been riding shotgun on the Benson stage—pursued Holliday to Denver with a warrant for the Stilwell murder. Bounty hunter Perry M. Mallon was also on his trail. However, he had no powers to arrest Holliday and had to get the local sheriff to take him into custody.

Learning of Holliday's fate, Wyatt Earp got Bat Masterson, who was in Denver, to

The feverish features of Doc Holliday, as portrayed by Val Kilmer in the 1993 movie *Tombstone*.

DOC HOLLIDAY'S SELF-HELP PROGRAM OF ALCOHOL AND OPIUM

In the nineteenth century, there were no such things as antibiotics, and aspirin wasn't invented until the 1890s. The recommended treatment to manage the cough and pain of tuberculosis was alcohol and opium.

Doc Holliday would have self-medicated with laudanum, a formulation containing opium and wine, flavored with cinnamon or saffron. Primarily used as a pain killer and tranquilizer, laudanum could be taken orally, and was the only potent treatment available at the time. Doc may also have taken bugleweed which has sedative and mild narcotic properties.

Known by many names, including Virginia water-horehound, archangel, green wolf's foot, and gypsy wort, it is a common plant in North America.

Doc Holliday's level of alcohol intake is legendary, but considering that he was an accomplished gambler, gunfighter, and horseman, it is difficult to believe that he spent much time being inebriated. However, he probably kept alcohol in his blood 24 hours a day as a pain suppressant, undoubtedly becoming intoxicated at times when he overdid the dosage.

intercede. Masterson visited Governor F.W. Pitkin who then refused to sign Holliday's extradition papers. To ensure that Holliday could not be sent back to Arizona, Masterson made up a false charge against Holliday—that he had cheated a Denver man out of $100. The bail was set at $300 and paid, but the case was prolonged indefinitely so that Holliday could not be removed from Colorado.

THE FINAL SHOWDOWN

Doc Holliday moved on to Leadville, Colorado, though the altitude was not good for his condition which he self-medicated with whiskey and laudanum. Also in Leadville was Billy Allen, a friend of Sheriff Behan from Tombstone. He worked as a bartender in the Monarch Saloon where Holliday gambled.

Down on his luck, Holliday borrowed $5 from Allen. When he could not pay it back, Allen called Holliday a "welsher." Doc was waiting for Allen when he came into Hyman's Saloon. He pulled a gun he had hidden behind the bar. The first bullet missed and Allen went running for the door. A second shot hit him in the elbow and knocked him down. Holliday was just about to finish him off with a third shot when Henry Kellerman, the bartender at Hyman's, stopped him. Holliday was disarmed and arrested. Charged with assault with intent to kill, he was acquitted as Allen had also been armed and had been looking for Holliday.

Prematurely aged, Holliday moved to Glenwood Springs, Colorado, possibly to take the waters there. He died in Hotel Glenwood in 1887 after his nurse refused him a final glass of whiskey. Having always figured that he would be killed in a gunfight, he looked down at his bootless feet and said: "This is funny." He was just thirty-six.

DOC HOLLIDAY: A VOLATILE MAN

Doc Holliday was physically impaired by tuberculosis throughout his fourteen years as a professional gambler. He was too weak to fight with his fists, so he became one of the most deadly gunmen of the era. John C. Jacobs, a fellow gambler and casino operator, described him as a volatile man of violent mood swings:

"This fellow Holliday was a consumptive and a hard drinker … He could at times be the most genteel, affable chap you ever saw, and at other times he was sour and surly, and would just as soon cut your throat with a villainous-looking knife … or shoot you with a .41-caliber double-barreled derringer …"

A dancehall girl of the 1890s.

DANCEHALL GIRLS

Around 1850, saloon houses began to appear in the West offering a wide array of not only gambling tables, but pretty women as well. While the games of chance were popular in these saloons, the chief attraction was dancing with the girls. The customer generally paid a dollar for a dance, with the proceeds being split between the dancehall girl and the saloon owner. After the dance, the girl would steer the gentleman to the bar, where she would make an additional commission from the sale of a drink. A popular girl could average fifty dances a night, sometimes making more than a working man could make in a month, and certainly more than she would earn as a prostitute.

GAMBLING IN THE WEST

Being a professional gambler was highly dangerous—losing players were often drunk and ready for a fight. It was no accident that many of the top gunfighters were hired as dealers in the gambling establishments across the West. Tough, steel-nerved, young men with reputations as gunslingers not only attracted customers, but also protected the large piles of cash that were openly displayed on the table. In towns such as Deadwood, Dodge City, and Tombstone, gamblers played with their back to the wall and their guns at their sides, as dealers dealt games with names such as chuck-a-luck, three-card monte, high dice, and faro.

Doc Holliday was working as a faro dealer in Leadville, Colorado, when his health began to dramatically fail. His Stage-2 tuberculosis caused severe weight loss, fatigue, and mental confusion, and he could no longer deal cards or work as a gambler. He became bedridden, lapsed into a coma and died on November 8, 1887.

Faro players in an Arizona saloon in 1895.

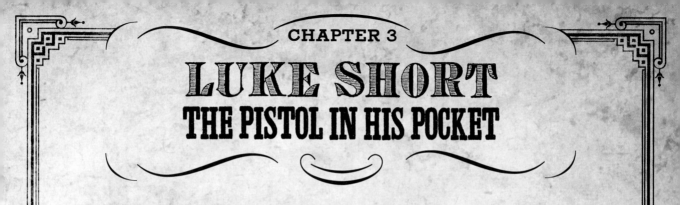

CHAPTER 3

LUKE SHORT
THE PISTOL IN HIS POCKET

"QUICKER THAN A FLASH, LUKE HAD JAMMED HIS PISTOL INTO THE BAD MAN'S FACE."

Bat Masterson about Luke Short

Born in Mississippi in 1854, Luke Short moved to East Texas via Arkansas with his family two years later. Having little education as a youth, he worked on the family farm before hiring out as a cowhand on the cattle drives to Kansas. But this was too much like hard work, so he moved north to Nebraska-Dakota Territory border where he peddled whiskey to the Indians. Known as the "White Indian," he traded a gallon of a poisonous brew called "Pine Top" worth ninety cents for an Indian robe worth $10.

Selling whiskey to the Indians was a federal crime. But a more immediate danger was drunken and disgruntled Sioux braves. Short claimed to have killed six of them, burying their bodies in remote places.

According to his friend Bat Masterson, the federal authorities finally caught up with Short and he was arrested by the Army. When told to collect his things, he said: "I have nothing that I care to take along, except what I have on."

"That mostly consisted of a pair of Colt's pistols and belt of cartridges," said Masterson, "the officer soon had them in his custody."

Short was taken to Sidney, Nebraska, though no record of this has been found. Masterson said that he escaped. However, during the Cheyenne Uprising of 1878, Short worked briefly for the Army as a dispatch rider and scout.

TROUBLE IS MY MIDDLE NAME

Next Luke Short arrived in the mining town of Leadville, Colorado, and almost immediately got himself into an argument with a well-known villain in a gambling house. Short's appearance was deceptive. He was a small man, five feet six, weighing around 140 pounds. But despite his stature he was more than capable of standing up for himself in a fight with an ever-ready fast gun. Luke Short was trouble. Masterson described him:

It was a small package, but one of great dynamic force. In this connection it will not be out of order for me to state that, though of small build, it required a $7\frac{1}{8}$ hat to fit his well-shaped, round head.

Masterson gave an account of the fracas in Leadville:

The bad man, who had a record of having killed someone somewhere, attempted to take some sort of liberty with one of Luke's bets and, when the latter politely requested the bad man to keep his hands off, the bad man became very angry and made some rude remarks.

Fearing that Short was about to be shot full of holes, the dealer offered to make good the bet. Short refused. The villain then called Short an "insignificant little shrimp," threatened to shoot his hand off if he touched the bet, and went for his gun. Masterson continued the story:

Quicker than a flash, Luke had jammed his own pistol into the bad man's face and pulled the trigger, and the bad man rolled over on the floor. The bullet passed through his cheek but, luckily, did not kill him.

Luke Short, around 1880.

Short was not even arrested, as such things happened all the time in Leadville in those days. However, the incident gave Short some standing in the town. He found himself in big demand by the proprietors of the gambling houses who wanted his gun skills to keep order. He started to deal faro and took to wearing dapper tailor-made suits and a derby hat—though the most famous picture of him shows him wearing a top hat and sporting a cane. He had the right-hand pocket of his trousers cut extra long and lined with leather. While Short appeared unarmed, with no visible firearm, he concealed his pistol in his pocket.

SHOOTING CHARLIE STORMS

In the spring of 1881, Luke Short moved on to Tombstone where he, Wyatt Earp, Bat Masterson, and Doc Holliday—the premier gunfighters of their day—were known as the "Dodge City Gang."

Short dealt faro at Earp's Oriental Saloon. There he came up against Charlie Storms, one of the best-known gamblers in the West and the victor in several gunfights. Once more, Short's stature worked in his favor and made Storms underestimate him, judging him to be insignificant-looking. When the inevitable confrontation came, pistols were pulled, but Bat Masterson, who was friends with both men, jumped between them.

He grabbed Storms and begged Short not to shoot. Bundling Storms outside, Masterson advised him to go home and have some sleep. He had been up all night and had already been in quarrels with other people. Masterson walked him home to his apartment. Thinking Storms had gone to bed, he walked back to talk to Short.

Masterson was just explaining to Short that Storms was a decent fellow, when Storms burst in. Without saying a word, Storms pulled his .45 single-action Colt. Before he could fire, Short stuck the muzzle of his pistol against Storms' heart and pulled the trigger. As he fell, Short shot him again. He was dead before he hit the ground. At a preliminary hearing

before a magistrate, Short was exonerated. It was a simple case of self-defense ... but Short also had friends in high places.

FACE OFF WITH THE MAYOR

Moving to Dodge City, Luke Short became a partner in the Long Branch Saloon. It was known as one of the vilest haunts in the city. Con man and convicted robber Jack McCarty was employed as house gambler, and Short would subdue rowdy customers by hitting them over the head with a chair. However, his partner, Will Harris, was also the vice-president of the Bank of Dodge City.

Around that time a number of moral ordinances were passed that resulted in a conflict between the authorities and the saloon owners. This became known as the Dodge City War. It began when Mayor Alonzo B. Webster instituted a vagrancy act.

His successor, Mayor Larry Deger, enacted an ordinance closing the brothels and, as prostitutes and pimps had no visible means of support, they were subject to the vagrancy act. Three female "entertainers" at the Long Branch Saloon were arrested. However, establishments owned by the Deger faction were allowed to keep their "entertainers." This was particularly galling as next door to the Long Branch was a saloon and gambling house run by Alonzo Webster.

According to Masterson, an ordinance was then passed banning music in gambling houses and saloons.

"That suits me," Short told the marshal. "I don't need music in my house in order to do business, and besides, maintaining a band is quite an item of expense."

However, when Webster's adjoining saloon continued playing music, Short rehired the band. The band was then arrested. While Short was looking for someone competent to accept a bail bond, he saw Special Police Officer Lewis Hartman standing on the sidewalk which was a foot or so above the street. He was one of the officers enforcing the ordinances.

Seeing Short coming, Hartman pulled his gun and fired. Short shot back. As Hartman

THE DODGE CITY PEACE COMMISSION

The Dodge City Peace Commission came to town threatening a war, so the title of "peace commission" was ironic. According to a biography of Wyatt Earp, this photo was taken in the Conkling Studio, Dodge City, June 1883. Left to right, standing: W.H. Harris, Luke Short, and Bat Masterson. Seated: Charlie Bassett, Wyatt Earp, Frank McLain, and Neal Brown.

THE WICKEDEST CITY IN AMERICA

From its founding, Dodge City, Kansas had a reputation for corruption and was often called "the Wickedest City in America." The Dodge City Gang dominated law enforcement and monopolized the whiskey trade, but in 1879, anti-gang supporters won a closely fought election for Ford County, defeating popular gang member Bat Masterson. The new political faction called themselves reformers, but they only wanted to reap the profits of the whiskey trade. Mayor Alonzo B. Webster, elected in 1881, owned two saloons himself. The new mayor lost no time in firing Bat Masterson's brother, Jim, as city marshal and tensions built between the Mastersons and the mayor.

In 1883 a friend of the Mastersons, gambler and gunfighter Luke Short, settled in Dodge and purchased a half interest in the Long Branch Saloon. The mayor passed a law making prostitution illegal in Dodge City and arrested several girls who worked in Short's saloon. Short was also arrested and banished from the town as an "undesirable."

Short and Masterson called in favors from some old friends including Wyatt Earp, Charlie Bassett, Johnny Millsap, Shotgun John Collins, Texas Jack Vermillion, and Johnny Green. The men marched up Front Street into Short's saloon. The mayor was intimidated by the show of force and negotiated peace. Short returned to the Long Branch Saloon in exchange for a promise that there would be no violence. Later that same year, Short got out of Dodge completely, selling his interest in the saloon and moving south to Fort Worth, Texas.

turned to flee, he fell off the sidewalk. Thinking he had hit Hartman, Short grabbed a shotgun and got out of Dodge.

The following morning, he was persuaded to surrender his guns. He was told that if he went to the police court, pleaded guilty to creating a disturbance, and paid a fine, that would be an end of the matter. Instead, when he surrendered himself, he was locked in the city jail. At noon, he was taken to the railroad depot and told to pick a train, either going east or west. He took the east-bound train to Kansas City.

THE WAR IN DODGE CITY

From Kansas City, Short wired Bat Masterson in Denver. The two of them decided to go to Topeka to petition Governor George Washington Glick, who denounced the conduct of the authorities in Dodge City, but refused to interfere. However, he wished Short luck in re-establishing himself in Dodge City.

Masterson went to Silverton, Colorado, to get Wyatt Earp, while Short headed for Caldwell, Kansas, to recruit a couple of friends. It was decided that Earp would go to Dodge City first with, what Masterson said were, "several desperate men:"

It finally became whispered about, that Wyatt Earp had a strong force of desperate men already domiciled in town in the interest of Luke Short. The mayor called a hasty meeting of his friends, and after they had all assembled in the council chamber of the city hall, informed them solemnly of what he had heard about the Earp invasion.

They decided to send a committee to invite Earp to attend one of their meetings and explain his position in the matter. Earp

Men relaxing in the Long Branch Saloon in Dodge City, Kansas, 1880. Lo Warren is the bartender.

accepted the invitation and warned the mayor and city council that Short and Masterson were expected on the noon train the following day—Earp's warning went on:

> *... and on their arrival we expect to open up hostilities. Moreover, thinking that perhaps something might happen where I would need assistance, I brought along some other gentlemen who signified a willingness to join in whatever festivities might arise.*

The mayor took fright. He said that they had had enough fighting in Dodge. Earp assured him that there would be no bloodshed if Short was allowed to return and "conduct his business unmolested as heretofore."

The mayor and city council quickly agreed. When Short returned to Dodge, he summoned the mayor and the sheriff and insisted that the law officers who had been enforcing the ordinances were dismissed. He also wanted the ban on music lifted. His bail bond was to be returned and all record of it destroyed. The authorities caved in to all his demands and they had a drink to settle the matter.

However, afterward, the mayor and his cronies wired the governor and asked him to send the militia. Glick refused.

BEHIND CLOSED DOORS AT THE WHITE ELEPHANT

Soon after, Short sold up and moved to Fort Worth, Texas, where he lived with a woman named Hettie Buck, and became proprietor of the White Elephant gambling house. It was one of the largest and costliest establishments of its kind in the south-west and Short would have become a wealthy man, if he had not been imposed upon by what Bat Masterson called "professional cadgers." Masterson recalled:

> *While he made fortunes in his gambling establishments, he died a comparatively poor man. He perhaps owed less and had more money due him when he died than any gambler who ever lived.*

When gambling became illegal in Fort Worth, Short continued his business behind closed doors and many of his customers were among the elite of society. However, he fell prey to Timothy Isaiah "Longhaired Jim" Courtright. He had been city marshal in Fort Worth in 1876, but when reports of corruption circulated, he left to become a drifter. He had killed a couple of men in Fort Worth, and two more in New Mexico before hiding out in South America for two years. In the mid-1880s, he returned to Fort Worth where he started a detective agency which essentially blackmailed local businesses for protection money. Naturally, Luke Short refused to pay, saying that he was happy to personally protect his own saloon. Courtright was furious.

SHORT STANDS HIS GROUND

In the spring of 1887, Bat Masterson visited his good friend Short in Fort Worth and said that Courtright was a dangerous gunman who was also notorious for intimidating the entire community. According to Masterson, Courtright had asked Short to install him as a special officer in the White Elephant. Short, Masterson said, had been a "substantial friend" of Courtright's during his troubles at Fort Worth, but told him he could not think of such a thing. Luke said:

> *Why Jim, I would rather pay you a good salary to stay away from my house entirely. You know that the people about here are all afraid of you, and your presence in my house as an officer would ruin my business.*

Courtright, who was a sullen, ignorant bully, with no sense of right or wrong, could not see Short's point of view, and would not understand that it was purely a matter of business. Masterson said:

> *At any rate Courtright got huffy at Luke and threatened to have him indicted and his place closed up. Courtright could not get it through his head how it was that Luke had dared to turn him down. He knew that he had everybody else in town "buffaloed" and could see no reason why Luke should be different from the others.*

SHOWDOWN WITH JIM COURTRIGHT

Masterson and Short were sitting together in the billiard room of the White Elephant one evening, when one of Luke's associates, named Jake Johnson, came in. He told Luke that Courtright was in the outer lobby and would like to have a talk with him.

"Tell him to come in," said Short.

"I did invite him in," replied Johnson, "but he refused and said that I was to tell you to come out."

"Very well," said Short, "I will see what he has to say." He got up and accompanied Johnson to where Courtright was waiting. Bat Masterson remembered the scene:

It did not take Short very long to discover that his mission was anything but one of peace. He brought along no olive branch, but instead a brace of pistols, conspicuously displayed. It was not a parley that he came for, but fight, and his demeanor indicated a desire that hostilities open up forthwith. No time was wasted in the exchange of words once the men faced each other.

SHORT'S GUN SPOKE FIRST

It was plain that Courtright had been drinking. He warned Short not to go for his gun. Short replied that he never carried a pistol at his place of business. But when Courtright went for his gun, Short pulled his revolver from his trouser pocket. Bat Masterson was there:

Both drew their pistols at the same time, but, as usual, Short's spoke first and a bullet from a Colt's .45-caliber pistol went crashing through Courtright's body. The shock caused him to reel backward; then he got another and still another, and by the time his lifeless form had reached the floor, Luke had succeeded in shooting him five times.

As Short had to reach under his coat to pull his gun, Courtright beat him to the draw. However, the hammer of Courtright's six-shooter had snagged on his watch chain, giving Short time to pull his gun and fire at close range. The first bullet broke the cylinder of Courtright's gun. Two more shots went wild. Three others hit his thumb, his shoulder, and his heart.

JUSTIFIABLE HOMICIDE

Short was arrested on the spot by a deputy sheriff and taken to the county jail, where he was held overnight. The next day he was taken before a justice of the peace, who held him for the grand jury on a $2,000 bond. In the end, the grand jury refused to indict on the evidence, finding that it was a case of justifiable homicide.

"This ended Luke Short's shooting scrapes with the exception of a little gun dispute three years later at Fort Worth which had no fatal results," said Masterson.

The event took place on December 23, 1890, when Short had a gambling dispute with Charles Wright, a local saloon owner. Wright ambushed Short, blasting him from behind with a shotgun. He was wounded in the left leg and part of his left thumb was blown off. Nevertheless, Short managed to turn and draw, hitting Wright in the left wrist, breaking it, as he fled.

GENTLEMAN GUNSLINGER

Though he was not yet forty, Short suffered from edema, then called dropsy. In August 1893, he went to Geuda Spring, a mineral spa in Kansas. This did no good and he died there the following month. His body was returned to Fort Worth where he was buried in Oakwood Cemetery. This was a relatively uneventful end for one of the deadliest gunfighters in the West.

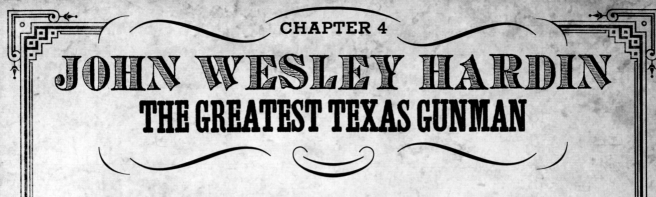

CHAPTER 4

JOHN WESLEY HARDIN
THE GREATEST TEXAS GUNMAN

"THERE ALWAYS SEEMED TO BE A MAN WITH A CHALLENGE ... AND I NEVER REFUSED ONE."

John Wesley Hardin (1853–95)

Thought to be the greatest of all Texas gunmen, John Wesley Hardin is credited with forty killings in stand-up gunfights, ambushes, and running battles on horseback, with a history of violence starting from a young age. He was just ten when he accepted the challenge to a wrestling match by schoolmate Charles Sloter, who was older and bigger. After Hardin pinned him down, Sloter attacked him with a knife. Someone tossed Hardin a blade and Sloter went home bleeding.

BORN A REBEL

Born in 1853, in Bonham, Fannin County, Texas, Hardin was named by his father, Methodist preacher James C. Hardin, after John Wesley the founder of Methodism. Hardin himself said his mother Elizabeth Dixon Hardin was "a cultured woman from an educated and comfortable family."

They moved to Sumpter, Texas, where Hardin was educated at a school established by his father. Tall and handsome, he used to arrange races, wrestling matches, and shooting contests. "We all carried guns in those days," he said. By the time he was twelve he was an accomplished hunter of possum, raccoon, deer, and wild cats. By fifteen, he was one of the best marksmen in the county.

During the Civil War, Trinity County was determinedly pro-Confederacy. His father organized a company of men to join the fight, but was persuaded to resign as captain on the grounds that he would be more useful teaching at home than off fighting Yankees.

The young Hardin and his cousin, Manning Clements, then ran off to join his father's erstwhile company, but were brought back by the Reverend Hardin who administered a "sound thrashing." This did not diminish Hardin's enthusiasm for the cause. He said he saw Abraham Lincoln as "a devil incarnate who was waging a relentless and cruel war on the South to rob her of her sacred rights."

"I grew up," he said, "a Rebel."

The young John Wesley Hardin.

JOHN WESLEY'S FIRST KILL

Hardin's father became a lawyer during the war, then bought a plantation on Long King Creek near Livingston, Texas, though he handed it over to his brother, Barnett. In 1865, when he was helping his uncle with the sugar cane harvest, Hardin and a cousin challenged an African-American freedman, known only as Maje, to a wrestling match. This ended in a brawl.

The following day, Hardin shot and killed Maje. On the advice of his father, Hardin fled, becoming a fugitive from the "Yankee courts." He was hiding out on a friend's farm when he heard that a Union patrol was coming to arrest him. Hardin decided to ambush the troopers, killing three at a river crossing.

Hardin then fled to Pisgah, Navarro County, where his father had been appointed head of the Old World School. John Wesley became a replacement teacher there and the teenage killer taught reading, writing, and arithmetic to a class of twenty-five boys and girls, some older than him. He was offered a permanent job there, but teaching was not a life for Hardin. He longed for the freedom of the open range.

DEADLIEST GUN IN THE SOUTH-WEST

With his cousins, Manning Clements and Tom Dixon, Hardin took to rounding up and selling wild longhorn. Still teenagers, they spent their money in gambling halls and saloons. He bet on poker, euchre, and his favorite game seven-up—as well as any other sporting contest he could find.

"I like fast horses and would soon bet on any kind of a horse race, a chicken fight, a dog fight, or anything down to throwing crackaloo, or spitting at a mark," he said.

He was also adept with a Colt .44.

Still on the run from Union troops, Hardin was named as the accomplice of Frank Polk, who had killed a man in Corsicana, Texas, though Hardin could prove he was not there. He then teamed up with his nineteen-year-old cousin, Simp Dixon, whose mother,

John Wesley Hardin from a tintype made in Abilene, 1871.

brother, and sister had been killed by a Union patrol. Simp had sworn to kill Yankees for the rest of his life. Hardin retold the story later:

There was a big reward for Simp, and so, of course, I sympathized with him in every way and was generally with him. On one occasion in the Richland bottom a squad of soldiers ran up on us and a pitched battle immediately ensued. It was a free and fast fight. When the battle was over, two soldiers lay dead. Simp killed one and I killed the other, while the rest escaped. Simp was afterwards killed by a squad of United States soldiers at Cotton Gin, in Limestone County. He was undoubtedly one of the most dangerous men in Texas.

But it was the sixteen-year-old Hardin who got the reputation of being the deadliest gunfighter in south-west Texas. After his election, Governor Edmund J. Davis publicly vowed to have Hardin killed, jailed, or hanged. Hardin then became one of the principal targets for the Texas State Police, but family and friends never failed to warn him when policemen were in the area.

TROUBLE IN TOWASH

In December 1869, Hardin was hiding out in the lawless town of Towash, where the saloons and brothels were run by the desperado Jim Bradley and his band of fugitives and gunslingers.

Celebrating Christmas with a day-long card game, Hardin cleaned out Bradley, who then refused to pay up. Hardin was unarmed. Threatening him with a knife, Bradley took his boots and ran him out of the saloon. Fearing trouble, the owner of Hardin's boarding house would not return his gun, but Hardin managed to borrow another. Hardin recounted the vicious confrontation with Bradley that followed in the street:

[Bradley was] getting in front of me with a pistol in one hand and a Bowie knife in the other. He commenced to fire on me, firing once, then snapping and then firing again. By this time we were within five or six feet of

each other, and I fired with a Remington .45 at his heart and right after that at his head. As he staggered and fell, he said: "O, Lordy, don't shoot me any more." I could not stop. I was shooting because I did not want to take chances on a reaction.

After the killing Hardin rode out of town.

A KILLER ON THE LOOSE

Traveling on to Brenham, he stopped at a circus to warm himself by their camp fire, where he accidentally struck a man on the hand. Hardin apologized, but the man pulled a gun. Hardin was too quick and put a .45-caliber round through the man's head.

Then at Kosse, he met a pretty girl who invited him to call on her that night. When he did, a man she claimed was her sweetheart turned up and demanded $100. Plainly it was a scam. Hardin handed over the money. As he did so, he deliberately dropped some of it. Hardin said:

He stooped down to pick it up, and as he was straightening up I pulled my pistol and fired. The ball struck him between the eyes and he fell over, a dead robber. I stopped long enough to get back most of my money and resumed my journey to Brenham.

Finally reaching the gambling halls of Brenham, he met John King Fisher and Ben Thompson, who would die together in San Antonio, and Phil Coe, who gave Hardin the nickname "Little Seven Up" after his favorite poker game. Coe would die at the hands of Wild Bill Hickok in Abilene. Hardin moved on when he heard that the State Police were on their way with a murder warrant for him.

STAYING AHEAD OF THE LAW

Hardin was getting tired of drifting and his father urged him to attend Professor Landrum's academy in Round Rock where his elder brother, Joe Hardin, was studying law. He rode there and enrolled. But one day his father sent word that the State Police were on their way.

Hardin left the school in a hurry, but continued his studies around the campfire at one of his many hideouts with his brother. Eventually Professor Landrum agreed to let him sit an academy examination. He passed the exam, but had to pick up the diploma on horseback with a State Police posse just a few miles behind him, and hot on his trail.

Joe Hardin then moved on to the town of Comanche, in north central Texas, where he set up as a lawyer. His wife, daughter, parents, and the rest of the Hardin clan—including cousins Tom and Buddy Dixon—joined him there. But John Wesley could not stay.

"My father always told me that when the Democrats regained power I could get a fair trial," he said, "but I could never expect that under carpet-bag rule."

RESISTING ARREST

Hardin was in Longview, Texas when "they arrested me for another party, on a charge of which I was innocent." The State Police decided to take him to a robust prison in Waco. However, he managed to buy "a .45 Colt with four barrels loaded," from a fellow prisoner, for $10 in gold and a $25 overcoat.

He tied the gun under his arm so his two guards would not find it when they searched him. On the second night out, one of the guards went to a nearby farmhouse to get some feed for the horses. Hardin shot and killed the remaining guard, and made off on horseback.

After visiting his parents in Comanche again, he headed for Mexico. On the way, he was arrested again by three other lawmen. That night they got drunk and, when they fell asleep, he killed them.

"I took an oath right there never to surrender at the muzzle of a gun," he said.

LITTLE ARKANSAW

Hardin met up with his cousin, Manning Clements, in Gonzales County, south central Texas. With several other cowhands, they stopped to play monte. The dealer fell out with Hardin, who hit him on the head with a gun barrel. Two Mexican players went for their knives. Hardin pulled a gun, wounding one in the chest, the other in the arm.

Clements persuaded Hardin to join him on a cattle drive on the Chisholm Trail to Abilene, Kansas, in the summer of 1871. While they were waiting for the ranchers to round up their cattle, they attended a wedding party where Clements introduced Hardin to Jane Bowen, the pretty, dark-haired, sixteen-year-old daughter of a local cattleman. Before he left for Kansas, they became engaged.

Broadway Avenue, Abilene, Kansas, 1875.

Love did not calm him though. Along the way, in Indian Territory, Hardin killed two Indians, who tried to tax the herd at ten cents a head. Then at a bend in the Arkansas River, a Mexican herd of cattle that was trailing them, came up too fast and the cattle got mixed up. As they tried to separate them, a dispute broke out. There was gunfire and six Mexican *vaqueros* lay dead, five of them killed by Hardin. This earned him the new nickname "Little Arkansaw"—though at five feet ten, he was far from small for the time.

ABOVE THE LAW IN ABILENE

Arriving at Abilene, Hardin refused to take off his two six-shooters. This brought him into conflict with Wild Bill Hickok, the city marshal. Hardin told the tale of pulling the "Road Agent's Spin" on Hickok. Some historians scoff, but Hickok and Hardin became firm friends during Hardin's stay. They seemed to have had some kind of mutual respect, drinking, gambling, and chasing girls together.

Hardin quarreled with Charles Cougar over a card game and shot him dead. He also killed a prowler who he found going through his clothes one night. The two stories became conflated and it was said that Hardin had killed Cougar for snoring. Anyway, Hickok did nothing.

Hardin told of another incident in Abilene, showing his supposed immunity to the law:

I had been drinking pretty freely that day and towards night went into a restaurant to get something to eat. A man named Pain was with me, a Texan who had just come up the trail. While we were in the restaurant several drunken men came in and began to curse Texans. I said to the nearest one: "I'm a Texan."

He began to curse me and threatened to slap me over. To his surprise I pulled my pistol and he promptly pulled his. At the first fire he jumped behind my friend Pain, who received the ball in his only arm. He fired one shot and ran, but I shot at him as he started, the ball hitting him in the mouth, knocking out several teeth and coming out behind his left ear. I rushed outside, pistol in hand and jumped over my late antagonist, who was lying in the doorway. I met a policeman on the sidewalk, but I threw my pistol in his face and told him to "hands up." He did it.

WANTED DEAD OR ALIVE

Hardin left for Cottonwood, about thirty-five miles away "to await results." There he learned that his friend, Bill Cohron, had been shot and killed by a Mexican named Bideno. Hardin remembered what happened:

Many prominent cow men came to me and urged me to follow the murderer. I consented, if they would go to Abilene and get a warrant for him. They did so, and I was appointed a deputy sheriff and was given letters of introduction to cattle men whom I should meet.

Accompanied by Bill Cohron's brother, Jim, and two other cowboys, Hardin caught up with Bideno in the small hamlet of Bluff City. While the three others surrounded the café where Bideno was eating, Hardin walked in and ordered him to surrender. When he tried to resist, Hardin shot him in the head at point blank range. They left $20 to bury him.

But being on the right side of the law did not suit John Wesley. When he returned to Texas to prepare for his wedding, he was in Smiley when he saw two African-American State Policemen, named Green Paramore and John Lackey, eating cheese and crackers in a general store. Knowing that the State Police were still hunting him, he walked up to them and asked them if they knew John Wesley Hardin. They said they had never seen him, but were duty bound to seek him out and arrest him.

"Well," said Hardin drawing his pistol. "You see him now!" And he emptied the gun into the two officers, killing Paramore and wounding Lackey in the mouth. He ran from the store and survived to see Hardin on another occasion. When Hardin made off, he was pursued by a fifteen-man posse. He killed three of them and drove the rest off. Governor Davis now ordered his policemen to bring in Hardin, dead or alive.

CARPETBAGGERS AND SCALAWAGS

Returning to Gonzales, Hardin swore to stay out of the way of the "carpetbaggers and scalawags" that made up Davis's police force. On February 29, 1872, he married Jane Bowen. They went on to have two daughters and a son.

Now a married man, Hardin planned to settle down and become a horse trader. But he could not stay out of trouble for long. In June 1872, he had gone to Hemphill, Texas, to sell a herd of horses and got into a quarrel with a State Policeman named Spites. Not recognizing Hardin, Spites told him to back off or face arrest. Hardin pulled a derringer and shot Spites in the shoulder, then made his way out of town with a posse on his heels.

Manning Clements, cousin of John Wesley Hardin.

BLASTED WITH BUCKSHOT

In August 1872, Manning Clements and John Wesley Hardin were in Trinity City, Texas, to inspect a mare that was doing well at the local racetracks. In a bar, a man named Phil Sublette watched as Hardin lost at bowling and challenged him to a series of matches at $5 a set. When Hardin won six games in a row, Sublette figured that he had been set up. There was an argument. Hardin made him finish the game at gunpoint, then, generously, bought him a drink.

Sublette left and returned with a shotgun. He blasted Hardin with buckshot and fled. Hardin hit him in the back with one shot as he went.

Hardin was carried unconscious to his hotel bed where doctors dug out the buckshot. When Jane arrived, she was told that her husband would probably die. A few days later, Clements heard that state troopers were on their way. Against the protest of the doctors, Hardin was dressed and put on a horse.

He was moved out to Angelina County where his friend Dave Harrel lived. After two days, he was warned that the State Police had tracked him there. Tired of running, Hardin had acquired a double-barreled shotgun and "resolved to sell my life dearly if they did come."

Two men rode up armed with Winchesters. As they approached, Hardin crawled to the back door and shot at them. He killed one and wounded the other. In return fire, he received another wound in the thigh. But he managed to mount a horse and ride on to the home of another friend.

THE MOST BLOODY DESPERADO

With a fresh wound and the old wounds still giving him trouble, Hardin was in no state to continue his flight. He sent Harrel to see Cherokee County Sheriff Richard B. Reagan, an old friend of his father's, and tell him he wished to surrender on the condition that he received medical attention and could keep one-half of the reward.

When Sheriff Reagan arrived, Hardin had fresh conditions.

"I told him I did not want to be put in jail," said Hardin. "I wanted half the reward; I wanted medical aid; I wanted protection from mob law; I wanted to go to Austin as quickly as possible and from there to Gonzales."

According to Hardin, Reagan agreed to this, but Hardin was just reaching for one of his pistols to surrender it, when one of Reagan's men shot him in the right knee.

"I first thought, on the impulse of the moment, that I would kill the sheriff," Hardin said, "but it flashed across me at once that it was a mistake and that in him was my only protection."

Good to his word, Reagan and his family tended Hardin in the family's hotel in Rusk. But it was clear that he would be charged with killing Paramore and wounding Lackey, though he thought that a "sympathetic" jury—that is, a white jury—might consider his actions as self defense. Nevertheless, the *Lone Star Reporter* emphasized the number of men he had killed:

> *... less than 21 [years] of age ... He is said to have killed 24 men in Texas, and four in Kansas—making 28 in all. He is the most bloody desperado we ever heard of. His father is a Methodist minister, and is said to stand quite high in the estimation of the public.*

SHACKLED AND CHAINED

Once well enough to be moved, Hardin was imprisoned in the notoriously filthy and vermin-infested Travis County Jail, which Austin's *Daily Democratic Statesman* described as "a disgrace to the age and a crime against humanity." However, an attorney got him a transfer to Gonzales County, where he felt he might find that "sympathetic" jury. Indeed, when he arrived citizens denounced the treatment of Hardin, who was shackled and chained. The Gonzales County Sheriff William E. Jones had his irons removed. Soon

after, probably with the sheriff's blessing, Hardin escaped.

THE SUTTON TAYLOR FEUD

At the time in Gonzales and DeWitt Counties, a savage feud was being fought between the Taylor family and the Suttons, who had the backing of Governor Davis and his State Police. Jane Hardin begged her husband not to get involved, but this was hardly possible, especially as Governor Davis now put a $1,000 reward on Hardin's head.

In April 1873, Hardin visited Cuero, Texas, to sell some cattle. In a saloon, he was approached by a half-drunk deputy of Sheriff Jack Helm named John Morgan, who demanded that Hardin buy him a bottle of champagne. Hardin ignored him and left, but Morgan followed him outside and tried to arrest him. When Morgan pulled a gun, Hardin drew and fired, hitting Morgan just above the left eye and killing him.

THE END OF JACK HELM

Jack Helm (sometimes Helms), a leading man in the Sutton faction, sent a posse after Hardin. When they could not find him at his spread, they abused his wife, Jane. Hardin now threw his gunfighting weight behind the Taylors in the feud. There are various stories of how Jack Helm met his end. This is Hardin's version of what happened in Albuquerque when he went looking for Helm on May 17, 1873:

> *On the 17th I was to meet Jack Helms at a little town called Albukirk in Wilson County. I went there according to agreement, a trusty friend accompanying me in the person of Jim Taylor. We talked matters over together and failed to agree, he seriously threatening Jim Taylor's life, and so I went and told Jim to look out, that Jack Helms had sworn to shoot him on sight because he had shot Bill Sutton and because he was a Taylor. Jim quickly asked me to introduce him to Helms or point him out. I declined to do this, but referred him to a friend that*

would. I went to a blacksmith shop and had my horse shod. I paid for the shoeing and was fixing to leave when I heard Helms' voice:

"Hands up, you d— s— of a b—."

I looked around and saw Jack Helms advancing on Jim Taylor with a large knife in his hands. Some one hollered: "Shoot the d—d scoundrel." It appeared to me that Helms was the scoundrel, so I grabbed my shot gun and fired at Capt. Jack Helms as he was closing with Jim Taylor. I then threw my gun on the Helms crowd and told them not to draw a gun, and made one fellow put up his pistol. In the meantime, Jim Taylor had shot Helms repeatedly in the head, so thus did the leader of the vigilant committee, the Sheriff of DeWitt, the terror of the country, whose name was a horror to all law-abiding citizens, meet his death. He fell with twelve buckshot in his breast and several six-shooter balls in his head. All of this happened in the midst of his own friends and advisors, who stood by utterly amazed. The news soon spread that I had killed Jack Helms and I received many letters of thanks from the widows of the men whom he had cruelly put to death. Many of the best citizens of Gonzales and DeWitt counties patted me on the back and told me that was the best act of my life.

SHOOTING CHARLES WEBB

In 1874, Hardin was in Comanche, celebrating his twenty-first birthday with Jim Taylor and cousin Bud Dixon, when Deputy Sheriff Charles M. Webb approached down the street, stopping around fifteen paces away. Hardin noted that he was wearing two six-shooters. He introduced himself and asked Webb if had any papers for his arrest.

Webb said he hadn't, but Hardin was in a provocative mood.

"I have been informed that the sheriff of Brown County has said that Sheriff Karnes of this county was no sheriff or he would not allow me to stay around Comanche with my murdering pals," he said.

Webb replied: "I am not responsible for what the sheriff of Brown County says. I am only a deputy."

Another deputy tried to intervene, but Hardin asked Webb what he had in the hand behind his back. It was a cigar.

"Mr. Webb, we were just going to take a drink or a cigar," said Hardin, indicating Jack Wright's Saloon. "Won't you join us?"

"Certainly," Webb replied.

As Hardin turned around to go into the saloon, Dixon shouted: "Look out, Jack."

Hardin turned and saw Webb drawing a pistol. As he raised it , Hardin jumped to one side, drew his own pistol, and fired.

Webb got off the first shot, "hitting me in the left side, cutting the length of it, inflicting an ugly and painful wound," said Hardin. His own shot was better. He hit Webb in the left cheek. As he fell, Webb loosed off another wild shot. Meanwhile, Dixon and Taylor pumped bullets into Webb as he was falling.

The three outlaws were then attacked by a mob who chased them out of town. Hardin escaped, but his brother Joe and cousins Bud and Tom Dixon were caught and lynched.

TRACKED BY TEXAS RANGERS

The reward on Hardin's head was now increased to $4,000, making him the most wanted fugitive in Texas. He moved to Pollard, Alabama, under the name James W. Swain. His brother-in-law, Brown Bowen, who was under an indictment for murder, joined them. But Bowen wrote home to Hardin's father-in-law in Gonzales County, where he had taken in a young boarder named John Duncan, an undercover agent for the Texas Rangers.

Duncan saw Bowen's letter and Texas Rangers were sent to Pollard to check out Swain, who was quickly identified as Hardin. After moving east, Hardin had hardly mended his way. One reported incident involved Hardin and a friend, named Gus Kenedy, traveling to Mobile and Pensacola, Florida to gamble. When a waiter brought wine rather than beer in a saloon in Mobile, Hardin kicked over the table and a gunfight started. After two were killed and another wounded, Hardin and Kenedy were arrested, but were discharged after a hearing.

But the Texas Rangers were on their case. Captain John Armstrong and Duncan tracked down Hardin to Alabama. He was away in Florida at the time so, with other lawmen, they took the train to Pensacola.

By then, Hardin and his companions were ready to go back. On August 23, 1877, they boarded the train bound for Alabama. But so did the Texas Rangers. Once the train was underway, Captain Armstrong came into the smoking car and pulled a Colt revolver with a seven-inch barrel. Seeing it, Hardin said: "Texas, by God!"

Because of his old wounds, he could not wear a gun belt. His pistol was in a shoulder holster. He tried to draw and his pistol snagged on his clothing. Other lawmen grabbed him.

Nineteen-year-old Jim Mann, who was sitting next to Hardin, put a bullet through Armstrong's hat. Armstrong shot him in the chest. Mann then jumped out of the window, ran several steps, then fell dead. Armstrong then cracked Hardin over the head with the barrel of his Colt. When Hardin woke up two hours later, tightly handcuffed, he asked Armstrong if he had a warrant for his arrest. Armstrong said no, but he would get one.

DOING TIME FOR HIS CRIMES

Hardin was taken back to Comanche, where he was convicted for the murder of Charles Webb, despite witnesses who said that Webb had tried to shoot him in the back. He was sentenced to twenty-five years hard labor in Huntsville State Penitentiary.

He tried to escape several times and was severely beaten for his pains. Then he began to cooperate. He took Sunday-school class, ran a debating team, and completed his studies in law. He also wrote copious letters to Jane until she died in 1892. A little over a year later, after serving fifteen years in jail, he was pardoned.

Hardin returned to Gonzales County to practice law and see his children, though relations were strained. The following year, the 41-year-old Hardin married 15-year-old Callie Lewis. The marriage lasted less than a week—some say an hour—before Hardin returned her to her parents.

GUNNED DOWN IN EL PASO

After standing for sheriff of Gonzales—and losing—Hardin moved to El Paso where he opened a law office. But he only attracted one client, a cattle rustler named Martin McRose, whose wife, a former prostitute named Beulah, interceded. A relationship blossomed between Beulah and the attorney, Hardin. When McRose crossed the border to surrender, he was shot dead by two law officers.

With Beulah, Hardin began dictating his autobiography *The Life of John Wesley Hardin as Written by Himself*. The relationship was drunken and violent.

On August 19, 1895, Hardin had a quarrel with gunman-turned-lawman John Selman. That night, around eleven o'clock, Hardin was playing dice in the Acme Saloon when Selman walked in and shot him in the back of the head, firing three more times as he fell.

Selman claimed that he had shouted a word of warning and the bullet that the coroner said exited through Hardin's eye went in through it. Hardin's guns had not been fired. Selman was acquitted and went on to wear the tin star again. However, a few months later, he was killed in a gunfight with a U.S. marshal.

Texas Ranger John Armstrong.

WES HARDIN IS KILLED

San Antonio Herald-Post
Tuesday, August 20, 1895
Justice Howe issued a warrant for John Selman's arrest this afternoon and ordered him held under arrest until bail was fixed.

The wounds on Hardin's body were in the back of his head, coming out just over the left eye; another shot in the right breast, just missing the nipple, and another through the right arm. The body was embalmed by Undertaker Powell and will be interred at Concordia at 4 p.m.

Post-mortem picture of John Wesley Hardin, in which bullet holes can be seen above his left eye and next to his right nipple.

SAMUEL COLT

An American inventor and industrialist born in 1814, Samuel Colt's Patent Fire-Arms Manufacturing Company made assembly line production of the revolver commercially viable. His business expanded rapidly after 1847, when the Texas Rangers ordered 1,000 revolvers during the American war with Mexico. During the American Civil War, his factory in Hartford, Connecticut, supplied firearms both to the North and the South. Colt's guns were part of a larger technological revolution in the last four decades of the nineteenth century that transformed the United States. When more than two million people flooded into the American West almost all of them relied on firearms in one way or another.

COLT'S NEW MODEL ARMY METALLIC CARTRIDGE REVOLVING PISTOL.

The Drawing is one-half the size of the Pistol.

cal. .45 inch.   PRICE $20,00.

SAMUEL COLT'S REVOLVERS

In 1846, Captain Samuel Walker, a former Texas Ranger, helped Samuel Colt redesign the features of the Colt Paterson including replacing the folding trigger with a conventional enclosed trigger. The result, in 1847, was the Colt Walker, a massive .44 caliber, six-shot "hand cannon," weighing 4 pounds 10 ounces with a 9-inch barrel. It was to be the most powerful handgun for 100 years to come.

In 1848, Colt produced a lighter version of the Colt Walker for use on horseback, called the Colt Dragoon along with a series of smaller .31 caliber pocket pistols. In 1850, he developed the .36 Colt Navy with a 7½-inch octagonal barrel, weighing just two pounds ten ounces. Then in 1860, changing to a round barrel design, Colt upgraded the .36 Navy to the .44 Colt Army Model 1860. With a six-shot,

rotating cylinder, the Colt Single Action Army (SAA) became the most widely used revolver of the Civil War.

The Colt SAA was manufactured in three major barrel lengths; 7½-inch, 5½-inch, and 4¾-inch. The shorter the barrel, the quicker the draw, and the 4¾-inch became the gunslingers weapon of choice. Colt went on to produce revolvers in many different barrel lengths, and legend has it that the 16-inch "Buntline" long-barrel Colt was used by Wyatt Earp at the O.K. Corral.

Samuel Colt died in 1862, but his company continued. In 1873, it produced the .45-caliber metallic cartridge New Model Single Action Army revolver, the "Peacemaker," which became the most famous sidearm in the West.

1. Colt .45 Peacemaker.
2. 4¾-inch engraved Colt .45 and holster.
3. Colt Baby Dragoon 1848.
4. Colt Pocket Revolver 1849.
5. Colt Army Fluted 1860.
6. Colt Army 1860.
7. Colt Police 1862.
8. Colt Walker 1847.
9. Leather holster.
10. Colt Dragoon 1848.
11. .36 Colt Paterson 1838.
12. Colt Navy 1851.
13. .28 Colt Paterson 1836.
14. Deluxe Engraved Colt Army 1861.
15. Colt Pocket Revolver 1849.
16. 16-inch barrel Colt Buntline.
17. 4-inch Colt .45 Sheriff's Model.

On a gathering storm comes
A tall handsome man
In a dusty black coat with
A red right hand.
Lyrics from Red Right Hand
by Nick Cave & the Bad Seeds (1994)

PART TWO

OUTLAWS AND VIGILANTES

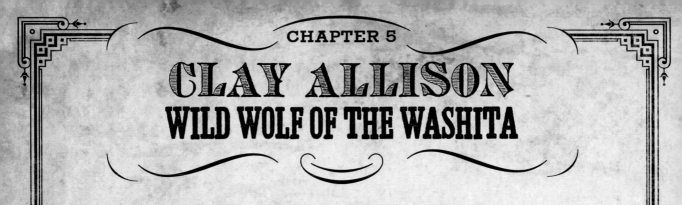

CHAPTER 5

CLAY ALLISON
WILD WOLF OF THE WASHITA

"MANY OF HIS STERN DEEDS WERE FOR THE RIGHT ... AS HE UNDERSTOOD THAT RIGHT TO BE."

Globe Live Stock Journal *about Clay Allison*

From his youth, Clay Allison was known for his violent mood swings and his quick temper. Enlisting in the Tennessee Light Artillery during the Civil War, he was discharged from the Confederate Army after three months because, his service record said, he was "incapable of performing the duties of a soldier because of a blow received many years ago. Emotional or physical excitement produces paroxysmal of a mixed character, partly epileptic and partly maniacal. He is suffering from such a paroxysmal caused by an attack of [illegible] during which he manifested an exact [illegible] to commit suicide ... "

Born in 1840 in Waynesboro, Tennessee, Clay Allison was six feet two with an athletic build and black wavy hair. His eyes were a fierce-looking blue and his right eye was slightly cocked. He also had a crippled right leg and walked with a limp. Later he accidentally shot himself in the foot and had to walk with a stick.

More often drunk than sober, alcohol increased his bloodlust. His first victim was thought to have been a corporal of the Third Illinois Cavalry who broke one of his mother's favorite serving pitchers during a Union raid on their farm in Wayne County. Such incidents were not uncommon.

REBEL SCOUTING AND SPYING

Allison re-enlisted in the Ninth Tennessee Cavalry, where he served as a scout. He claimed to have been captured and sentenced to death as a spy, but escaped from Johnson Island in Sandusky Bay, off Lake Erie, on the eve of his execution after killing a guard and swimming ashore. There is no record of this and the story may be apocryphal.

After the war, he set out for a new life in the West with two of his brothers, his sister, and her husband. During a dispute on the Brazos River in Texas, he beat a ferryman named Zackery Colbert to a pulp, stole his boat and ferried the family across himself. Then he became a wrangler in Texas and New Mexico. Allison considered himself to be more of a shootist than gunman.

WEIRD NAKED TALES

Until Clay Allison arrived in New Mexico, his reputation as a hell-raiser was based on legend and has since been embellished with further yarns and myths. Examples include the oft-quoted story of his bare-assed horseback ride through Canadian, Texas, and the anecdote of his naked knife fight in a grave.

Legend has it that one day in 1866, Allison was said to have ridden into the town of Canadian, naked except for a gun belt, firing his revolver. When the town marshal tried to arrest him, he turned his pistol on the peace officer, marched him to the saloon, and forced him to buy a drink. Sometime later he is said to have fought a naked duel with Bowie knives in an open grave the contestants had dug for the loser. A challenge along these lines seems to have been issued in Pecos, Texas, but the grave had not been completed by the time of

Allison's death. The truth of both stories is highly questionable.

LYNCH MOB IN ELIZABETHTOWN

Allison became a rancher in his own right. Then one night he was drinking in a saloon in Elizabethtown, New Mexico, with a Texan named David Crockett, when the wife of one Charles Kennedy came in, saying that her husband had killed their infant daughter, as well as several other people.

Allison and Crockett went to investigate. There was no evidence of foul play and Kennedy was too drunk to answer questions, nevertheless they brought him into town and jailed him. When the local judge ordered that Kennedy's property be searched, two sackfuls of bones were found—though five medical men could not agree whether there were any human bones among them.

Nevertheless, Allison and Crockett broke into the jail, took Kennedy to the town slaughterhouse, and lynched him. It was said that Allison got carried way, cut Kennedy's head off, and displayed it on a spike in his favorite bar, Henri Lambert's saloon in Cimarron, New Mexico.

DINNER WITH A KILLER

The well-known gunman Chunk Colbert decided to kill Allison. To lure him away from his home turf, he challenged Allison to a horse race at Clifton House, an inn and store on the Canadian River in Colfax County. The race was declared a dead heat. The two men then went to have dinner together.

Afterward, Colbert still intended to kill Allison. As he reached for the coffee pot with one hand, he gripped his pistol with the other. Allison spotted what was coming and drew his own revolver. Colbert rushed his shot and hit the table-top. Allison's shot hit him just above the right eye.

Asked why he had accepted a dinner invitation from someone who was trying to kill him, Allison replied: "Because I didn't want to send a man to hell on an empty stomach."

Colbert's friend Charles Cooper who witnessed the event made no move to draw his gun. Later he rode off toward Cimarron with Allison and was never seen again.

DRAWING AGAINST MASON T. BOWMAN

Mason T. Bowman sought out Allison to see who was quickest on the draw. Witnesses said that Bowman beat him to the draw nearly every time. Tiring of this game, the two drunken gunmen stripped down to their underwear and began dancing with each other. Then they took turns to shoot at each other's feet to see who was the better dancer. Somehow the competition ended without bloodshed.

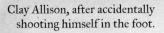

Clay Allison, after accidentally shooting himself in the foot.

SAMUEL B. AXTELL
(1819 – 1891)

Born near Columbus, Ohio, Samuel Beach Axtell spent most of his youth in New Jersey. After attending college, he graduated as a lawyer in 1843 and practiced law in Michigan until 1851. He moved to California and was elected to Congress in 1866. He became governor of Utah in 1874 and subsequently governor of New Mexico in 1875.

However, during his New Mexico term of office, violent feuding broke out between two groups of Lincoln County settlers, the recently-arrived Tunstall-McSween group and the more established Murphy-Dolan group. Axtell sided with Murphy and Dolan and their backers, the corrupt local businessmen of the "Santa Fe Ring." He was blamed for failing to stop the escalating civil unrest and was suspended from office in 1878.

Despite his controversial governorship, Axtell was appointed Chief Justice of the New Mexico Supreme Court in August 1882, a position he held until May 1885 after which he returned to practicing law. He died in 1891, and was buried in Morristown, New Jersey.

THE SANTA FE RING

In the late 19th century, New Mexico had a governor appointed by the U.S. president. From 1875 to 1878, Samuel B. Axtell was Santa Fe governor but was also part of a political clique—the Santa Fe Ring—that had considerable power over the territory. Allison opposed the Santa Fe Ring, and when fellow opponent, the Reverend F.J. Tolby, was murdered, local ne'er-do-well Cruz Vega was suspected. Clay was a man who went to extreme lengths to extract retribution when he felt he had been wronged. His upbringing demanded a settling of scores for the death of Reverend Tolby.

A masked mob including Allison strung up Vega from a telegraph pole. Vega told his assailants that it was another Mexican named Manuel Cardenas who had murdered the minister. This did not save his life. Left dangling, someone put a bullet in his back, then Allison allegedly tied the lynching rope around the pommel of his saddle and dragged the corpse through the greasewood.

Vega was a friend, or possibly a relative, of *pistolero* Francisco "Pancho" Griego, who had killed three soldiers in a saloon brawl six months earlier. Pancho let it be known that he blamed Allison and would avenge Vega's murder. He met Allison outside the St. James Hotel at Cimarron with some friends. They went inside for a drink.

When the two men stepped aside for a private conversation, Allison drew his pistol and shot Griego three times. He fell dead. The lights then went out as Allison made his escape in the darkness. According to *The Daily New Mexican* of November 5, 1875:

> *Francisco Griego was well known in Santa Fe where his mother resides. He has killed a great many men, and was considered a dangerous man; few regret his loss.*

Manuel Cardenas was arrested, but before he could be tried he was killed by vigilantes. Allison was blamed.

STOP PRESS

Allison was plainly out of control. He threatened to kill his brother-in-law, but was pacified by his sister. In a raid on a mule corral, Allison accidentally shot himself in the foot. When the doctor delayed coming, out of fear, Allison promised to deal with him, once the foot had healed.

He made knife attacks on the Colfax County court clerk and an attorney, pinning them to the wall by the sleeve. Another man who had a drunken argument with Allison fled the town when he heard that Clay was looking for him.

Governor Samuel B. Axtell put a $500 reward on Allison's head. When still no one tried to arrest Clay, the editor of the *Cimarron News and Press* wrote a caustic editorial. Allison trashed the newspaper office and dumped the type and presses in the Cimarron River. As the front page had already been printed, Allison marked these the "Clay Allison Edition" and sold them at twenty-five-cents a copy. The following day, when he sobered up, he paid the newspaper $200 in damages.

SENDING THE CAVALRY

When three African-American soldiers were shot dead as they walked into Lambert's Saloon, Allison was suspected. A detachment of cavalry then came to the aid of Colfax County Sheriff Isaac Rhinehart, who had been too afraid to arrest Allison on his own. Clay only submitted to being arrested if he was allowed to keep his firearms.

It seemed that two of Allison's friends were responsible for shooting the soldiers. Nevertheless, he was charged with the murders of Chunk Colbert, Charles Cooper, and Francisco Griego, but was acquitted due to lack of evidence. Later he boarded a stagecoach carrying Governor Axtell and told him what he thought of his reward.

DANCEHALL SHOOT-OUT

On December 21, 1876, Allison and his brother John were celebrating in the Olympic Dancing Hall at Las Animas, Colorado. Deputy Sheriff Charles Faber asked them to check their guns. They refused. Soon there were complaints from other customers. Faber armed himself with a shotgun and returned with two special deputies.

As he entered the dancehall, Faber leveled the shotgun. Someone cried: "Look out!" As John Allison turned, Faber fired, hitting him with buckshot in the shoulder and chest.

Clay Allison drew his six-shooter and loosed off four shots. The first hit Faber in the chest. As he fell dead, the shotgun went off again, the second barrel hitting John in the leg. The special deputies fled with Clay shooting after them. He then dragged the body of the dead or dying Faber over to where his brother lay to show him he had been avenged.

The brothers put up no fight when they were arrested at their lodging house. Both were charged with murder, though John was released for medical treatment. But again, at separate hearings, the charges against both of them were dismissed due to lack of evidence.

CONFRONTING WYATT EARP

On his way back from St. Louis, Allison stopped by in Dodge City, Kansas, after a young Texan named George R. Hoyt, who had worked for Clay, had been shot by members of the local police force. The lawmen concerned were thought to be Assistant Marshal Wyatt Earp and Bat Masterson's younger brother James.

Allison was intent on confronting Earp and Masterson. There are various versions of what happened. One was that Allison and Earp had a scrap; another was that Allison was arrested for being drunk and disorderly.

However, according to George T. Hinkle, bartender at ex-Mayor George M. Hoover's saloon, a meeting was arranged between Allison and Ford County Sheriff Bat Masterson, Earp, and City Marshal Charles E. Bassett. It passed off peacefully and Allison left town. By then in his forties, Allison seems to have been calming down.

WILD WOLF OF THE WASHITA

He moved to Hemphill County, Texas, where he married and had two children. Although this had a sobering effect on him, he was still known locally as the "Wild Wolf of the Washita."

Proud of his "Wild Wolf" reputation, Allison rode to Pecos, Texas, to confront Jen Clayton, who had cast aspersions on his fighting ability. Meanwhile, later in New Mexico, friends had to talk him out of killing two young cowhands who had made similar remarks about him.

When a dentist extracted the wrong tooth, Allison pulled one of the dentist's with a pair of forceps, and was about to pull another, along with part of the man's lips, when his screams attracted a crowd and Allison desisted.

But despite his wild man reputation, Allison didn't die with a gun in his hand. On July 1, 1887, he was carrying supplies home from Pecos, Texas, when a sack of grain fell from the wagon. When he made a grab for it, he fell. A wagon wheel ran over him and broke his neck. He died soon after the accident.

CLAY ALLISON KNEW NO FEAR

In the *Globe Live Stock Journal* of Dodge City, July 26, 1887, Clay Allison's obituary read:

Clay Allison ... knew no fear ... To incur his enmity was about equivalent to a death sentence. He contended always that he never killed a man willingly; but that the necessity in every instance had been thrust upon him. He was expert with his revolver, and never failed to come out first best in a deadly encounter. Whether this brave, genteel border man was in truth a villain or a gentleman is a question that many who knew him never settled to their own satisfaction. Certain it is that many of his stern deeds were for the right as he understood that right to be.

GUNFIGHT
N.C. WYETH
(1882 – 1945)

Wyeth's illustrations were designed to be understood quickly; his style was realistic, direct, and dramatic. *Gunfight*, an up-close, desperate saloon shoot-out, is a 1916 illustration for Frank H. Spearman's western novel *Nan of Music Mountain*.

JESSE JAMES
THE RISE AND FALL OF A LEGEND

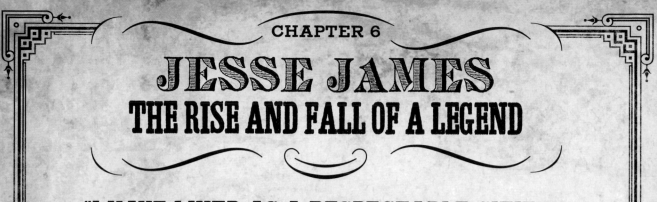

"I HAVE LIVED AS A RESPECTABLE CITIZEN AND OBEYED THE LAWS OF THE UNITED STATES TO THE BEST OF MY KNOWLEDGE."

Jesse James (1847 – 82)

Jesse Woodson James was born in Clay County, Missouri, on September 5, 1847. His brother and fellow outlaw Alexander Franklin "Frank" James was four and a half years older. Their father Robert S. James, a Baptist preacher, died in the California Gold Rush in 1850. To make ends meet, in 1852, their mother Zerelda Cole James married wealthy farmer Benjamin Simms. But Simms was apparently abusive to Frank and Jesse, so Zerelda left him and, when he died, married a gentle soul named Dr. Reuben Samuel in 1855. Zerelda and Reuben Samuel owned seven slaves who worked as farmhands.

RIDING WITH QUANTRILL'S RAIDERS

When the Civil War started, as a border state, Missouri was ripped apart by split loyalties. With the state riven by a vicious guerrilla war between Confederate secessionist "bushwhackers" and Unionist "jayhawkers," the James family allied themselves with the Confederate cause. Frank James joined a local band of Confederate guerrillas and fought at the Battle of Wilson's Creek. In 1863, he was identified as a member of a guerrilla gang that operated in Clay County and was hunted down by Union militia. Frank evaded arrest, but the militia raided the James-Samuel farm, tortured Reuben Samuel and whipped young Jesse. Frank went on to join the Confederate guerrillas led by William C. Quantrill, and legend has it that he and

the Younger brothers, Cole and Jim, second cousins by marriage, took part in the notorious Lawrence Massacre, when over two-hundred Union supporters were slaughtered in Kansas.

They rode with Quantrill's Raiders to Texas during the winter of 1863 – 64, but returned to Clay County in the spring of 1864 in a gang of raiders led by Fletch Taylor. Sixteen-year-old Jesse joined his brother in Taylor's gang, seeking cold-blooded revenge against the Unionists.

Fletch Taylor was shot in the summer of 1864 and his right arm was amputated, so the James boys joined up with "Bloody Bill" Anderson's pro-Confederate bushwhackers. Jesse was badly wounded twice but continued looting and killing with the Raiders until the end of the Civil War. It was reported that both Frank and Jesse James took part in the atrocities at Centralia, Missouri on September 27, 1864, when twenty-four unarmed Union troops were captured and executed. Legend has it that some of the dead were scalped and dismembered.

TURNING TO CRIME

Toward the end of the Civil War, on April 15, 1865, Jesse and six other Confederate guerrillas were heading for Lexington, Missouri, under a white flag of surrender, when they were attacked by a column of Union cavalrymen. Jesse was shot through the right lung, but managed to escape. When he was eventually picked up by the authorities, it was assumed he was going to die, so they allowed him to return to his mother and stepfather. During his convalescence, he met his future wife, his cousin Zerelda "Zee" Mimms.

After he recovered, Jesse took to drinking and gambling, gathering around him a band of war-hardened former guerrillas including brother Frank and the Younger brothers. Unable or unwilling to go back to farming, they decided to employ the terror tactics they had learned during the war in the lucrative business of bank robbing. Although Jesse was the youngest of the gang, he was undoubtedly the leader.

DAYLIGHT ROBBERY

On the morning of February 14, 1866, a dozen men of the James-Younger gang rode into Liberty, Missouri. Two then walked into the Clay County Savings and Loan Bank and produced revolvers. The cashier and his son were locked in the vault, while the robbers took $15,000 in gold coins and $45,000 in bonds. These were no good to them and were later thrown away.

Outside, the rest of the gang shot randomly into the air and at windows to frighten off any opposition. The robbers emerged with the loot in a wheat sack, having pulled off

Jesse Woodson James, age 17, from a tintype made in 1864. He is armed with three Colt 1860 Army revolvers, two are worn reversed in his belt in typical Civil War guerilla style.

the first armed daylight robbery of a bank in U.S. history. As they made off, they shot a nineteen-year-old student who crossed the street at the wrong time—adding to the gang's notoriety. A posse chased the outlaws, but returned after a few hours, saying that the trail had been covered by a fresh fall of snow.

The robbers then had the problem of disposing of the gold coins without attracting attention. So they rode south to San Antonio, Texas, where they exchanged the gold for silver coins and greenback dollar bills. Dividing the spoils, the gang members got $1,000 each.

Jesse (left), age 25, and Frank James, age 29, in 1872.

For the James brothers and the Youngers this easy money was compelling. On October 30, they hit another bank in Lexington, Missouri. Then in Richmond, Missouri, the citizens put up a fight. A banker was wounded and three others, including the mayor, were killed, but the robbers made off with $4,000.

Other banks were robbed. No one could say whether the James or the Younger boys were involved, but they were usually blamed.

SHOOTING NIMROD LONG

On March 21, 1868, the James and Younger brothers rode into Russellville, Kentucky, with four other men. Jesse led the way into the bank, but a number of warning shots had to be fired before the cashier, Morton Barkley, would hand over the money.

The shots alerted the bank's President, Nimrod Long, who was eating lunch at his nearby home. He ran back to the bank, sounding the alarm as he went. Entering through the back door, he ran into Jesse in the hallway. During the scuffle, Jesse managed to fire two shots. One grazed Long's head and knocked him to the floor.

Jesse ran out to the front, shouting that he had killed the bank president. The robbers scrambled for their horses. As they made off, Long staggered out of the front door. Galloping away, the outlaws fired a couple more shots at the wounded Long as he called for help.

JESSE JAMES THE LEGEND

Fame came when the gang robbed the Daviess County Savings Association in Gallatin, Missouri, on December 7, 1869. Jesse shot the proprietor, John W. Sheets, a former army officer. He had mistaken him for Samuel P. Cox, also a businessman in the town, who had been the Union colonel responsible for the death of Bloody Bill Anderson. The clerk, William McDowell, was also shot in the arm, but managed to make his way out onto the street where he raised the alarm.

WILLIAM C. QUANTRILL

Born in Canal Dover, Ohio in 1837, William C. Quantrill was a schoolteacher and a farmer, before turning to thieving and murder. In 1860, he was charged with being a horse thief and began a life of crime on the run, sometimes profiting from capturing runaway slaves. At the outbreak of the Civil War he became a Kansas Jayhawker, freeing slaves and, at the same time, freeing slaveholders of their cash. However, he was none too particular about who he shot and, as the killings mounted, the Union outlawed him and the military were ordered to shoot him down.

He fled to Richmond, Virginia, where he was commissioned as a Confederate officer and learned guerrilla tactics with the First Cherokee Regiment. After fighting at the Battle of Wilson's Creek, Quantrill then formed his own band.

In August 1863, they attacked Lawrence, Kansas, home of Senator James H. Lane, head of the Jayhawkers, killing over 150 men, often in front of their families, and burning down the town. Two months later, Quantrill's men slaughtered ninety soldiers at Baxter Springs, Kansas. As Union forces took reprisals, Quantrill rode south to Texas where the guerrillas broke up into smaller bands. One of them, under William T. "Bloody Bill" Anderson, returned to Missouri, where they became the state's most feared guerrilla band.

At Centralia, Missouri, they massacred twenty-four unarmed Union soldiers. Jesse James was credited with shooting the Union commander, Major A.V.E. Johnson. In the ensuing battle, another 125 were killed. Anderson was killed in October 1864, at age twenty-four, charging a Union detachment, under Lieutenant Colonel Samuel P. Cox, sent to kill or capture him.

A month after the Confederate surrender, Quantrill was mortally wounded in a Union ambush and died four weeks later. He was twenty-seven.

Charcoal drawing of William C. Quantrill by A.L. Dillenbeck, 1890.

The robbers then fled with a small haul of loot. One had trouble mounting his unruly horse and had to double up on horseback as they made their escape through the middle of a posse. Later they stole an extra horse from a farmer and made their way back to Clay County.

After the Gallatin robbery, the name of Jesse James appeared in the newspapers for the first time. Noting the power of the press, Jesse then began to use the newspapers to protest his innocence. Soon after the Gallatin raid, the *Kansas City Times* ran a "report" that Jesse had written for them:

> *Miss Susie James, a sister of the accused, swears that her brother Jesse and herself attended preaching in Greenville, Clay County, on Sunday, December 5th, and after their return, Jesse sold her bay mare Kate (the one left by the murderer at Gallatin) to a stranger who said he was from Topeka, Kansas. She further testifies that her brother was at home on the 7th.*
>
> *Zerelda Samuel, mother of the accused, swears that her son Jesse was at home December 6th, 7th, and 8th, and that he sold his sister's mare to a man from Topeka, Kansas, for five $100 bills on Sunday, the 6th, Reuben Samuel, step-father of the accused, testifies to the same thing.*

ASSAULT ON SAMUEL'S FARM

The James brothers were officially declared outlaws and Missouri Governor Thomas T. Crittenden offered a reward of $3,000. On December 15, 1869, four men led by Deputy Sheriff John Thomason approached Samuel's farm. Alerted, Frank and Jesse came bolting out of the barn astride swift mounts.

Thomason and his men headed after them. Fearing they would get away, the deputy stopped and dismounted. Resting his gun across the saddle, he took careful aim and fired at the fleeing brothers. But his horse bolted. Riderless, it caught up with the James brothers. One of them shot it dead and they made good their escape.

CREATING HAVOC AND MAYHEM

During the early 1870s, the James-Younger gang caused chaos wherever they went, in an unprecedented crime wave of hold-ups and robberies.

On September 26, 1872, at the crowded Kansas City Fair, three mounted men robbed the cashier and ticket seller, Ben Wallace. One of them, said to be Jesse James, grabbed the cashbox, pocketed the contents, and threw the box aside. Wallace grappled with the robber, who drew a gun and fired a shot. The bullet hit a small girl in the legs, and the robbers escaped into the nearby woods.

Bloody Bill Anderson photographed shortly after his death on October 27, 1864, in Richmond, Missouri. Dramatically posed with gun in hand.

By that time, the banks were getting tired of being robbed and had called in the Pinkerton's National Detective Agency, so the James boys took to robbing trains instead. On the night of July 23, 1873, they derailed the Rock Island Express, fifty miles east of Council Bluffs, Iowa, by ripping up part of the track. The train rolled over and the boiler exploded, scalding the engineer to death. But the gang, it seems, had hit the wrong train and made off with just $7,000.

To make up the deficit, they held up a stagecoach near Malvern, Arkansas. Two weeks later, they robbed the Iron Mountain Express at Gads Hill, Missouri. Instead of derailing the train, they held the entire population of Gads Hill hostage until the robbery was over.

The gang next robbed a train on the Kansas Pacific Railroad near Muncie, Kansas, on December 8, 1874. It was one of the outlaws' most successful robberies, netting them $30,000. Gang member William "Bud" McDaniel, was captured by a Kansas City police officer after the robbery, and later was shot during an escape attempt.

HUNTED DOWN BY THE PINKERTONS

In 1874, the James boys had enough money to marry and settle down. By all accounts they were attentive husbands and fathers. However, Jesse kept up a stream of letters to the *Kansas City Times*, denying the latest robbery was theirs.

This made little difference to the men of the Pinkerton's Detective Agency who were determined to build a reputation for bringing outlaws to justice. Two Pinkerton agents, named Louis J. Lull (a.k.a. W.J. Allen) and John Boyle (a.k.a. James Wright), engaged John and Jim Younger in a gunfight on a Missouri road on March 16, 1874. Boyle fled the scene, but both John Younger and Louis Lull were killed.

Another Pinkerton agent, W.J. Whicher, who was tracking the James brothers, was abducted and later found dead at the side of

a rural road in Jackson County, Missouri. By the time the body was discovered, hogs had eaten away part of his face.

The Pinkertons were now out for revenge, and in January 1875, they heard that the James brothers were visiting their family on Samuel's farm. Two men thought to be Pinkerton agents fire-bombed the place, mutilating the arm of their mother, killing their eight-year-old half-brother Archie, and injuring their African-American servant.

Newspapers denounced the savagery of the attack. Feelings ran high among those of the local population who still held deep feelings for the Confederacy, and the Pinkertons eventually dropped the case.

RETURN OF THE CONFEDERATE HERO

With Southern public opinion running in their favor, the James brothers returned to their old robbing ways. On September 1, 1875, during the hold-up of the Huntington National Bank in West Virginia, Bud McDaniel's brother, Tom, was shot and killed, and another new gang member, Tom Webb, was captured.

The James brothers moved on to Nashville, Tennessee, possibly to avoid any further problems from the Pinkertons. Jesse's letters to the press grew increasingly political. He asserted that he was a Confederate hero being persecuted by vindictive Radical Republicans who, following Reconstruction, were being driven from office by traditionally pro-slavery Southern Democrats.

Following the gang's successful robbery of the Kansas Pacific Railroad, they took on the Missouri Pacific. They stacked cross-ties on the line at a sharp turn in the track at Rocky Cut near Otterville, Missouri, and waited for the engineer to bring the train to a grinding halt. The outlaws made off with $8,000. However, Hobbs Kerry, a new man with the James-Youngers, was arrested soon after and betrayed the gang by identifying his accomplices.

Founded by former deputy sheriff of Cook County, Illinois, Allan Pinkerton in 1850, the agency became famous when Pinkerton claimed to have foiled an 1861 plot to assassinate Abraham Lincoln, who later hired Pinkerton agents as his bodyguards during the Civil War. At the behest of General George B. McClellan,

Pinkerton also organized a system of obtaining military information in the Southern states which developed into the U.S. Secret Service.

In 1866, Pinkerton's captured the principals in the theft of $700,000 from the Adams Express Company safes on a train of the New York, New Haven & Hartford Railway, and recovered all but $12,000 of the stolen money.

Five years later, the agency was employed by the new Department of Justice for "the detection and prosecution of those guilty of violating federal law." It also hired itself out to banks and railroads as security. At one time it was thought to have more personnel than the U.S. Army.

Later the agency got involved in strike-breaking and in 1893 the Anti-Pinkerton Act banned the federal government from hiring private investigators. These days, Pinkertons still exist as a division of the Swedish company Securitas.

THE GREAT NORTHFIELD, MINNESOTA RAID

For weeks, gang member Bill Chadwell had been trying to persuade Jesse James that the banks they had been robbing were not worthwhile. There were richer pickings in Minnesota, he said, even though he was already a wanted man in that state. Jesse was eventually reluctantly persuaded.

But Bill Chadwell had left out one simple, obvious fact—Minnesota was not Missouri. Legends in their own time, popular in Missouri for actively trying to further the Confederate cause, the gang had never operated in the North before. Their bank and train robbery exploits had all been in old Confederate states where the people were still full of Southern hospitality. Minnesota had suffered badly in the Civil War, losing many men at Gettysburg. Minnesotans did not take kindly to Confederate outlaws and "Johnny Reb" bank robbers.

Oblivious to the coming catastrophe, the gang went ahead and planned a big-time bank raid in Minnesota. To avoid attracting too much attention, Jesse and Frank James, Cole Younger, Jim Younger and Bob Younger, Clell Miller, Bill Chadwell, and Charley Pitts quietly rode north out of Missouri in pairs.

They met up in St. Paul, Minnesota and then turned south-west to check out the bank at Mankato. However, that bank was undergoing reconstruction work, making a robbery problematic. So they split up again and, posing as cattle buyers, moved onto Northfield. Approaching the town from different directions, they checked out escape routes and the routine of the law officers, and cased their new target—the First National Bank.

THE PLAN STARTS TO UNRAVEL

The plan was for Jesse, Bob Younger, and Charley Pitts to amble into town, have lunch, then hang around outside the bank, before robbing it. The others would create a diversion. Using the old Quantrill swoop and hurrah tactics, Cole Younger and Clell Miller would come charging into town from the north, while Frank James, Jim Younger, and Bill Chadwell would charge in from the south.

At two o'clock in the afternoon of September 7, 1876, the squad hit the town, shooting and screaming rebel yells. However, the robbers outside the bank had already been spotted and the element of surprise had gone. Local citizens, recognizing what was happening, had armed themselves and were ready to resist the robbery.

When the three men rushed into the bank, cashier Joseph Lee Heywood refused to cooperate. He was cracked over the head with a revolver and a Bowie knife was held to his throat. Another teller, Alonzo E. Bunker, who tried to lock the back door, fled with a bullet in his shoulder. He survived.

By this time, there was a full-scale battle going on outside. Up for the fight, two hardware stores had handed out guns. Clell Miller was shot and killed by a medical student, who later displayed his skeleton in his office once qualified. Meanwhile, Cole Younger shouted at a seventeen-year-old boy to get off the street. He was an immigrant from Sweden and understood no English. Younger killed him. Wounded in the shoulder, Younger, lurched into the bank shouting: "Let's get out of here! They're killing us!"

THE FINAL SHOWDOWN

The robbers grabbed what money they could. Cashier Heywood tried to close the till drawer and got a bullet in the head for his pains. Every one of the outlaw gang was wounded. Cole Younger was hit in the thigh, Jim in the shoulder, and Bob's elbow was shattered. Frank and Jesse James were peppered with shotgun pellets. Pitts was wounded in the leg and his horse had also been shot. Cole Younger pulled him up behind him and rode fast out of town.

Minnesotans joined posses and set up picket lines by the hundreds, as the entire male population of Northfield spread out in pursuit. The heavens opened and the countryside turned into a quagmire. Because the Youngers were badly injured and were slowing them down, the James brothers made off, but Pitts remained behind with the Youngers.

A contemporary drawing shows Northfield citizens responding to the bank robbery attempt by Jesse James and his gang.

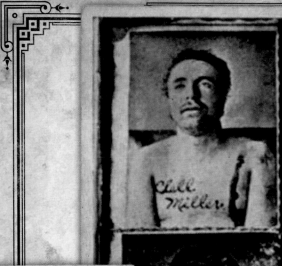

Composite photographs of the James-Younger gang members killed or captured in Northfield were popular for years following the robbery in 1876. Clockwise from top left: Clell Miller, Bill Chadwell, Jim Younger, Bob Younger, Cole Younger, and Charley Pitts.

NORTHFIELD BANK ROBBERS.

THE YOUNGER BROTHERS

There were four Younger brothers—Cole (1844 – 1916), Jim (1848 – 1902), John (1851 – 74), and Bob (1853 – 89). They were born and brought up in Lee's Summit, Missouri. When Kansas Jayhawkers raided their farm and killed their father, Cole and Jim joined Quantrill's Raiders and were present at the Lawrence massacre.

After the Civil War, they joined Frank and Jesse James to form the James-Younger gang. Later, John and Bob joined the gang and took part in a series of bank and train robberies. On March 16, 1874, John and Jim Younger were involved in a shoot-out with Pinkerton agents. During the fight, Jim took a bullet in the thigh while shooting one of the agents. John managed to shoot another of the agents but was killed by a bullet in the throat. Jim buried him by the roadside to avoid the law digging him up. John Younger was later re-buried in the Yeater-Cleveland Cemetery in St. Clair County, Missouri.

On September 7, 1876, the remaining three Younger brothers participated in the disastrous James-Younger bank raid in Northfield, Minnesota during which Cole and Bob were both badly wounded. Pursued by the local posse into a nearby swamp, Cole, Bob, and Jim Younger surrendered, while Frank and Jesse James escaped.

Pleading guilty to robbery and murder, the Youngers were sentenced to life imprisonment in the state prison at Stillwater, Minnesota.

Bob died of tuberculosis in prison in 1889. Cole and Jim were released in 1899 on condition they remained in Minnesota. Jim, who was in poor health, tried to settle down and get married. When the woman concerned refused him, he put a bullet through his brain in 1902.

Cole Younger went on to sell tombstones and insurance, and wrote his autobiography, *The Story of Cole Younger by Himself*. Returning to Missouri in 1903, he and Frank James played in Wild West tribute shows and carnivals for a few years. Then he retired to Lee's Summit, where he died of a heart attack in 1916.

Frank and Jesse James were on one horse. In the darkness, near Lake Crystal, they were spotted by a posse. One lucky shot passed through Frank's thigh, killed the horse, and lodged in Jesse's inner thigh. The two wounded men fled on foot across a cornfield. Then they stole two plow-horses from a nearby farm and escaped into Dakota territory.

Pitts and the Youngers shot their way across Blue Earth River Bridge at two o'clock that morning. They stole some chickens to eat, but were soon cornered. Pitts was cut down by a fusillade and the badly wounded Youngers surrendered. They refused to answer any questions and pleaded guilty to murder to avoid the hangman's rope.

Ironically, these Confederate outlaws who had robbed, hijacked, and ransacked their way across the Southern states during the 1870s, had finally fallen apart in the Unionist North. The days of the James-Younger gang were done. Sometimes classified by historians as postwar terrorists, the gang's failed raid is often referred to as the last major event of the American Civil War. Meanwhile, in Minnesota, every year in September, Northfield hosts *Defeat of Jesse James Days*, a re-enactment and celebration of the town's victory over the James-Younger Gang.

THOMAS B. HOWARD

But Frank and Jesse James knew no other way of life and weren't ready to retire. Recovered from their injuries, they went undercover and assumed false identities—Jesse became Thomas B. Howard, and Frank was known as B.J. Woodson. Robberies began to be attributed to Howard and Woodson, who had now assembled a whole new gang of outlaws. Two stores were hit in western Mississippi, at Washington in Adams County and Fayette in Jefferson County.

The population of Glendale, Missouri, were held hostage in the depot while a train of the Chicago & Alton Railroad was robbed at gunpoint of $35,000 on October 7, 1879. Two years later, the outlaws turned their attention to the Chicago, Rock Island & Pacific Railroad.

On July 15, 1881, Frank James and Jesse James, and another unidentified bandit boarded the evening train from Kansas City at Cameron, Missouri. They had grown thick beards to conceal their identity further. Sixty miles further on, at Winston, four more bearded men boarded the train, just as darkness fell.

As the train left the station, conductor William Westfall was collecting fares in the smoking car. He found the aisle blocked by a bearded gunman who told the conductor to get his hands up. But Westfall turned and the bandit shot him in the back. He staggered to the door and a second slug sent the conductor tumbling off the rear platform of the train onto the tracks.

The passengers began to panic and scramble for the exit. The outlaws fired shots overhead and ordered them back to their seats. One man, a stone mason named Frank McMillan, was shot and killed.

The robbers ordered the engineer at gunpoint to stop the train and then forced their way into the express car. They pistol-whipped the guard, took his keys, and opened the safe. Having escaped with $10,000, Governor Crittenden increased the rewards on Frank and Jesse's heads to $5,000 each.

MURDERED BY A COWARD

While other members of the gang were arrested, Frank and Jesse James continued to elude the law. They were living in St. Joseph, Missouri, planning new robberies. Constantly in need of new men, gang member Charley Ford introduced his younger brother Bob, who was still only twenty.

At the time, the James brothers were planning to rob the Platte City Bank, but the Fords realized that their cut would be small compared to the $5,000 bounty on each of Frank and Jesse's heads. They consulted Governor Crittenden and asked whether he wanted the James brothers dead or alive. Crittenden said that it did not matter. So they dreamed up a plan to collect the bounty. When the end came, it would be fate that

Jesse James's body in 1882.

played a hand in the assassination of Jesse James.

On April 3, 1882, the Ford brothers were having breakfast with Jesse James in his home in St. Joseph. The robbery was planned for the next day. When they went through into the parlor, the notorious gang-leader decided to straighten a picture on the wall. He stepped up onto a chair and turned his back. Bob Ford seized his moment in history and shot Jesse James in the back of the head, killing him instantly.

James's body was identified, photographed, and viewed by hundreds. It was then taken back to the Samuel's farm for burial. The inscription on the tombstone read:

Devoted husband and father, Jesse Woodson James. September 5, 1847, murdered April 3, 1882 by a traitor and coward whose name is not worthy to appear here.

After his mother Zee died, Jesse's son, Jesse Edwards James, had Jesse's body disinterred and buried alongside Zee in the Mount Olive Cemetery in Kearney, Missouri.

WHAT HAPPENED TO FRANK JAMES?

Five months after the murder of Jesse James, Frank James gave himself up to Governor Crittenden on the understanding that he would not be extradited to Minnesota to stand trial for the Northfield raid. He stood trial in Missouri for robbery and murder, but was acquitted. To many, the James brothers were heroes who had stood up to the Yankees. Frank lived for another thirty years doing a number of odd jobs, including running the James-Younger Wild West Show in partnership with Cole Younger. He died in 1915.

Frank James, age 55, in 1898.

WHERE DID BOB FORD GO?

After receiving a small portion of the reward, Charley and Bob Ford fled Missouri. Sheriff James Timberlake and Marshal Henry H.Craig, who were the law enforcement officials active in the plan, took the majority of the bounty. Later the Ford brothers starred in a touring tribute stage show in which they re-enacted the shooting of Jesse James. Suffering from tuberculosis (then incurable) and a morphine addiction, Charley Ford committed suicide on May 6, 1884, in Richmond, Missouri. Bob Ford went on to operate a tent saloon in Creede, Colorado. On June 8, 1892, Edward O'Kelley went to Creede, loaded a double-barrel shotgun and entered Ford's saloon. He shot Bob Ford in the throat at point blank range, killing him instantly. O'Kelley was sentenced to life in prison, but the sentence was subsequently commuted because of a 7,000-signature petition in favor of his release. The governor pardoned him on October 3, 1902.

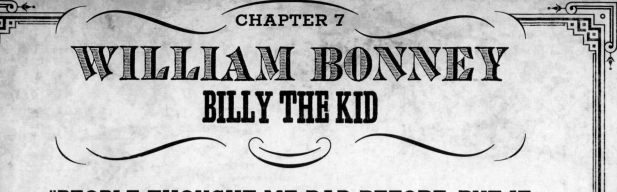

CHAPTER 7
WILLIAM BONNEY
BILLY THE KID

"PEOPLE THOUGHT ME BAD BEFORE, BUT IF EVER I SHOULD GET FREE, I'LL LET THEM KNOW WHAT BAD REALLY MEANS."

William Bonney alias Billy the Kid (1859 – 81)

WHO WAS BILLY THE KID?

William Bonney came out of nowhere—little was known about where he was born. Early in 1881, he was interviewed by a Secret Service agent about a mail fraud. His interrogator left a barely legible note saying that he "talked like he came right off the streets of New York where he was born." However, a year earlier Bonney told a census taker in Fort Sumner that he was born in Missouri.

It was not clear when he was born either. The authoritative *American National Biography* gives the date as September 15, 1859. The *Encyclopedia Americana* says November 23, 1859, while the *Encyclopedia Britannica* says November 23, 1859/60.

Then there is the question of his real name. He told the Fort Sumner census taker that his name was William Bonney. The *Encyclopedia Americana* concurs. The *American National Biography* says Henry McCarty, while the *Encyclopedia Britannica* states:

"William H. Bonney, Jr., original name Henry McCarty (?)"

All three agree that Bonney/McCarty was born in New York, rather than Missouri. However, it is perhaps somewhat fitting that there is a mystery about what the name and the date and place of birth of a person who, in some people's eyes, is the American version of Robin Hood. It is not even clear how many people he killed—somewhere between four (*American National Biography*) and

THE UPHAM TINTYPE

The first authenticated tintype image of William Bonney was taken by a traveling photographer on the street in Fort Sumner, New Mexico in 1880. It was sold at auction in 2011 to billionaire William Koch for $2.3 million.

twenty-seven (*Encyclopedia Britannica*). The *Encyclopedia Americana* says:

> By 1877, when he became a cowhand in the Pecos Valley of New Mexico, twelve murders had been charged to his account ... A total of twenty-one killings is traditionally ascribed to Billy, but there is no reliable evidence for this figure.

THE KID FROM NOWHERE

The source of much of this confusion is Marshall "Ash" Upson's book, *The Authentic Life of Billy the Kid* (ghostwriter for Sheriff Pat Garrett):

> William H. Bonney, the hero of this history, was born in the city of New York, November 23rd, 1859. But little is known of his father, as he died when Billy was very young, and he had little recollection of him. In 1862 the family, consisting of the father, mother, and two boys, of whom Billy was the eldest, emigrated to Coffeyville, Kansas. Soon after settling there the father died, and the mother with her two boys removed to Colorado, where she married a man named Antrim, who is said to be now living at, or near, Georgetown, in Grant County, New Mexico, and is the only survivor of their family of four, who removed to Santa Fe, New Mexico, shortly after their marriage. Billy was then four or five years of age.
>
> These facts are all that can be gleaned of Billy's early childhood, which, up to this time, would be of no interest to the reader. Antrim remained at and near Santa Fe for some years, or until Billy was about eight years of age.

HENRY MCCARTY A.K.A. WILLIAM BONNEY

It seems that his mother's name was Catherine McCarty and Billy's—or Henry's—younger brother was named Joseph McCarty. She met William Henry Antrim in Indianapolis. They moved to Wichita, Kansas, where she opened a laundry and they lived in a log cabin. She contracted tuberculosis. Seeking a dry climate to ease her condition, they moved to Silver City, New Mexico. On the way, Catherine and William Antrim got married. Henry, then fourteen, and Joseph were witnesses.

But soon their mother was dead. Henry was constantly at her bedside during her last four months. After his mother's death, Henry was taken in by Mrs. Truesdell, the mother of a friend. He worked in her hotel and was, she said, polite and hardworking. However, he fell in with a small-time thief, Sombrero Jack, nicknamed after the large Mexican hat he wore.

Sombrero Jack stole some clothes from a Chinese laundry which Henry hid for him. While Jack skedaddled, Henry was arrested, giving the name William Bonney, probably to avoid disgracing the family name. He escaped from jail by climbing up a chimney. Mrs. Truesdell fed him, gave him some money, and put him on the stagecoach to Globe, Arizona. Over the coming months William Bonney a.k.a. Henry McCarty, a.k.a. William Henry Antrim, kept on the move.

BECOMING THE KID

Two years later, William Bonney, calling himself Billy, appeared in a cantina outside Fort Grant, Arizona. Barely out of his adolescence, he became known as the Kid. He tangled with a bully named Frank "Windy" Cahill in Fort Grant who pulled a gun. The Kid shot him, stole a horse, and hightailed it out of town.

The teenage killer now became a wanderer, drifting around the cow camps on the New Mexico-Arizona frontier, and occasionally stopping for a time in mining camps and towns to gamble, drink, and work at odd jobs. During that period it is thought that he broke a friend, Melquiades Seguara, out of jail in San Elizaro, Texas.

Eventually, he made his way to Lincoln County, New Mexico. It was the nation's largest county, 150 miles east and west and 170 miles north and south. That was where the legend of Billy the Kid began.

LINCOLN COUNTY WAR

When Billy arrived in Lincoln County, he walked right into a war. His first stop was at the cow camp of Jimmy Dolan. The two men soon fell out and Billy moved on. Then he stopped by the ranch belonging to Frank and George Coe and their cousin Ab Saunders. There he met Dick Brewer, who was foreman on the spread of English rancher John Tunstall. Frank Coe recalled:

> *Tunstall saw the boy was quick to learn and was not afraid of anything ... he made Billy a present of a good horse, and a nice saddle and a new gun ... my, but the boy was proud ... said it was the first time in his life he had ever had anything given to him.*

To Billy's ears, Tunstall had a funny accent and, unusually in the Old West, a library valued at $3,000. Nevertheless, he became a father figure, and Billy the Kid quickly became the head of Tunstall's hired hands. He was happy and friendly. He laughed a lot and spent his time dancing with the local Mexican girls. But friends noticed that his pale blue eyes could suddenly become cold when strangers approached the Tunstall spread.

Lieutenant Colonel Fritz, the business partner of local boss Lawrence Murphy, had died in Germany, leaving a $10,000 life insurance policy in the name of his brother and sister who lived in Lincoln County. They retained Tunstall's partner, lawyer Alexander McSween, to collect it from the insurance company in New York. While he was away, Jimmy Dolan persuaded them to sue McSween for failing to return promptly with the money.

The Murphy-controlled sheriff of Lincoln County, William Brady, then sent a posse of

Billy the Kid and the Regulators cut loose out of John Tunstall's ranch, Lincoln, New Mexico, 1878.

Murphy's men to seize Tunstall's herds, on the grounds that he was McSween's business partner. They found the ranch had been fortified. Billy, who disliked interlopers, was ready to shoot it out.

However, Tunstall persuaded Billy and the ranch hands to back down, saying that all the cattle in the West were not worth a man's life. He would fight it out in court. But as they left the ranch, a large number of Dolan's men followed and began firing. Billy galloped to a small hill where they could make a stand. Tunstall remained behind to talk to their pursuers who shot him down dead.

THE REGULATORS

Matters soon escalated when the United Kingdom's minister to Washington insisted that the killers of a prominent British subject

be brought to justice. With the approval of President Rutherford B. Hayes, assistant U.S. attorney in New York, Judge Frank Warner Angel, was sent to investigate. He took sworn statements. One of them was from *William H. Bonney, Known as "the Kid."*

Billy was more upset than anyone at the death of his mentor, Tunstall. Plainly there was no legal remedy as Sheriff Brady had deputized the killers and given them tin star badges. A drunken Jim Riley, an associate of Murphy and Dolan, barged into a town meeting at Lincoln. Billy pulled a gun, but McSween got between them. Riley was then ejected, but he left behind a notebook containing the coded names of men who had been supplying stolen beef.

Lincoln's Justice of the Peace, John B. Wilson, deputized Dick Brewer, who was head of a band calling themselves "The Regulators." But like the sheriff's posse they were little more than vigilantes.

Wilson issued warrants, charging the members of the posse with murder. Billy the Kid was one of those deputized to go and arrest them. When he did, he was arrested himself by Sheriff Brady for "disturbing the peace." Brady further incurred Billy's wrath by refusing to release him until after Tunstall's funeral.

LAWLESS VIGILANTES

When Billy was released, he joined Brewer and a half-Cherokee named Fred Waite, who were searching for Billy Morton and Frank Baker, two members of the posse who had killed Tunstall. After an exchange of shots, Morton and Baker were arrested. But they never made it to justice. Legend has it that they were killed trying to escape that night.

Governor Sam Axtell, who was a Murphy-Dolan partisan, declared that The Regulators were now lawless vigilantes. Sheriff Brady, along with troops of the Ninth Cavalry, set off after them.

Hearing that Sheriff Brady and George Hindman, one of the posse who had shot Tunstall, were coming into Lincoln, Billy led a small group of Regulators who took up position behind the gates at the end of Tunstall's store. Brady and Hindman left the Wortley Hotel and were walking down the street when there was a volley of gunfire. Brady turned and fell dead. Hindman was hit, but made it to cover.

Billy Mathews, who had led the posse that killed Tunstall, heard the shots. As the Kid emerged from behind the gate, Mathews fired, creasing his side. More shots were exchanged, but Billy and Fred Waite managed to mount their horses and ride out of town to San Patricio, seven miles away.

"I KILLED HIM"

Three days later, Billy led a band of Regulators to find other members of the posse. They found some at the sawmill belonging to Dr. Joseph H. Blazer on the Mescalero Apache Reservation. A Regulator, named Charley Bowdre, called for them to surrender. The reply was a rifle shot that tore off his gun belt, also taking off George Coe's thumb.

The Regulators' reply hit crippled buffalo hunter Andrew "Buckshot" Roberts in the stomach and wounded Frank Middleton. As the Regulators crept up on the sawmill, there was a boom. Billy and Waite found Dick Brewer with the top of his head blown off.

"I killed the son of a bitch," shouted the dying Roberts, "I killed him."

Billy wanted to storm the sawmill, but Roberts was dying. Meanwhile Coe and Middleton needed medical attention. They were taken back to Lincoln. The following day when they returned to the sawmill, Roberts was found dead, his buffalo gun beside him.

The coroner's jury then charged "William Antrim, alias the Kid," with killing Roberts, although Bowdre had shot him. The acting sheriff, George Peppin, a Dolan associate, announced that Billy would soon be in custody. The Kid told Peppin to come and get him. Meanwhile a Lincoln County jury found in McSween's favor in the insurance case.

THE BATTLE OF LINCOLN

Tom Catron, head of the Santa Fe Ring and Murphy's principal backer, identified McSween and Billy as the main trouble-makers in Lincoln County and appealed to his friend and fellow Santa Fe Ring member, Governor Sam Axtell, to send the army to restore order. Under a new federal law, Axtell was not allowed to send in troops, but he appointed George Peppin as his full-time Sheriff of Lincoln and ordered him to hire a new gang of outlaws under notorious horse thief John Kinney to reinforce his posse. They ambushed three of Billy's friends in the Regulators. One was killed, a second badly wounded, the third, Frank Coe, was captured.

FORENSIC EVIDENCE

After close scientific investigation, world famous forensic artist Lois Gibson has come up with compelling evidence, through her scientific photo comparison methods, that the young man in the photo is truly the same William Bonney as in the first known Billy the Kid tintype. Not only do all the facial features match but the neck, hands, and body shape appear identical.

The Regulators needed more men and reinforcements arrived when a band of some thirty native New Mexicans led by Billy's friend Martin Chavez rode into town. With both sides escalating their numbers, the situation was getting out of control. Despite the new federal law, Governor Axtell increased the stakes by requesting that Colonel Nathan Dudley of the U.S. Army, from nearby Fort Stanton, assist Peppin's men to restore law and order in the town.

Dudley arrived in Lincoln with troopers, a howitzer, and a Gatling gun. During what became known as The Battle of Lincoln or "The Five-Day Battle," Dudley's men besieged McSween, Billy, and the Regulators, who had retreated to McSween's house. Shots were exchanged, one of the sheriff's men was killed and one of the Regulators wounded. A stand-off ensued for the next four days.

On the fifth day, the house was set on fire, even though McSween's wife and two daughters were still inside. Under cover of dusk, Billy and the Regulators burst out of the back door and made a dash for the horses in the corral, firing their guns as they went. But as soon as they were outside they found themselves sitting targets silhouetted against the burning building. McSween was hit five times and died. Harvey Morris, a young student who had been reading law in his office, also perished. The Regulators were defeated but Billy escaped to Fort Sumner, where he vowed to return to Lincoln one day to extract his revenge.

After taking statements from all concerned, Judge Angel returned to New York where he wrote his report. It came down on the side of McSween and alleged that Governor Axtell had taken a $2,000 bribe from Riley. Axtell was suspended from office and replaced by Lew Wallace, a former Civil War general and friend of Abraham Lincoln who was, at the time, working on his great novel *Ben Hur*.

A WEDDING PHOTOGRAPH

This tintype photograph found by Frank Abrams is only about four by three inches in size but, if authentic, could be worth millions. The men are said to be, far left: Pat Garrett; middle: Barney Mason; second from right: Billy the Kid; far right: "Dirty" Dave Rudabaugh. The man to the right of Garrett is unidentifiable. The photo is thought to have been taken at the double wedding of Garrett and Mason, that Billy the Kid was known to have attended in 1880.

ENCOUNTERING PAT GARRETT

Back in Fort Sumner, Billy became friends with Pat Garrett, then the bartender at Beaver Smith's saloon and gambling hall. Though Garrett was ten years older, they shared similar interests—drinking, gambling, and girls.

With the Regulators out of the way, Lincoln County was taken over by an even more vicious band of gunmen and rustlers under Texan John Selman, the sometime lawman who later killed John Wesley Hardin. Though the numbers under his command were now depleted, Billy bid farewell to Pat Garrett and headed back to Lincoln with his latest recruit, Tom O'Folliard.

DEATH BY PERSONS UNKNOWN

Billy and O'Folliard rode into Lincoln under a hastily arranged truce. They met Dolan in the saloon and everything was peaceable enough, until they left together late that evening.

In the street, they met Houston J. Chapman, a one-armed lawyer from Las Vegas, who was representing Mrs. McSween and who had denounced Dudley, Catron, and the Santa Fe Ring to the Secretary of the Interior. Words were exchanged. Then one of Dolan's men, named Bill Campbell, pulled a gun and shot Chapman in the chest. Dolan fired two more shots into the dying man. His men poured whiskey on the corpse and set fire to it. Billy and O'Folliard were forced to watch.

When, back in the saloon, someone pointed out that Chapman had been unarmed, Dolan gave Billy a gun and told him to plant it on Chapman's body. O'Folliard went with him. The two seized the opportunity to run to their horses and make off.

The following day, Dolan's men packed the coroner's inquest on the death of Chapman. The verdict: death at the hands of persons unknown.

SERENADING THE KID

Governor Lew Wallace was outraged. He wrote to General Hatch at Fort Sumner, asking for the removal of Dudley and the arrest of Dolan, Campbell, and Jesse Evans, another Murphy man. However, he also posted a reward of $500 for the capture of Billy the Kid.

Billy wrote to Wallace saying that he was willing to be a witness in a trial on the murder of Chapman provided all charges against him were dropped. Wallace wrote back offering a secret meeting, which Billy attended. After talking for an hour, Billy agreed to testify before a grand jury. Wallace promised immunity from prosecution, plus protection against Dolan, Campbell, Evans, and others who would want to kill him.

The Kid and O'Folliard contrived to be captured. Wallace wrote to the Secretary of the Interior that he was surprised to find local musicians "actually serenading" the Kid when he was in jail.

Governor Lew Wallace, author of *Ben Hur*.

DOUBLE-CROSSED

The Kid quickly found he had been double-crossed. He was going to be tried for the murder of Sheriff Brady. O'Folliard urged him to escape, but he still wanted to take the witness stand against his enemies. It did no good.

First Dudley was exonerated by a court of inquiry—a case of the Army defending its own—though his career on the frontier was curtailed. Bill Campbell and Jesse Evans escaped to Texas, while Jimmy Dolan stood trial, but the venue was moved so he would find a sympathetic judge.

As a result, one night in June 1879, Billy slipped the handcuffs from his slender wrists and walked out of jail. Tom O'Folliard and another old Regulator named "Doc" Scurlock were waiting with horses and they headed back to Fort Sumner.

A DEADLY GAME OF TWO

A young tough named Joe Grant swore to kill Billy. Some time in January 1880, they were in Jose Valdez's saloon when the drunken young gunslinger pulled a gun and fired at him. Grant's shot missed, but Billy's didn't. In the blink of an eye, Grant was dead.

Asked about the incident, Billy said: "It was a game of two and I got there first."

Billy also joined up with wanted robber and killer Dave Rudabaugh and two young gunslingers named Billy Wilson and Tom Pickett. A posse was soon after them. They escaped, though the Kid and Wilson had their horses shot from under them. The leader of the posse, Jimmy Carlyle, was also killed. Billy wrote to Governor Wallace explaining that there had been a mistake.

CAPTURE AT STINKING SPRINGS

When Billy and his growing gang of outlaws rode into Fort Sumner on December 19, 1880, the newly appointed sheriff, Pat Garrett, was waiting. He ordered them to stop. O'Folliard, who was in the lead, went for his gun. Garrett opened fired. O'Folliard fell, dying two hours

later. The rest turned tail. It was a foggy night and they escaped easily, taking refuge in a deserted house at Stinking Springs about four miles away.

It had been snowing and it was easy for Garrett and his posse to track them there. At daybreak, Charley Bowdre, who wore a hat like the Kid's, came to the door and stepped out. Garrett raised his rifle and two bullets hit Bowdre, knocking him back into the house.

The men inside called out that Bowdre was dying and wanted to come out. The Kid shoved him out of the door with the words: "Kill some of the sons-of-bitches before you die."

Bowdre came out with his pistol still hanging in front of him, but with his hands up. When he recognized Garrett, he said: "I wish ... I wish ... I wish ... I'm dying." Garrett laid him gently on his own blankets and he died almost immediately.

To prevent the others escaping, Garrett shot one of their horses and shot through the ropes tying another two, allowing them to walk away.

That afternoon, the posse brought up provisions. Soon the smell of roasting meat proved too much for the hungry outlaws. A handkerchief that had once been white appeared on the end of a stick from a window. Rudabaugh came out and said they would surrender, if Garrett would guaranteed their safety—which, of course, he did.

BACK IN SANTA FE

As there were U.S. warrants outstanding against the prisoners, Garrett took them to Santa Fe, taking the train from Las Vegas. Both the authorities and a lynch mob there wanted Rudabaugh for the murder of Deputy Sheriff Antonio Lino Valdez. But Garrett insisted that he knew only of the federal charges. Meanwhile Billy gave copious interviews to the *Las Vegas Gazette*.

From Santa Fe, Billy wrote four letters to Governor Wallace, reminding him of his bargain. But *Ben Hur* was now a bestseller and Wallace was on his way to Turkey where he was to become U.S. minister to the Ottoman Empire. Billy was transferred to Mesilla where he was tried by Justice Warren Bristol who had connections to the Santa Fe Ring. He was found guilty of the murder of Sheriff Brady and sentenced to hang.

BREAKING OUT

The sentence was to be carried out in Lincoln. On April 28, 1881, Garrett was away buying lumber to make the gallows, leaving deputies Bob Ollinger and James Bell guarding the Kid. Ollinger left his shotgun in the gun cabinet while he took some of the prisoners across the road to feed them in the Wortley. Billy remained behind with Bell, playing cards.

Billy then asked to go to the downstairs privy. On the way back, he pulled a gun which was thought to have been hidden there. He shot Bell. Finding the key in Bell's pocket, he undid his handcuffs, then took Ollinger's shotgun from the cabinet. When Ollinger came up the stairs, Billy reportedly said: "Hello, Bob." Then gave him both barrels.

With a miner's pick, he managed to remove the shackle from one leg and tied the chain to his belt. Riding out of town, he visited a friend who fed him and helped him knock off the other leg iron. Then, instead of heading to Mexico, Billy rode to Fort Sumner. There he was tended by Deluvina, a Navajo slave, bought by the Maxwell family years before for $10.

"¿QUIÉNES ES?"

In May 1881, Garrett had hired a deputy, John William Poe, a Kentuckian who had once cleaned up Fort Griffin. Early in July, at White Oaks, Poe met an old bar-room derelict who told him that he had been sleeping off the drink in a livery stable when he heard two men discussing Billy the Kid, saying that he was living in Fort Sumner.

Poe sought out Garrett and, with Deputy Sheriff Thomas C. "Kip" McKinney, they rode into Fort Sumner in the afternoon of July 13. They scouted around until well after

dark. It was late when Poe suggested that they consult leading citizen Pete Maxwell, who seemed to know everyone in town.

Garrett left Poe and McKinney on the porch while he went into Maxwell's house. Half-a-minute later, Poe saw a man only partially dressed—hatless and shoeless—approaching. Poe thought Maxwell's was the last place in Fort Sumner that would be harboring the Kid, so he was not on his guard. He assumed the man was a guest staying there.

When the man saw Poe, he pulled a six-shooter and asked: "¿Quiénes es? ¿Quiénes es?"—"Who is that? Who is that?"

Poe moved forward to reassure him and the man pulled back into the doorway to Maxwell's room where he was protected by a thick abode wall. He then disappeared into the darkness inside, saying: "Pete, who are those fellows outside?"

Then there was a shot, followed by another. A third report came from its ricochet. Garrett came out and brushed past Poe.

"That was the Kid that came in there onto me and I think I have got him," Garrett said.

Poe said that Billy the Kid would not come to a place like that. Garrett must have shot the wrong man.

"I am sure it was him," said Garrett. "I know his voice too well to be mistaken."

Maxwell fetched a candle. The man lying dead on his back in the middle of the room was, indeed, Billy the Kid. He had a six-shooter in one hand and a butcher's knife in the other—and there was a bullet hole in his chest, just above his heart.

For Billy the Kid, his violent death came too soon—the *American National Biography* shone a light on the other side of his life story:

Billy the Kid did not marry. However, he was extremely popular with young women, especially the Hispanics who idolized him because he spoke their language and did not patronize them. Almost certainly he left an unrecorded progeny. His brother survived him by nearly fifty years and died a Denver derelict.

SHERIFF PAT GARRETT

Patrick Floyd Garrett was born in Alabama on June 5, 1850, and raised in Louisiana. Leaving home at nineteen, he headed for the buffalo ranges of Texas. There he shot and killed fellow buffalo hunter Joe Briscoe, but the authorities at nearby Fort Griffin, Texas, declined to prosecute.

After Comanches attacked the buffalo hunter's camp near present-day Lubbock, Texas, he moved onto Fort Sumner where he met Billy the Kid. They became friends and were known as Big Casino and Little Casino, due to their respective sizes. Garrett was six feet four; Billy was five feet eight.

Garrett married and fathered eight children. Following the Lincoln County War, Garrett was elected sheriff to restore order in the area. This brought him into conflict with his old friend who he pursued relentlessly, eventually shooting him down in 1881. Garrett was asked if he was nervous when he shot the Kid. "No," he answered quickly, "A fellow with nerves wouldn't last long in the business I'm in."

Immediately, Billy the Kid became a folk hero, with Garrett the villain of the tale. Even publication of *The Authentic Life of Billy, the Kid*, written with Ash Upson, did little to restore Garrett's prestige. He could not even get re-elected sheriff of Lincoln County and had to hire a lawyer to get the reward posted for Billy.

He continued a checkered career, alternately as a lawman and rancher. President Theodore Roosevelt appointed him collector of customs in El Paso in 1901. On February 29, 1908, Garrett was heading to Las Cruces, New Mexico, to sell his ranch. On the road, he was shot in the back of the head by local cowboy Wayne Brazel, who claimed it was self-defense and was acquitted.

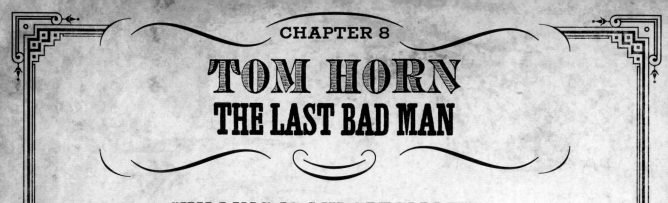

CHAPTER 8

TOM HORN
THE LAST BAD MAN

"KILLING IS MY SPECIALTY ... I LOOK ON IT AS A BUSINESS."

Tom Horn (1861 – 1903)

Tom Horn was one of a surprising number of gunfighters who left memoirs. His was called *Life of Tom Horn, Government Scout and Interpreter*. What it does not say—how could it?—was that he died at the end of a hangman's rope, after the murder of a fourteen-year-old boy. He is thought to have committed seventeen murders as a hired killer—"my stock-in-trade," he boasted.

The son of a wealthy farmer in Missouri, he left home at fourteen following a disagreement with his father. After working on the railroads in Kansas, a job with a team of freighters got him to Santa Fe, where he drove a stage. Then a year as a night herder near Camp Verde, Arizona, left him fluent in Spanish and Apache.

Meeting the famous Indian scout Al Sieber at Fort Whipple, he was taken on as an interpreter at $75 a month. Still a teenager, he lived in the village of Pedro, home of the old war captain Chief Victorio, hunting with the bucks and having the young women throw sticks at him—this was the way Apache women showed they were ready for courting.

However, after a scandal involving kickbacks from trading posts in the Indian Territory, civilians were banned from Indian agencies, so he was fired. In his memoirs, Horn claims he and Al Sieber were with Ed Schieffelin when he founded Tombstone. However, they were recalled to Fort Whipple to help the Sixth Cavalry bring in Geronimo.

APACHE WAR SCOUT

With civilians back in business with the Indian agencies, Horn began supplying the reservation at San Carlos with beef. When the Chiricahua Apache killed the agent and war broke out in May 1880, Horn had to make a thirty-two-mile ride and swim the swollen Gila River to alert the Army at Camp Thomas.

During the Apache War, Horn served as a scout under Captain Adam R. Chaffee, who

Tom Horn, circa 1880, age 19.

was well-known for his order issued during the earlier Kiowa-Comanche war: "Forward! If any man is killed, I'll make him a corporal."

They found themselves climbing the walls of Devil's Canyon "by our fingernails" to outflank the enemy. The resulting firefight was halted by a heavy rain and hailstorm, the worst he had ever seen in the West, Horn said.

HUNTING GERONIMO

In the summer of 1885—after a spree on tiswin, a corn beer—the fifty-seven-year-old Geronimo led a large number of warriors into Mexico. Horn was sent as chief scout on Captain Emmett Crawford's expedition to track them down.

Horn claims to have found Geronimo's camp on the Aros River. But during the fighting, they were attacked by Mexican irregulars and Captain Crawford was killed.

With the expedition over, Horn and Sieber were fired again—and recalled once more when it was realized that experienced scouts

Geronimo, in 1887, after the Apache surrender.

were still needed. Eventually, when Geronimo surrendered, Horn claimed that he had persuaded him to talk to the Army.

With the Apache War at an end, there was again no need for scouts.

THE HIRED GUN

Horn worked as a lawman and a rodeo rider—he was particularly adept at roping steer. In Arizona's Pleasant Valley he fought in a war between the cattlemen and gangs of rustlers. Then he became a Pinkerton detective, tracking the notorious train robbers "Peg Leg" Watson and Joe McCoy to their lair.

"While Pinkerton's is one of the greatest institutions of its kind in existence, I never did like the work, so I left them in 1894," said Horn.

He went to Wyoming and worked for the Swan Land & Cattle Company as a "stock detective"—that is, a hired gun. During his time in the Army, Horn had been used to tracking down and killing Apache raiders. Now he switched his allegiance to the cattle barons and, this time, the enemy were supposed to be rustlers, though they also turned out to be the sodbusters and sheepherders who were taking over the range.

He worked alone. The big solitary man on horseback silhouetted against the sky or squatting by a camp fire became a figure of fear. His fee was between $300 and $600 a head.

Horn stalked his victims with all the skill of an Apache. In the morning, there would be a shot from cover using a high-powered rifle. The body would be left to be found by his friends, his wife, or his children. He would collect the shell casings and other incriminating evidence. There is a legend that he left two small stones under a dead man's head as a calling card.

SPANISH-AMERICAN WAR

When the Spanish-American War broke out in Cuba in April 1898, Horn enlisted. He joined the Rough Riders—the First U.S.

Volunteer Cavalry under Teddy Roosevelt—as packmaster at $133 a month. In Cuba, he caught malaria.

The war was over quickly and, in August 1898, Horn was discharged in New York, but drifted back to the West and resumed his career as a gun for hire. His first target was suspected rustler Matt Rush. Under the assumed name James Hicks, Horn tracked Rush down to Cold Springs Mountain in Routt County, Colorado.

One afternoon, Rush had just finished a meal of meat and potatoes, and stepped outside his cabin. He was hit by three bullets; a fourth killed his sorrel mare. It was a sloppy assassination. Horn galloped off toward Denver to establish an alibi, but Rush was not dead. He staggered inside and collapsed on his cot. With his own blood, he began to write a note, but died before he could leave anything legible.

That October, still posing as James Hicks, Horn returned to Routt County. This time his mark was an African-American cowboy "Nigger Isom" Dart. His hideout was in Brown's Hole, once the home of Butch Cassidy. Horn set up a sniper position with a .30-30 rifle two-hundred yards from Dart's cabin. After breakfast, Dart and five companions came out of the cabin. Horn fired twice and Dart fell with a head wound, while his friends rushed back inside. They cowered there until dark.

Around the same time, Horn tangled with a hard case named Neut Kelley, who knifed him in the stomach. Although he recovered, it was said that Horn was never the same again.

THE OLD FRONTIERSMAN

In the spring of 1901, Horn went to work for an old friend named John Coble. On his horse ranch, north of Laramie, Wyoming, Horn tracked down the rustlers who were preying on his Iron Mountain herds. Coble was a romantic and Horn entertained him and his guests at the Cheyenne Club with tales of the Old West.

Similarly enthralled was a Missouri schoolmarm named Glendolene Myrtle Kimmell. She had come to see the Wild West and was staying with the Millers, a homesteading family. The Miller boys were like the hired hands she had met back in Missouri and hardly filled the bill of the Western hero. But Tom Horn was six feet two inches tall, straight as an arrow, with broad shoulders and a slim waist. She said, he "embodied the characteristics, the experiences and the code of the old frontiersman."

Through Kimmell, Horn learned of a long-running feud between the Millers and Kels P. Nickell, who had also tried to slash Coble with a knife. Wyoming was cattle country and the cattle farmers turned against Nickell when the stubborn Kentuckian started farming sheep, standing guard over his flock with a shotgun.

SHOOTING WILLIE NICKELL

Around 3:30 p.m. on July 18, 1901, Nickell was out tending his flock when his fourteen-year-old son Willie hitched up a team of horses to the hay wagon to take it to Cheyenne. He was wearing his father's hat and coat. A tall lad, he resembled his father from a distance.

As he got down to open the gate, a bullet hit him in the head, knocking him down. He got up and staggered back toward the wagon when he was hit again. His two younger brothers found the body.

Because of his reputation, Horn was immediately a suspect, but he produced an alibi proving he was on a train between Laramie and Cheyenne on the day of Willie's killing. Miss Kimmell testified to the coroner's court that Tom was at home at the time of the killing. Reward posters went up offering $500 for the apprehension of the killer.

Then on August 4, Kels Nickell was shot in an ambush. His arm was shattered. While he was in the hospital, he heard that masked men had clubbed his sheep to death. When he left the hospital, he sold his spread and moved to Cheyenne where he opened a steam laundry. For the time being, the cattle barons had won.

TOM HORN'S DIRTIEST TRICK

Horn was on a drinking spree in Denver, when Miss Kimmell wrote to him warning that Joe LeFors, deputy U.S. marshal from Cheyenne, was looking for him. But in 1901, Denver was no longer a frontier town where the cowboy was king. With his high-heeled boots and sombrero, Horn was an anachronism. In a bar, he picked on a smaller man beside him. This was local boxer "Young" Corbett who broke his jaw and put him in the hospital for three weeks.

Meanwhile, LeFors had visited Laramie where he was told that, on the day of Willie Nickell's murder, Horn had arrived "on a steamy shaken horse," which had obviously been ridden hard. He also left a bloodstained sweater at a cobbler's shop.

LeFors said that he would set a trap for Horn. On the pretext of arranging a job as stockman's detective for him, they went out drinking together during the frontier celebration in Cheyenne. Half drunk, the hired killer boasted that he had been paid "twenty-one hundred dollars for killing three men and shooting five times at another." According to LeFors, Horn also bragged that he had killed the Nickell boy from three-hundred yards, saying it was "the best shot but the dirtiest trick I have ever done ... killing is my specialty ... I look on it as a business."

These remarks were thought to have been said in LeFors' office. Behind the door were Deputy Sheriff Leslie Snow and district court stenographer Charles Ohnhaus who took down everything. Afterward, LeFors swore out a warrant for murder and Horn was arrested in the lobby of the Inter-Ocean Hotel, Cheyenne.

COURT CASE

The court case attracted nationwide publicity. It was perceived as the struggle of the cattle barons against the small farmer. The vested interest gave Horn the best defense attorneys money could buy. The streets were thronged with homesteaders who wanted their presence felt, while Eastern newspaper sent reporters in Derby hats and celluloid collars.

Fourteen-year-old Willie Nickell, who was killed by Tom Horn in 1901.

The trial hinged on Tom Horn's so-called confession behind closed doors to Joe LeFors, and the defense's allegation that the notes had been falsified by LeFors to get the reward.

On the morning of October 23, 1902, the jury returned a verdict of guilty and Horn was sentenced to hang. There was a plot to blow the jail up; dynamite was found, along with a length of lead piping in Horn's trousers.

ESCAPE ATTEMPT

On the morning of August 9, 1903, Horn's fellow prisoner Jim McCloud told Deputy Sheriff Richard Proctor that he felt ill. When Proctor returned with medicine, he was overpowered by McCloud and Horn, who demanded the keys. Although Proctor had them on him, he said they were in the safe.

Ordered to open the safe, Proctor pulled a gun from it. In the resulting tussle, Proctor fired four times, wounding McCloud slightly. Grabbing a shotgun, Horn and McCloud left Proctor bound, and escaped through the rear door.

McCloud leapt on the only horse. It did him no good. Sheriff Edward Smalley then turned up and, after a short chase, recaptured McCloud.

Horn had made off on foot in the other direction. O.M. Eldrich, who ran the amusement stand across the street, chased after him. He fired several shots, grazing Horn's neck. Horn had a revolver, but it had a new lock that he was unfamiliar with and he was unable to fire. Eldrich beat him into submission and Horn was returned to jail.

HANGING TOM HORN

Cheyenne filled up with Horn's friends and there were fears that they would storm the jail and free him, but Kels Nickell kept watch outside the jail with a shotgun.

"Let Horn make another break for it and I'll blow his head off," he said. "He's going to hang if I have to stay here for the rest of my life."

Even Governor Fenimore Chatterton received death threats and sent in the militia.

Soldiers patrolled the streets and Gatling guns guarded the entrance to the jail.

Horn's attorneys, who had been hired by prominent men in the cattle industry, made a last desperate attempt to save him. Miss Kimmell gave last-minute affidavits that she had heard two men talk of how they had shot the boy "on three different occasions." Governor Chatterton dismissed her attempts to shield Horn. The prosecutor indicated that his death sentence might be commuted if he talked. He scorned the offer. A plot to free him if the sentence was commuted came to light. The train taking him to the penitentiary would be derailed, but no commutation was forthcoming.

On November 20, 1903, Tom Horn was duly hanged. In the mortuary, Kels Nickell checked that they had killed the right man. Coble paid for his funeral in Boulder, Colorado. Two thousand followed his cortege to the grave.

NOT GUILTY RETRIAL

It is still debated whether Horn committed the Nickell murder or not. In 1993, the case was retried in a mock trial in Cheyenne, and Horn was "acquitted."

Some historians believe he did it, but that he didn't realize he was shooting an underage boy. Some such as Professor Larry Ball of Arkansas State University are convinced of his guilt, while renowned Tom Horn expert Chip Carlson continues to support his innocence. The circumstances of Horn's alleged confession to Joe LeFors were definitely unconvincing, but the prosecution made no effort to interview any other suspects. The consensus of historians is that regardless of whether Horn committed that particular murder, he had certainly committed many others. Horn's reputation as a bad man who liked violence made him an easy target. He was also his own worst enemy—Horn liked to talk about himself. Consequently, during his trial, the more he talked about his brutal life, the tighter the hangman's noose became.

WHO WAS JOE LEFORS?

Joseph "Joe" S. LeFors (1865 – 1940) was born in Paris, Texas, and grew up to be a cowboy. After going on a cattle drive from Texas to Wyoming in 1885, he stayed there and became an inspector-detective responsible for tracking stolen cattle. In the process, he was involved in a number of gunfights in Wyoming and Montana.

In 1899, he rode with the posse tracking the Hole-in-the-Wall Gang, led by outlaw Butch Cassidy, after the Wilcox Train Robbery. The robbers eventually escaped into the Big Horn Mountains. He was appointed as a U.S. deputy marshal the same year.

LeFors was not a particularly impressive lawman. He led several posses in pursuit of train robbers and outlaws in the north-west, but more often than not, returned home empty handed, capturing no one.

In 1901, LeFors became famous for arresting Tom Horn, for the shooting of fourteen-year-old Willie Nickell. But legend has it that he falsified Horn's confession to get the reward money. In 1902, LeFors was working for the Iron Mountain Ranch Company in Helena, Montana, but his attempt to infiltrate a gang of cattle rustlers was unsuccessful and he was fired in 1904.

After that he disappeared from sight, and little is known about him other than that he died on October 1, 1940, at age seventy-five, and is buried in the Willow Grove Cemetery in Buffalo, Wyoming.

The 1969 film *Butch Cassidy and the Sundance Kid* featured Joe LeFors as a character.

REMINGTON
AMERICA'S OLDEST GUNMAKER

Founded in Ilion, New York, in 1816 by Eliphalet Remington, the Remington Arms Company claims to be America's oldest gunmaker. It began making barrels, then rifles. In 1858, it introduced the Remington Model 1858, a six-shot, single-action percussion revolver designed by Fordyce Beals. The Remington Army revolver was .44 caliber with an eight-inch barrel. The .36-caliber Remington Navy revolver was slightly smaller. Small modifications were made. The Remington-Beals Army & Navy was produced from 1860 to 1862, the 1861 Army & Navy from 1862 to 1863, and the New Model Army & Navy from 1863 to 1875, due to continual improvement suggestions from the U.S. Ordnance Department. Slight differences in hammers, loading levers, and cylinders help identify each model.

The Remington had a solid frame with a metal top strap above the cylinder, unlike

the early Colts, which made it more durable. Another advantage was that the cylinder could be removed, though this had to be done by detaching the barrel. However, a gunman could carry one or more spare cylinders for quick reloading. It became popular when a fire in 1864 closed the Colt factory for some time.

Remington percussion revolvers were very accurate and capable of considerable power with muzzle velocities up to 1,300 feet per second, depending upon the charge. It was used throughout the American West, both in its original percussion configuration and as a metallic cartridge conversion.

Remington Model 1875 Single Action Army (a.k.a. Improved Army or Frontier Army) was a revolver based upon the successful Remington Model 1858. Both guns were the same size and appearance with a removable cylinder. The new 1875 Remington differed mainly from the older 1858 percussion model by having a bored-through cylinder chambered for metallic cartridges. This big-frame, army style revolver was intended to compete with the Colt Peacemaker. This design was followed by the Model 1888 and the Model 1890.

1. Remington New Model Army Percussion.
2. Remington New Model 1861 Navy Percussion.
3. Remington Model 1875 Single Action Army.
4. Remington New Model Army Percussion de-assembled.
5. Remington Model 1867 Rolling Block Pistol.
6. Remington Model 1861 Army Single Action Percussion.
7. Remington Single Action New Model Pocket.
8. Remington Smoot New Model No. 3.
9. Remington New Model Pocket.
10. Remington Model 1890 Single Action Army.

Mama, take this badge off of me,
I can't use it anymore.
It's gettin' dark, too dark for me to see,
I feel like I'm knockin' on heaven's door.

Lyrics from Knockin' On Heaven's Door
by Bob Dylan (1973)

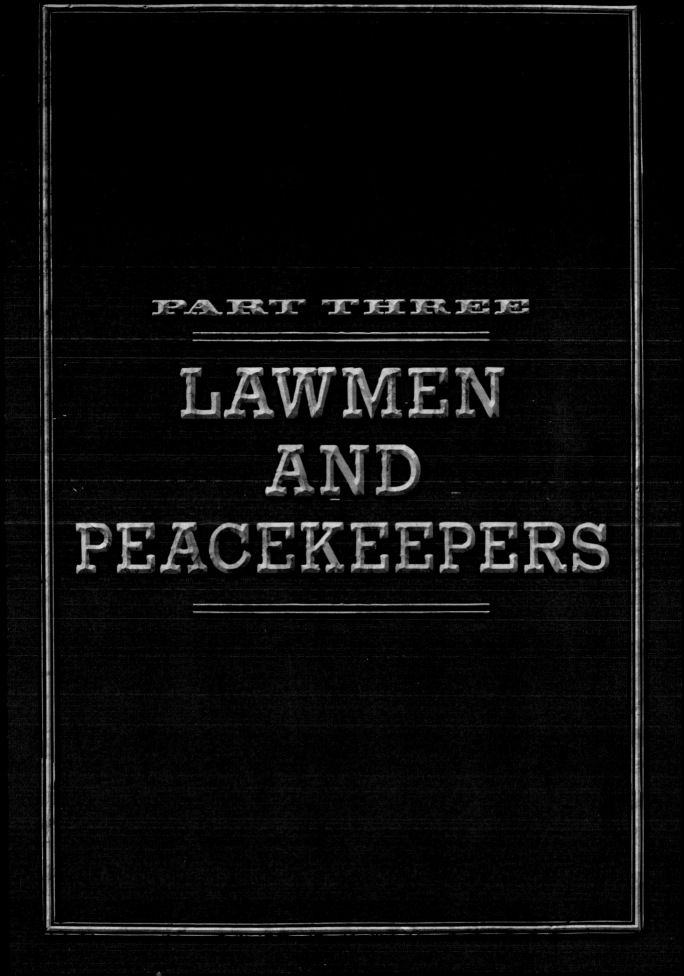

PART THREE

LAWMEN AND PEACEKEEPERS

CHAPTER 9

WILD BILL HICKOK
THE DEADLIEST PISTOL SHOT ALIVE

> "WHENEVER YOU GET INTO A ROW BE SURE AND NOT SHOOT TOO QUICK. TAKE TIME. I'VE KNOWN MANY A FELLER SLIP UP FOR SHOOTIN' IN A HURRY."

Wild Bill Hickok (1837 – 76)

In 1867, not yet thirty, "Wild Bill" Hickok was already something of a media star. Earlier that year, he had met Colonel George Ward Nichols, who had quit Sherman's army at the end of the Civil War to become a correspondent for *Harper's New Monthly Magazine*. Nichols was in Springfield, Missouri when he met "the famous Scout of the Plains." Writing in *Harper's* February issue, Nichols said:

Bill stood six feet and an inch in his bright yellow moccasins. A deer-skin shirt, or frock it might be called, hung jauntily over his shoulders, and revealed a chest whose breadth and depth were remarkable. These lungs had grown strong in some twenty years of the free air of the Rocky Mountains. His small, round waist was girthed by a belt which held two of Colt's Navy revolvers.

His legs sloped gradually from the compact thigh to the feet, which were small, and turned inward as he walked. There was a singular grace and dignity of carriage about that figure which would have called your attention to it where you would. The head which crowned it was now covered by a large sombrero, underneath which there shone out a quiet, manly face; so gentle is its expression as he greets you as utterly to belie the history of its owner, yet it is not a face to be trifled with.

The lips thin and sensitive, the jaw not too square, the cheek bones slightly prominent, a mass of fine dark hair falls below the neck to the shoulders. The eyes, now that you are in friendly intercourse, are as gentle as a woman's.

In truth, the womanly nature seems prominent throughout, and you would not believe that you were looking into eyes that have pointed the way to death to hundreds of men. Yes, Wild Bill with his own hands has killed hundreds of men. Of that I have not a doubt. He shoots to kill, as they say on the border.

In vain did I examine the scout's face for some evidence of murderous propensity. It was a gentle face, and singular only in the sharp angle of the eye, and without any physiognomical reason for the opinion, I have thought his wonderful accuracy of aim was indicated by this peculiarity. He told me, however, to use his own words:

"I allers shot well; but I come ter be perfeck in the mountains by shootin at a dime for a mark, at bets of half a dollar a shot. And then until the war I never drank liquor nor smoked," he continued, with a melancholy expression; "war is demoralizing, it is."

HEADING WEST

Born in Troy Grove, La Salle County, Illinois, on May 27, 1837, young Jim Hickok was fascinated by stories of the Western frontier. Kit Carson was his boyhood idol. At the age

THE FAMOUS SCOUT OF THE PLAINS

In April 1867, four years before Henry Morton Stanley found fame with the phrase "Dr Livingstone, I presume?" he tracked down James Butler "Wild Bill" Hickok in darkest Kansas for the *Weekly Missouri Democrat*. Their conversation was nothing if not frank.

"I say Bill, or Mr Hickok, how many white men have you killed to your certain knowledge?"

After a little deliberation, he replied, "I would be willing to take my oath on the Bible tomorrow that I have killed over a hundred, a long ways off."

"What made you kill all those men; did you kill them without cause or provocation?"

"No, by Heaven! I never killed one man without a good cause."

"How old were you when you killed your first white man, and for what cause?"

"I was twenty-eight years old when I killed the first white man, and if ever a man deserved killing he did. He was a gambler and counterfeiter, and I was in a hotel in Leavenworth City then, and seeing some loose characters around, I ordered a room, and as I had some money about me, I thought I would go to it. I had lain some thirty minutes on the bed when I heard some men at the door. I pulled out my revolver and Bowie knife and held them ready, but half concealed, pretending to be asleep. The door was opened and five men entered the room. They whispered together, "Let us kill the son of a b***h; I bet he has got money."

"Gentlemen," he said further, "that was a time, an awful time. I kept perfectly still until just as the knife touched my breast; I sprang aside and buried mine in his heart and then used my revolvers on the others, right and left. Only one was wounded, besides the one killed; and then, gentlemen, I dashed through the room and rushed to the fort, procured a lot of soldiers, came to the hotel and captured the whole gang of them, fifteen in all. We searched the cellar and found eleven bodies buried there—men who had been murdered by those villains."

Turning to us, he asked, "Would you have not done the same? That was the first man I killed and I was never sorry for that yet."

Wild Bill Hickok in 1869, with Navy Colts and a Bowie knife.

of eighteen, Hickok, thinking he had killed local bully Charles Hudson in a fistfight, left Illinois, fled West, adopting his father's name, William.

He arrived in Kansas during the infamous Missouri-Kansas border wars over the issue of slavery known as "Bleeding Kansas." He joined an irregular army of "Free-Staters" as one of the personal bodyguards of its leader Jim Lane. He then became the elected constable of the village of Monticello, Kansas, where he set up home with Miss Mary Jane Owen, without benefit of a preacher.

Domestic life proved too dull for him and he moved to Leavenworth, Kansas, to work as a teamster on the Santa Fe Trail. At Leavenworth, he met the teenaged William Frederick Cody, later known as "Buffalo Bill." And at Santa Fe he met his idol Kit Carson.

ROCK CREEK REPUTATION

In March 1861, Hickok took a job with the Pony Express at the Overland Stage and Express Station at Rock Creek, Nebraska Territory. The station superintendent there, Dave McCanles, disliked him, mocking his slender, feminine looks—even calling him a hermaphrodite. Because of Hickok's protruding lower lip, usually hidden behind a luxuriant mustache, McCanles called him "Duck Bill." This possibly innocent teasing turned sour when Hickok began courting McCanles's mistress Sarah Shull.

When McCanles fell out with the backers of the Pony Express—Russell, Majors, and Waddell—over payments on the station, he came with his son William, cousin James Woods, and employee James Gordon to confront the new superintendent, Horace Wellman. The door was answered by Hickok. When McCanles stepped inside to find Wellman, Hickok shot him from behind a curtain.

Mortally wounded, McCanles stumbled out and collapsed in the yard. Then Woods and Gordon entered the station through separate doors. Hickok shot both of them. They fled. Woods fell in a weed patch and was beaten to death with a hoe. As Gordon ran off, Hickok emptied his pistol into him. Hickok, Wellman, and Pony Express rider James W. "Doc" Brink caught up with him and he was finished off with a shotgun.

Hickok, Wellman, and Brink were arrested, but released when Justice of the Peace T.M. Coutler found that they had acted in self-defense. McCanles's son, who was the only

The stagecoach and Pony Express station at Rock Creek, Nebraska, where Hickok shot Dave McCanles in 1861.

witness, had escaped, but was not called to testify. While no one took much notice at the time, this established Hickok's reputation as a gunman, who gunned down a handful of Western desperados.

BECOMING "WILD BILL"

Hickok left Rock Creek and signed up as a civilian wagon master in the Union Army. He seems to have served as a scout and a spy, though many of his reported exploits during the Civil War seem to have been spurious.

In 1864, he earned his living as a lawman again. The following year, he was given the sobriquet "Wild Bill," he said, by a woman in Missouri. At the time he was living in Springfield with a red-haired woman named Susannah Moore. He had met her during the war and he was making his living as a professional gambler.

It was then that he had a run-in with twenty-six-year-old gambler Davis Tutt,

formerly of the Twenty-Seventh Arkansas Infantry. It is thought that Hickok had lived with Tutt's sister in Yellville, Arkansas. When the family moved to Springfield, the illicit relationship renewed, while Susannah Moore took up with Tutt, causing bad blood.

SHOWDOWN IN SPRINGFIELD

The showdown came over a gambling debt. Hickok had lost a large amount of money to Tutt in a card game, but Tutt refused to take an IOU. Instead he seized Wild Bill's pocket watch. Hickok growled a threat that Tutt had better not use it.

On the morning of July 21, 1865, they had one of the earliest recorded "quick draw duels." In the town square in Springfield, Tutt was seen proudly wearing Hickok's prized pocket watch. With most of the town looking on, they approached each other, drawing their guns. At seventy-five yards, they fired almost simultaneously. Tutt missed.

Davis Tutt grabbing Wild Bill's pocket watch, as illustrated in *Harper's New Monthly Magazine*, February 1867.

GENERAL GEORGE A. CUSTER ON HICKOK

Whether on foot or on horseback he was one of the most perfect types of physical manhood I ever saw. Of his courage there could be no question; it had been brought to the test on too many occasions to doubt. His skill in the use of the rifle and pistol was unerring; while his deportment was exactly the opposite of what might be expected from a man of his surroundings. It was entirely free from all bluster or bravado. He seldom spoke of himself unless requested to do so. His conversation, strange to say, never bordered either on the vulgar or blasphemous. His influence among the frontiersmen was unbounded, his word was law; and many are the personal quarrels and disturbances which he has checked among his comrades by the simple announcement that "This has gone far enough," if need be followed by the ominous warning that when persisted in or renewed the quarreler "must settle it with me."

Wild Bill is anything but a quarrelsome man; yet no one but himself can enumerate the many conflicts in which he has been engaged, and which have almost invariably resulted in the death of his adversary. I have personal knowledge of at least half a dozen men whom he has at various times killed, one of these being, at the time, a member of my command.

Others have been severely wounded, yet he always escaped unhurt. On the plains every man openly carried his belt with its invariable appendages, knife and revolver, often two of the latter. Wild Bill always carried two handsome ivory-handled revolvers of the large size; he was never seen without them.

George Armstrong Custer, 1874

Wild Bill rested his gun barrel on his forearm and hit Tutt in the chest, killing him almost instantly. Hickok handed his guns to the sheriff and was charged with murder. Again he was acquitted on the grounds of self-defense.

BEING CUSTER'S SCOUT

After failing to be elected as chief of police of Springfield, Hickok returned to military duty, becoming a scout for General George Custer. They played poker together.

During that period, he spent time in Leavenworth and Ellsworth, Kansas, where he lived with a woman known only as "Indian Annie." But he was defeated when he stood to become sheriff there in November 1867. However, a month later, he was serving as deputy U.S. marshal and, the following March, he arrested eleven renegade soldiers, operating as horse thieves, and with Buffalo Bill Cody escorted them to jail in Topeka.

Returning to the army he was lanced in the foot by an Indian.

WILD BILL HICKOK'S MARKSMANSHIP

ROBERT A. KANE,
OUTDOOR LIFE, JUNE 6, 1906

When we arrived at his hotel Mr. Hickok treated us with great courtesy, showed us his weapons, and offered to do a little shooting for us if it could be arranged for outside the city limits. Accordingly, the early hours of the afternoon found us on our way to the outskirts of the city. Mr. Hickok's weapons were a pair of beautifully silver plated S.A. .44 Colt revolvers. Both had pearl handles and were tastefully engraved.

He also had a pair of Remington revolvers of the same caliber.

The more showy pair of Colts were used in his stage performance. On reaching a place suitable for our purpose, Mr. Hickok proceeded to entertain us with some of the best pistol work which it has ever been my good fortune to witness.

Standing on a railroad track, in a deep cut, his pistols cracking with the regularity and cadency of the ticking of an old house clock, he struck and dislodged the bleaching pebbles sticking in the face of the bank, at a distance of about fifteen yards.

Standing about thirty feet from the shooter, one of our party tossed a quart can in the air to a height of about thirty feet. This was perforated three times before it reached the ground, twice with his right hand and once with his left.

Standing midway between the fences of a country road, which is four rods wide, Mr. Hickok's instinct of location was so accurate that he placed a bullet in each of the fence posts on opposite sides. Both shots were fired simultaneously.

Located midway between two telegraph poles he placed a bullet in one of them, then wheeled about and with the same weapon planted another in the second. Telegraph poles in this country run about thirty to the mile, or one hundred and seventy-six feet distant from each other.

Two common bricks were placed on the top board of a fence, about two feet apart and about fifteen yards from the shooter. These were broken with two shots fired from the pistol in either hand, the reports so nearly together that they seemed as one.

His last feat was to me the most remarkable of all. A quart can was thrown by Mr. Hickok himself, which dropped about ten to twelve yards distant. Quickly whipping out his weapons, he fired alternately from left to right. Advancing a step with each shot, his bullets striking the earth just under the can, he kept it in continuous motion until his pistols were empty.

No matter how elusive the target, even when shooting at objects tossed in the air, he never seemed hurried. This trait was, of course, natural and in part due to his superb physique and superior mentality, which, combined and supplemented by his methods of practice and free wild life in the open, developed in him that perfect coordination of hand and eye which was essential to the perfect mastery of the one-hand gun.

SHOOTING BILL MULREY

In 1869, he ran for sheriff of Hays City, Kansas. Shootings there were common. Mrs. Custer said: "Every night in Hays sounded like the Fourth of July." When the city's old Boot Hill was razed, most of the corpses in it had suffered a violent death.

Wild Bill was elected interim sheriff at a salary of $75 a month. But it seems that he spent much of his time playing cards in Tommy Drum's saloon on North Main Street or with the "soiled doves" at Ida May's sporting house, while his deputy Peter Lanihan did most of the work. Nevertheless, soon after being elected he shot Bill Mulrey. When Mulrey cornered Hickok and threatened to kill him, Wild Bill looked past him and said: "Don't shoot him boys, he's drunk." When Mulrey turned to look who was behind him, Hickok shot him. He died the next day.

The following month, Hickok and Lanihan went to quell a disturbance at the saloon. Teamster Samuel Strawhim objected to his interference and went for his gun. Wild Bill put two slugs in him.

At the election in November, Hickok stood as an Independent, while Lanihan ran as a Democrat and won. But Wild Bill was allowed to serve out his term. By then Lanihan had been shot and killed.

Hickok fled Hays City after a bloody encounter with the Seventh Cavalry on July 17, 1870. Legend has it that Wild Bill fell out with Custer's younger brother, Tom, over one of Ida May's girls. At least five soldiers set on Hickok in Drum's saloon, knocked him to the ground, and started kicking him. Wild Bill drew his pistols from his belt —he never wore holsters—and killed one private, seriously wounding another. He quit as sheriff and grabbed the train for Ellsworth to recuperate.

ABILENE CITY MARSHAL

After a period hiding out in Ellsworth and Topeka, Wild Bill was invited by Mayor Joseph G. McCoy to become the city marshal of Abilene—the town was then just four years old. The rail head at the end of the Chisholm Trail, it was a lawless cow town. By then Hickok had a reputation and was paid $150 a month, plus one-fourth of all fines levied against those he arrested and fifty cents for every unlicensed dog he killed.

Again Wild Bill's deputies did most of the work, while Hickok spent his time gambling

HICKOK "REAL DEAD"

In March 1873, the *Missouri Democrat* prematurely reported Hickok's death:

It begins to look as if "Wild Bill," was really dead. The latest report is that the Texan who corraled the untamed William did so because he lost his brother by Bill's quickness on the trigger. When the Texan shot Wild Bill, he asked the crowd in the bar-room if any gentleman had any desire to "mix in;" if so, he would wait until he was "heeled," and then take pleasure in killing him. No gentleman expressed a desire to be killed, the Texan got on his horse, and remarking that he had business in Texas, slowly started for the Lone Star State.

Still very much alive, Hickok wrote in reply:

Springfield, Mo., March 13, '73

To The Editor of the Democrat:

Wishing to correct an error in your paper of the 12th, I will state that no Texan, has, nor ever will, "corral William." I wish you to correct your statement, on account of my people.

Yours as Ever,

J.B. Hickok

P.S. I have bought your paper in preference to all others since 1857.

J.B. Hickok or "Wild Bill"

at the Alamo Saloon and keeping company with local women. The *Abilene Chronicle* complained that "Hickok and McCoy's administration allowed Abilene to be overrun with gamblers, con men, prostitutes and pimps."

Wild Bill was now painfully afraid of being bushwhacked. He would not walk down the sidewalks, always entered a building by the back or side entrance, would not sit with his back to a door or window, and would never allow anyone to stand or sit behind him. When he was with one of the various women who shared his bed, he would always keep a pistol in easy reach and, if sleeping alone, he would surround his bed with crumbled newspaper on the floor so that no one could creep up on him.

AT THE SIGN OF THE BULL

There was good reason for Hickok to be afraid. A number of Texan gunslingers were in town. One of them was John Wesley Hardin who killed two men during his brief stay. But it was Ben Thompson and Phil Coe, the owners of the Bull's Head Saloon, he had trouble with. Their first clash came over a painting of a bull with a giant phallus on the sign outside the establishment, which the city council found obscene. Hickok stood by with a shotgun while painters masked the offending portions.

Coe then accused Wild Bill of arresting Texans on false charges to get his share of the fines. Hickok responded by accusing the Bull's Head of running crooked gambling games. The city council believed the marshal and Thompson and Coe were forced to sell up. Thompson left town, but Phil Coe stayed on as a freelance gambler with a grudge.

The feud between Hickok and Coe came to a head over Jessie Hazel. Jessie was a semi-nude dancer at the Novelty Theater and she was Wild Bill's favorite prostitute. One night, Mike Williams, who had been hired as a special policeman at the Novelty, told Hickok that Jessie was with Coe in the Gulf House Hotel. Hickok went along and there was a fight but no shots were exchanged, as Coe was unarmed.

CONFRONTING COE

However, Phil Coe was armed on October 5, 1871, when the Texans were celebrating the last night of the cattle-driving season. Coe was near the Alamo Saloon when he shot a vicious dog. Hickok rushed to the scene to confront him. They were just eight feet apart when Wild Bill pulled two pistols and fired at Coe, who was hit twice in the stomach. He returned fire and a bullet tore through Bill's coat. Hickok then heard footsteps coming up behind him. Thinking it was one of Coe's men, he turned and fired, killing his friend Mike Williams instantly.

Few survived stomach wounds in those days and Coe died three days later. Hickok paid for Williams' funeral. Abilene then put a stop to the Texan cattle drive celebrations and dismissed Wild Bill as the city was "no longer in need of this service."

GOING INTO SHOW BUSINESS

Showman Colonel Sidney Barnett persuaded Wild Bill to follow in his footsteps and go into show business. He gave exhibitions of marksmanship, then appeared in a "buffalo hunt" at Niagara Falls. The show was a disaster.

Hickok then joined Buffalo Bill Cody in his play *Scouts of the Prairies*. But Wild Bill had a high squeaky voice, rather than a deep manly voice. He substituted real whiskey for the cold tea used on stage, made up his own lines, and was troublesome to the female members of the cast backstage.

In 1874, he returned to the West. He was nearly forty, balding, and wore eyeglasses. Nevertheless, he was said to have killed three buffalo hunters in Dyer's Saloon in Sydney, Nebraska, in 1875.

The following year he married Agnes Lake Thatcher in Cheyenne. She had known Hickok since Abilene, and had run a circus after her husband was killed in a gunfight. After a brief honeymoon in Cincinnati, Hickok borrowed a grubstake and headed for the goldfields near Deadwood in the Black Hills of South Dakota. Along the way, he met Calamity Jane.

CALAMITY JANE

Born in 1852 in Princeton, Missouri, much of Martha Jane Canary's life is confused by the claims she made in an autobiographical booklet produced in 1896 when she was touring with Wild West shows. Traveling west on a wagon train when she was young, she lost both her mother and father at an early age. For the rest of her life she did whatever was necessary to survive—including, she said, bushwhacking and fighting Indians, earning the nickname for her skill at skirmishing.

A putative daughter claimed that Jane had married Wild Bill Hickok, but she probably met him only shortly before he died. Her story was enhanced by the magazine writers of the 1870s. Her career with the Wild West shows peaked in 1901 when she appeared at the Pan-American Exposition in Buffalo, New York.

An alcoholic, she returned West to South Dakota where she died in 1903, at age fifty-one, and was buried next to Wild Bill at the Mount Moriah Cemetery.

PLAYING A DEAD MAN'S HAND

Hickok had no luck at mining and quickly returned to gambling. On the afternoon of August 2, 1876, Wild Bill was playing poker in the Number Ten Saloon on Main Street, Deadwood, South Dakota, with the owner Carl Mann, Missouri River pilot Captain William R. Massie, and Charles Rich, a gunman and friend of Hickok's.

For once, Wild Bill violated his own rule and sat with his back to the door. Twice he asked Rich to change places with him, but he refused. At 4:10 p.m., twenty-five-year-old Jack McCall came in, pulled a pistol, screamed "Take that!," and shot Hickok in the back of the head. From Wild Bill's dead hands fell two black eights and two black aces. The fifth card is still in dispute. Since then, this has been known as "dead man's hand."

McCall claimed that Hickok had killed his brother and was acquitted. However, he was later re-arrested in Wyoming. As Deadwood was considered an illegal town in Indian Territory, he could be retried. Found guilty, McCall was sentenced to death and hanged.

WILD BILL'S GUNS

Hickok's favorite guns were a pair of Colt 1851 Navy Model (.36 caliber) cap-and-ball revolvers. They had ivory grips and silver plating, and were ornately engraved with "J.B. Hickok 1869" on the backstrap. He wore his revolvers butt-forward in a belt or sash, and seldom used holsters; he drew the pistols using a "reverse," "twist," or cavalry draw, as would a cavalryman. At the time of his death Hickok was wearing a Smith & Wesson Model 2 Army Revolver, a .32 rimfire with a six-inch barrel, blue finish, and varnished rosewood grips.

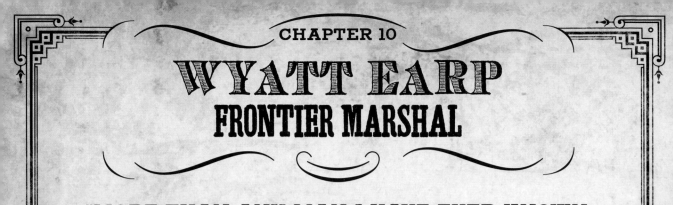

CHAPTER 10

WYATT EARP
FRONTIER MARSHAL

"MORE THAN ANY MAN I HAVE EVER KNOWN, HE WAS DEVOID OF PHYSICAL FEAR."

Bat Masterson about Wyatt Earp

Wyatt Earp has gone down in legend as the victor of the Gunfight at the O.K. Corral in Tombstone, Arizona. However, he had a long and interesting career as saloon keeper, horse thief, con man, gambler, buffalo hunter, farmer, section hand, prospector, lawman, and, of course, gunslinger.

Born March 19, 1848, in Monmouth, Illinois, Earp was the son of a Mexican-American War veteran. With his four brothers—James, born 1841; Virgil, 1843; Morgan, 1851; and Warren, 1855—Wyatt grew up in Illinois and Iowa. Then in 1864, the family moved to California. Five years later, they returned to Lamar, Illinois, where Wyatt was elected constable and married. His wife died the following year, probably of typhoid fever.

Wyatt then took off into the Indian Territory. In 1871, he and two other men stole two horses. They were arrested and taken to Fort Smith, Arkansas. Earp posted bail of $500, then absconded.

THE COW TOWNS OF KANSAS

For a couple of years, Earp hunted buffalo. Then he was drawn to the cow towns of Kansas, where he became a professional gambler, profiting from the Texan cowhands who were flush with money at the end of the trail. In Wichita, the biggest of the cow towns, Wyatt became a city policeman in April 1875, on a salary of $60 a month. His brother James was a bartender at W.W. Rupp's Keno House in Wichita and Jim's wife, or mistress, Bessie

Earp ran a bordello. One of her girls, Kate Elder, known as "Big Nose Kate," became the mistress of Doc Holliday. When he was not working as a lawman, Wyatt collected debts for prostitutes and gambling dens, a portion of which he kept.

The following year, during the election of the city marshal, Earp's appointment became an issue. Earp was arrested and fined for beating up the candidate standing against his boss, the incumbent. Without a job and threatened with prosecution for vagrancy after his salary had been withheld, Wyatt left Wichita under a cloud with his younger brother Morgan. They headed for Dodge City.

DODGE CITY

In Dodge, Morgan Earp became a deputy sheriff, while Wyatt became deputy city marshal, earning $75 a month plus $2 for every conviction. He spent his spare time gambling in Peter L. Beatty and James H. "Dog" Kelley's Alhambra Saloon on Front Street. This was Dodge City's main thoroughfare. It was divided by the tracks of the Atchison, Topeka and Santa Fe Railroad. South of the tracks, or "across the Dead Line," were the dancehalls, brothels, and most of the saloons.

Descriptions of Wyatt vary. He was known to be tall—between six feet and six feet two at a time when most men were five feet six. His weight was given between 165 and 185 pounds. In 1887, the *Los Angeles Herald* described Wyatt as:

... quiet, unassuming, broad-shouldered, with a large blonde mustache. He is dignified, self-contained, game and fearless, and no man commands greater respect ...

To curb gunfighting, City Ordinance Number 4, Section 7 was passed on December 24, 1875. It said:

No person shall in the city of Dodge City carry concealed about his or her person any pistol, Bowie knife, sling shot, or other dangerous or deadly weapons except United States, County, Township, or City Officers and any person convicted of a violation of this section shall be fined not less than three nor more than twenty-five dollars.

LOOKING FOR TROUBLE

While the cowboys were often rowdy, it was said that railroad men and drifters caused more trouble and, when it came to street fights, gamblers were the real culprits. Wyatt Earp himself was also a cause of trouble. He picked a fight over a dancehall girl with a cowboy named Red Sweeney. Standing six feet six and weighing 245 pounds, Sweeney beat Earp to a pulp, then fled town with his girl. He threatened to kill Earp on his next drive north, but was killed in a stampede.

Wyatt resigned as deputy marshal and sojourned in the Black Hills of Dakota. When he returned in July 1877, the *Dodge City Times* said:

Wyatt Earp, who was on our city police force last summer, is in town again. We hope he will accept a position on the force once more. He had a quiet way of taking the most desperate characters into custody which invariably gave one the impression that the city was able to enforce her mandates and preserve her dignity. It wasn't considered policy to draw a gun on Wyatt unless you got the drop and meant to burn powder without preliminary talk.

However, trouble soon came calling. He bumped into old acquaintance and dancehall girl, Frankie Bell, on Front Street. She cursed him and he slapped her. He was arrested and fined $1; she was jailed and fined $20, plus costs. Afterward, Earp left Dodge again and traveled the gambling circuit in Texas. Along the way, he met Doc Holliday and Celia Ann "Mattie" Blaylock, who became his common-law wife.

Within a week of returning to Dodge City, he was appointed assistant marshal by Dog Kelley, who was now mayor, on the same pay as before. Wyatt supplemented his income by taking protection money from the saloons and dancehalls across the Dead Line to keep order.

Wyatt Earp in 1869, age 21.

SHOOTING UP THE COMIQUE THEATER

In the early morning of July 26, 1878, George Hoy, a young cowboy, freed on a $1,500 bond on a charge of cattle rustling, and another cowhand, put a number of bullets through the thin walls of the Comique Theater after a dispute with the owner. They were both drunk.

Earp and fellow officer Jim Masterson gave chase. They exchanged a number of shots with Hoy and his accomplice. Other citizens joined in. A bullet hit Hoy and he fell from his horse, while his companion made good his escape. Hoy's arm was broken in two places. The surgeon at Fort Dodge amputated it, but Hoy died the following month, becoming one of the last people to be buried in Dodge City's Boot Hill.

More shots were fired at the Comique Theater in a dispute between the bartender and some cowhands. Several trail hands were pistol-whipped and James W. "Spike" Kenedy was arrested; Wyatt had arrested him before for carrying a gun. Two months later, Earp joined Sheriff Bat Masterson's posse that wounded and captured Kenedy for killing actress Dora Hand, a.k.a. Fannie Keenan.

MOVING TO TOMBSTONE

In September 1879, Earp resigned as assistant marshal of Dodge, and left for Las Vegas with Mattie Blaylock. On the way, Wyatt and "Mysterious Dave" Mather, a professional gambler he had known in Dodge City, were run out of Mobeetie, Texas, for a gold-brick scam, where a victim is sold what purported to be a gold ingot which turns out to be gold-coated lead.

From Las Vegas, Wyatt and Mattie moved on to Tombstone, Arizona, following reports of a silver strike there. They were joined by Jim, Virgil, Morgan, and Warren. There, Wyatt invested in several mining operations, one of which he and his partner sold for $30,000 in March 1880. He also worked as a Wells Fargo shotgun messenger, before becoming a deputy sheriff again. In that role, he pistol-whipped rustler William Graham, alias "Curly Bill" Brocius, after he had shot the city marshal. With Virgil and Morgan, he then rounded up several of Curly Bill's accomplices.

Wyatt was ousted from his job by John H. Behan, an associate of the Clanton brothers. The bitterness between the two men increased when Behan's young mistress, Josephine Sarah Marcus, left him for Wyatt, who also managed to maintain his relationship with Mattie Blaylock.

He also bought a stake in the Oriental Saloon owned by Milton E. "Mike" Joyce, installing as dealers Morgan Earp, Bat Masterson, Luke Short, and Doc Holliday, who also bought a share.

Morgan Earp (1851 – 1882).

THE MCLAURYS AND THE CLANTONS

The McLaurys and the Clantons were members of a loosely associated gang of outlaws known as "The Cowboys" who had ongoing feuds and arguments with the Earps.

Lieutenant Joseph H. Hurst enlisted Virgil Earp, now a U.S. marshal, to recover some stolen mules. One of Virgil's first acts as marshal was to arrest Wyatt for disturbing the peace. Nevertheless, along with Wyatt and Morgan, they tracked the missing mules to the ranch of Tom and Frank McLaury, but the brothers refused to give up the mules unless the Earps went back to Tombstone. They complied, but the McLaurys reneged on their part of the bargain. Later they threatened to kill Wyatt if he ever crossed them again.

When, in March 1881, there was an attempted hold-up of the Benson stage, where the driver and a passenger were killed, Ike Clanton accused Doc Holliday and implicated the Earps. Billy Clanton and Wyatt also fell out over the ownership of a horse.

On September 8, the Bisbee stage was held up. Marshal Virgil Earp and deputies Wyatt

Frank McLaury, 1876.

and Morgan arrested Pete Spence and Frank Stilwell, who were friends of Ike Clanton and Frank McLaury, further fueling the feud.

On the evening of October 25, 1881, Wyatt and Morgan Earp, and Doc Holliday confronted Ike Clanton. Though Holliday goaded him, Clanton refused to fight, saying he was unarmed.

Later, Ike Clanton confronted Wyatt, saying he was now armed and would welcome a fight in the morning. Ike passed the rest of the evening in a poker game with Virgil Earp, John Behan, and Tom McLaury. After the game, words were exchanged between Virgil and Ike.

THERE'S GONNA BE A SHOWDOWN

On the morning of October 26, 1881, Virgil Earp pistol-whipped and arrested Ike Clanton for carrying weapons within the city limits. In police court, Clanton was fined $25. More heated words were exchanged between

Tom McLaury, 1876.

Morgan and Ike. Tom McLaury turned up to support Ike, but as he was leaving he bumped into Wyatt who slapped and pistol-whipped him, though he was unarmed.

Ike and Billy Clanton, and the McLaury brothers gathered at a vacant lot on Fremont Street, near the O.K. Corral. Frank McLaury and Billy Clanton had apparently decided to leave town and saddled their horses. But it was too late. The Earps and Doc Holliday had already decided that there was going to be a showdown.

One witness testified that Virgil Earp told Sheriff Behan: "I will not arrest them, but will kill them on sight."

Behan tried to calm the situation. He went to the Clantons and McLaurys and asked them to give up their guns. Billy Clanton and Frank McLaury refused as they were leaving town. Tom McLaury opened his coat to show that he was unarmed, though he may have had a gun hidden in his waistband. Behan felt Ike Clanton's waistband and found no gun. Wyatt Earp later testified that Ike was unarmed. Behan returned to the Earps and begged them not to force a fight. They brushed him aside.

Wyatt, Virgil, and Morgan Earp, along with Doc Holliday who carried a double-barreled shotgun under his long coat, bore down on the Clantons and McLaurys.

"You sons of bitches, you have been looking for a fight. Now you can have one," yelled one of them, probably Wyatt.

Virgil told The Cowboys to put their hands up. Then the shooting started.

GUNFIGHT AT THE O.K. CORRAL

The "Gunfight at the O.K. Corral" did not happen at the O.K. Corral at all, but rather in a vacant lot between a boarding house and a private dwelling nearby. The O.K. Corral and Livery Stables were on the other side of the block.

There are conflicting versions of who fired first. However, Wyatt shot Frank McLaury in the stomach. Holliday killed Tom McLaury with a shotgun blast. Billy Clanton was fatally wounded and the unarmed Ike Clanton fled uninjured.

Although Virgil Earp had a bullet-hole in his right leg and a bullet also grazed Doc

Tombstone in 1881. An ore wagon at the center of the image is pulled by 15 or 16 mules.

Holliday's hip, they would recover. Wyatt and Morgan Earp emerged unscathed. Warrants were issued for the Earps and Doc Holliday. Virgil and Morgan were bonded, while Wyatt and Holliday remained in jail.

Hearings began on October 31, 1881, and, after listening to contradictory evidence, Justice of the Peace Wells Spicer ruled on November 30 that there was not enough evidence to indict the men.

FIGHTING AND FEUDING

The matter was far from over. When Virgil Earp walked into the Golden Eagle Brewery in the Cosmopolitan Hotel shortly before midnight on December 28, a shotgun blast shattered his left arm, leaving him crippled. Wyatt then applied to become a U.S. marshal and was immediately appointed. Along with Tombstone's acting police chief James Flynn, he broke up a confrontation between Doc Holliday and Johnny Ringo.

Ike Clanton swore out fresh warrants for the murder of his brother Billy at Contention, Arizona. After Wyatt and Virgil Earp resigned as U.S. marshals, they were arrested and taken there, but the judge found no reason to retry the matter.

Back in Tombstone, on the night of March 18, 1882, a bullet fired through the window of Campbell and Hatch's Billiard Parlor shattered Morgan Earp's spine. He died an hour later. Another bullet lodged in the wall just above Wyatt who was watching the game. A third man, George A.B. Berry, was hit in the thigh and died of heart failure.

Mrs. Marietta Spence said that her husband Pete Spence, Frank Stilwell, Florentino "Indian Charlie" Cruz, and others were responsible for the shooting.

SHOOTING IN TUCSON

Morgan Earp's body was sent for burial at Colton, California, now the family home. It was accompanied to Tucson, Arizona, by Morgan's widow, Virgil and his wife, Wyatt and Warren Earp, Doc Holliday, and two other Earp sidekicks—Jack "Turkey Creek" Johnson and Sherman McMasters.

They had another reason for traveling to Tucson. Stilwell was facing charges of robbing the Bisbee stage there and Ike Clanton was also in Tucson as a character witness. The Earps spotted Stilwell as the train pulled in and chased him in the evening gloom.

When they caught up with him, he tried to push the barrel of Wyatt's shotgun aside, but he was hit in the chest and thigh. The rest of the party opened up. Four rifle bullets were found in his body, though his own gun had not been fired.

Murder warrants were issued for the two Earps, Holliday, Johnson, and McMasters in Tucson. But they had left town. They were wired to Tombstone, but the telegraph operator there was persuaded to delay their delivery to Sheriff Behan until the Earp boys had time to leave town.

They went after Pete Spence. But fearing the Earps' vengeance, he had surrendered to Sheriff Behan and was in protective custody. However, they caught up with Indian Charlie Cruz. He was killed with a volley of five bullets. After a hearing over the death of Morgan Earp, Spence was released.

Five days later the *Tombstone Epitaph* carried the story that Wyatt Earp had killed Curly Bill Brocius. There is some dispute over the facts of the matter though.

THE DRIFTER YEARS

The Earps and their cronies were still wanted for the Stilwell slaying. Wyatt and Warren fled to Gunnison, Colorado, where the Governor F.W. Pitkin, a wealthy gambler, refused to sign the extradition papers.

Wyatt Earp then became a drifter, though he spent time with Josephine Marcus at her home in San Francisco. They may have married after the death of Mattie Blaylock from an overdose of laudanum in 1888. But the book *I Married Wyatt Earp* is thought to be a hoax as there is no record of the marriage.

In June 1883, Wyatt returned to Dodge City to help out his friend Luke Short. The

DODGE CITY

From 1847, a series of forts were built in Kansas, on the site of Dodge City, to protect travelers on the Santa Fe Trail from Indian attack. Then in 1871, rancher Henry J. Sitler built a sod house to the west of Fort Dodge to oversee his cattle operations. The following year, with the approach of the Santa Fe Railroad from the east, the town was staked out. While this was underway, a bar was opened in a tent to serve thirsty soldiers.

When the railroad arrived, Dodge City was open for business. However, the track had reached Wichita to the west first and it was already nicknamed "Cowtown." In 1872, Wichita shipped 70,600 head of cattle eastwards, after they had been driven up from Texas.

However, Dodge City soon became a serious rival. In 1876, Wichita shipped 14,643 head, while Dodge managed 9,540. But between 1875 and 1884 Dodge City shipped an estimated total of 349,097 head of cattle, a record for a Kansas cow town.

Famously lawless, it boasted a vast array of gambling halls, saloons and brothels, including the famous Long Branch Saloon and China Doll brothel. For a time in 1884, Dodge City even had a bullfighting ring where Mexican bullfighters would put on a show with specially chosen longhorn bulls. The gunfights brought fame to a succession of marshals and sheriffs, including Bat Masterson and Wyatt Earp and resulted in the establishment of its famous Boot Hill Cemetery. Of the thirty-three cadavers removed from Dodge City's Boot Hill, only one is generally accredited to Wyatt Earp's six-shooter.

Dodge City, the Cowboy Capital of the World. Front Street, in 1876, with the Long Branch Saloon on the left, and the railroad tracks in the foreground.

following year, Wyatt and Jim were in Eagle City, Idaho, where they did some mining as well as some claim-jumping. They also ran the White Elephant Saloon in Eagle City. It is also thought that Wyatt was in Lake City, Colorado, in September 1884, where he was reportedly shot in the arm after being accused of cheating at cards.

Between 1889 and 1890, he was living in San Diego with "Mrs. Wyatt Earp"— Josephine Marcus had been living there since 1886.

HEAVYWEIGHT CHAMPIONSHIP FIGHT

In 1896, Wyatt Earp was called upon to referee the heavyweight championship of the world in the Mechanics Pavilion in San Francisco, between Englishman Bob "Ruby Robert" Fitzsimmons, a former blacksmith, and Irish seaman Tom Sharkey. As Wyatt entered the ring, the police chief noticed a bulge in his coat and Earp was forced to hand over his six-shooter.

Fitzsimmons, the favorite, was ahead in the eighth round when he landed a left to the body and a right to the chin. Sharkey went down clutching his groin. Earp immediately declared him the winner on a foul and handed Sharkey the $10,000 winners' check. A riot broke out.

The athletic club stopped payment. Doctors were called in, but could not agree whether there had been a foul. Sharkey kept the purse, but his claim to the title was ignored and he returned to Ireland, while Fitzsimmons was acknowledged as world heavyweight champion after defeating James J. Corbett soon after.

Meanwhile Earp was arrested for carrying a concealed weapon and posted a $50 bond. At the hearing over the match outcome, Wyatt claimed to be destitute, owning only the clothes he stood up in, though the fight had brought him renewed notoriety.

BECOMING A LEGEND

In 1899, Wyatt Earp was running the Dexter Saloon in Nome, Alaska, after gold was discovered there. But he got into too many fights and was eventually arrested for interfering with an officer of the law. He moved on to Tonopah and Goldfield, Nevada, and Parker, Arizona, where he established mining interests.

Finally, after years of roaming the West, Wyatt and Josephine settled in Los Angeles. In 1911, he was arrested for fleecing a mark out of $25,000 in a bunco game, although there is no record of his conviction.

In Wyatt's later years, he was a technical advisor on several silent cowboy films. Legend has it that he became friends with a props-man and extra named Marion Morrison (John Wayne) and told him stories of the Old West. Wayne later claimed his portrayals of Western characters were based on Wyatt Earp's anecdotes.

Wyatt Earp died in Los Angeles on January 13, 1929, at age 80, two years before his purported memoirs, *Wyatt Earp: Frontier Marshal*, with Stuart N. Lake came out. The book has since been dismissed as fiction, but it changed history. Until the book was published, Earp had a dubious reputation as a sometime Western lawman and gunfighter who had been arrested nine times and left more than one town with warrants for his arrest. But *Wyatt Earp: Frontier Marshal* was responsible for the Gunfight at the O.K. Corral coming to public attention and for Earp becoming a symbol of American frontier justice. Since then, Wyatt Earp has featured in numerous films, TV shows, biographies, and works of fiction that have increased his mystique as a legend of the West.

CHAPTER 11

BAT MASTERSON
WESTERN LAWMAN AND GUNFIGHTER

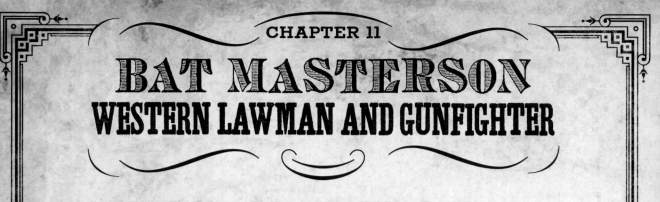

"NEVER RUN A BLUFF WITH A SIX-GUN."

Bat Masterson (1853 – 1921)

William Barclay Masterson—better known as Bartholomew or "Bat"—was one of the legendary lawmen of the Old West. But, like the others, he was not averse to working the other side of the law when it suited him.

Born in County Rouville, Quebec, Canada, in 1853, the second of seven children, he was not yet in his teens before his family moved

via Illinois and New York State, to Sedgwick County, Kansas. Bat soon realized that he was not cut out for the life of a mid-western farmer.

In 1872, he left home with his older brother Edward and a young friend named Theodore D. Raymond. Reaching Dodge City, they went to work for a private contractor named Raymond Ritter who was grading the railroad spur from Fort Dodge. When the job was done, Ritter ran off without paying them. Bat collected their wages at gunpoint when he came across Ritter the following year. Meanwhile he and his brothers took up buffalo hunting. He also lived with Lizzie Palmer, a former prostitute, who was said to have died after a brawl with another woman over Masterson.

BEING AN ARMY SCOUT

The Masterson brothers were at Adobe Walls in the Texas Panhandle when a full-scale Indian assault under Quanah Parker was repulsed by the buffalo hunters. They returned to Dodge City and, in August 1874, Bat enlisted as an Army scout at a salary of $75 a month with a bonus for every dispatch he carried through hostile territory—though this does not seem to have been paid.

At the time, Major General Nelson A. Miles of the Fifth U.S. Infantry was mounting a punitive expedition against the Southern Plains tribes. Bat was assigned to the scouting detachment of First Lieutenant Frank D. Baldwin, who became only the second man in the U.S. Army to be awarded two Congressional Medals of Honor.

THE BATTLE OF ADOBE WALLS

Adobe Walls was the name of a trading post in the Texas Panhandle, just north of the Canadian River. In 1845, an adobe fort was built there to house the post, but it was blown up by the traders three years later after repeated Indian attacks. In 1864, the ruins were the site of one of the largest battles ever to take place on the Great Plains. Colonel Christopher "Kit" Carson led three-hundred volunteers from New Mexico against a force of thousands of Native Americans. The results of the battle were indecisive, though Carson was acclaimed as a hero for successfully striking a blow against the Indians and for leading his men out of the trap with minimal casualties.

In the spring of 1874, Dodge City traders built a sod trading post there. This was soon followed by a saloon, a blacksmith shop, and a couple of stores. In June that year, the buffalo hunters from Dodge City moved out there. Around that time, braves from the Arapaho, Cheyenne, Comanche, Kiowa, and Kataka broke out of the reservations, beginning what became known as the Red River War.

During the first battle of Adobe Walls, the Indians had been led by the chief of the Kiowas, Satanta. He was now eclipsed by Quanah Parker, son of the Comanche chief Peta Nokoni and Cynthia Parker, a white captive. The Comanche medicine man Isatai claimed that his medicine would protect the tribes from the white men's bullets.

An Army scout named Amos Chapman rode out to Adobe Walls to warn the inhabitants that the Indians intended to attack. It was said that the saloon owner Jim Hanrahan had invested so much in his property that he did not tell the others.

Twenty-nine men and a woman named Mrs. Old were there when two-hundred Indians under Quanah Parker attacked at dawn on June 27. Two hunters asleep in a wagon near the corral were killed in the first assault. The men sleeping in the saloon were wakened by a loud crack from the ridgepole, though nothing was found to be wrong with it.

Billy Tyler was killed the first day, trying to protect the livestock, and George Olds was killed when his rifle went off accidentally while he was descending a ladder. The defenders suffered no other casualties.

The siege lasted for five days. When the battle was over, the bodies of ten Indians were found, along with that of one African-American, thought to be a deserter from the Ninth or Tenth U.S. Cavalry who blew a bugle to signal the advance and retreat of the Indians.

Bat Masterson was credited with killing one Indian. Using a .50 Sharps rifle, Billy Dixon reportedly felled an Indian at 1,538 yards. Quanah Parker was injured and both he and Isatai had their horses shot out from under them.

Bat Masterson (left), and Billy Dixon (center) at the Second Battle of Adobe Walls, 1874.

He was with Baldwin's scouting party near Adobe Walls when they engaged the Indians in light skirmishes. Masterson was then sent with a dispatch to General Miles. The rest of the scouts caught up with the main column near Antelope Hills in Indian Territory.

On August 30, 1874, General Miles committed his troops to the biggest battle of the campaign. This was spearheaded by Baldwin's men. A large number of Cheyenne were seen off by light artillery and Gatling guns. Reportedly Masterson distinguished himself by rescuing Julia and Adelaide German who had been seized by the Indians after their family had been massacred in Kansas two months earlier.

SHOOTING IN SWEETWATER

Afterward, Masterson did not re-enlist as a scout. He worked as a teamster before moving to Sweetwater, Texas, which changed its name to Mobeetie in 1879.

Deputies Bat Masterson (standing) and Wyatt Earp in Dodge City, 1876.

One night, Corporal Melvin King of the Fourth Cavalry fell foul of Masterson. A Civil War veteran, King had been discharged from the Army on a number of occasions for drunkenness and fighting, but had re-enlisted under various aliases. He had already been beaten in a confrontation with Wyatt Earp.

It seems that King was sweet on a dancehall girl named Molly Brennan, former lover of Ben Thompson's brother Billy and ex-wife of Ellsworth saloon owner Joe Brennan. One night, King found Molly alone with Masterson. He burst in with his six-gun blazing. Masterson shot him dead. Molly was also killed when she stepped between them and Masterson was shot in the leg. After that he walked with a cane. It has been suggested that this was the origin of his nickname. It may also have been short for "Battling"—the sobriquet then given to notorious scrappers.

BACK IN DODGE CITY

Bat returned to Dodge City where he bought a saloon and dancehall, which also seems to have operated as a brothel. Just a month after getting his saloon license, he stepped in on the side of right, if not the law.

City Marshal Larry Deger was a big guy. One day, he was escorting diminutive town tramp Robert Gilmore, a.k.a. Bobby Gill, to jail with more bullying force than Masterson thought necessary. For his pains, Bat was pistol-whipped by Deger while others held him down. Masterson was then disarmed, jailed, and, the following day, fined $25 plus costs by Police Judge Daniel M. Frost. Later, when his friend James "Dog" Kelley became mayor, he refunded $10. But Masterson held a grudge against Deger.

Soon after, Masterson became under-sheriff of Ford County when friend and fellow gambler Charlie Bassett was sheriff, and managed to oust Deger from his city marshal position. Mayor Kelley then appointed Bat special policeman at $2.50 a day.

A week after Bat had taken office, a Texan cowhand named A.C. Jackson rode into town and loosed off two or three shots in front of the Alhambra Saloon. Bat dashed out onto the street and ordered him to stop.

"I'm going to skip out for camp," shouted Jackson, firing a couple more rounds in the air.

Bat sent a couple of bullets after him as he raced out of town. Masterson's brother, Ed, who had been assistant marshal under Deger, joined in. Jackson's horse was hit, but carried him out of town before it died. Bat mounted his horse and rode after Jackson, but turned back when he realized he was out of ammunition.

EDWARD J. MASTERSON

Bat Masterson's older brother, Ed, left home with Bat to become a buffalo hunter. When Bat became under-sheriff of Ford County, Ed became deputy marshal of Dodge City. Seven months later, he was promoted to marshal, a position he held for just five months.

In November 1877, Ed intervened in a quarrel between Texas Dick Moore and Bob Shaw, the owners of the Lone Star Dancehall. Ed Masterson ordered Shaw to surrender his gun. Instead, Shaw took a shot at Moore. Ed clubbed Shaw on the head with his gun butt. Shaw turned and shot Ed in the chest. The bullet struck a rib and came out under the right shoulder blade. With his right arm paralyzed, Ed's six-gun thudded to the floor. Ed dropped down, grabbed the gun and shot Shaw in the left arm and left leg, knocking him to the floor. In the melee Moore was hit in the groin.

The following April, half-a-dozen cowboys were celebrating the end of the cattle drive at the Lady Gay. One of them, Jack Wagner, was carrying a gun in contravention of the city ordinance. Masterson and his deputy Nat Haywood went to disarm him. Ed gave the gun to the trail boss Alfred Walker with instructions not to give it back to Wagner until he was sober. But as soon as Masterson and Haywood had left, Walker handed the gun back to Wagner and they came out after them, along with the other four trail hands.

Ed again went to disarm Wagner who tried to shoot him in the face, but the gun misfired. Haywood stepped forward, but was forced back at gunpoint by Walker and the others. Wagner then squeezed off another shot. This time the gun did fire. Ed was hit in the stomach at such close range that the muzzle flash set his shirt on fire. Nevertheless, he got off four shots. One hit Wagner in the stomach. The other three hit Walker, shattering his right arm and piercing his lung after grazing the faces of two bystanders.

Wagner ran into A.J. Peacock's saloon where he collapsed, dying the following day. Walker made it out of the back door before he too collapsed, though he eventually recovered. With his clothes still on fire, Ed staggered across the railroad tracks to George Hoover's saloon where he said to bartender George Hinkle: "George, I'm shot."

He was carried to brother Bat's room where he died half-an-hour later, surrounded by his brother and friends. Bat then arrested the other four cowboys, but they were released for lack of evidence. Tom Masterson maintained that Bat had shot Wagner and Walker, but he was not there and this version has largely been discounted.

Edward Masterson (1852 – 1878).

ARREST AT CROOKED CREEK

In October 1877, Bat Masterson decided to run for sheriff of Ford County as Bassett was prohibited from serving a third term. Bat defeated Deger for the position by three votes. Meanwhile, Mayor Kelley appointed Ed Masterson as city marshal and Bat made Bassett under-sheriff. Later Jim Masterson also became a deputy.

Bat had been in office less than a month when five men tried to rob the Santa Fe Railroad at Kinsley, thirty-five miles northeast of Dodge City. Refusing to cooperate with the posse from Kinsley, Bat formed his own posse which tracked down two of the would-be robbers, arresting them at Crooked Creek, sixty miles south of Dodge City. Another two were arrested in Dodge City by Bat, Ed, and Charlie Bassett.

During the investigation, Bat also arrested his friend Bill Tilghman for complicity. He later arrested Tilghman for horse theft. Tilghman was discharged by the courts on both charges and later became city marshal in Dodge City, and after that a deputy U.S. marshal in Oklahoma Territory.

ARRESTS AND ACQUITTALS

Following the death of Ed Masterson in a street fight, Dodge City became an even more lawless place. However, the police force was shored up by the presence of Wyatt Earp. Along with Charlie Bassett and Bill Tilghman, Wyatt joined Bat Masterson's posse to track Spike Kenedy after he shot actress Dora Hand. On the afternoon of October 5, 1878, the posse shot Kenedy's horse out from under him near Meade City, thirty-five miles southwest of Dodge City. Kenedy was wounded in the left shoulder. He was taken back to Dodge City, but was later acquitted of the murder.

Hearing that his old friend, the notorious horse thief Henrich "Dutch Henry" Borne was in Trinidad, Colorado, Bat sent word for the authorities there to detain him. Masterson arrived in Trinidad on New Year's Day 1879, only to find that the authorities there wanted $500 to hand him over. After a great deal of legal red tape, Bat took Borne back to Dodge City, where he too was acquitted for lack of evidence.

Later Bat traveled to Fort Leavenworth to identify Cheyenne braves held by the Army.

Oriental Saloon, Tombstone in the 1880s with Wyatt Earp (second from the right) dealing faro and Doc Holliday as watcher to Wyatt's right.

They were members of Dull Knife's band of renegades and he had warrants for their arrest. He brought seven of them back to Dodge City, but they were granted a change of venue to Lawrence where they were acquitted for lack of evidence. The whole procedure had cost the county $4,000. This later counted against Bat in his re-election campaign.

FIGHTING PIMPS

On January 18, 1879, Bat Masterson was appointed deputy U.S. marshal. He also found the time to invest in South Side saloons, dancehalls, and brothels—though he left the running of them to trigger-happy younger brother Jim. As a result the Mastersons—and Wyatt Earp and Charlie Bassett who also owned bordellos—were called "fighting pimps" by Texas trail hands.

Bat also appeared as something of a dude to them. Five feet ten, he was a stocky man at 175 pounds with gray eyes and brown hair, but he wore tailor-made Eastern clothes and a white derby. His thick mustache was well trimmed—he did not allow it to droop, as was the custom of the time.

Disliked by trail hands, he also fell out of favor with his boss, George B. Cox, chairman of the board of Ford County commissioners, for his high-handed attitude to policing, but it was Cox who was forced to resign.

RAILROAD WARS

The Santa Fe Railroad and the Denver & Rio Grande Western Railroad contested the right of way through the Royal Gorge, also known as the Grand Canyon of the Arkansas River, near Pueblo, Colorado. In March 1879, Santa Fe officials in Canon City, Colorado, contacted Bat Masterson and asked for his help. He recruited thirty men, who left Dodge City on March 22. This was not official business and Masterson was working as a private citizen.

He returned to Dodge City on April 5, leaving Ben Thompson in charge. However, he went back to Canon City on June 9 to take command of the roundhouse there that blocked the Rio Grande's right of way through the gorge. But he surrendered the roundhouse when writs were served by U.S. marshals and he returned to Dodge City. The issue of the right of way was settled out of court.

SAVED FROM A LYNCHING

Bat was defeated in his bid for re-election as sheriff in November 1879 by George Hinkle. He was still living in Dodge City with his nineteen-year-old mistress Annie Ladue when he got a telegram from Ben Thompson asking him to rescue his brother Billy.

Billy Thompson and another Texan named Jim Tucker had fought a duel in Ogallala, Nebraska. Thompson had been wounded and, unable to flee, brother Ben feared that he was in danger of being lynched. Legend has it that Bat sneaked Billy out of Ogallala under the noses of the citizenry and hid him in North Platte, Nebraska, at the home of Buffalo Bill Cody who was famed for his hospitality.

After a sojourn in Kansas City, Bat returned to Dodge City before moving onto Tombstone, where he joined Wyatt Earp at the Oriental Saloon.

LADY GAY DANCEHALL AND SALOON

Jim Masterson and A.J. Peacock were partners in the Lady Gay Dancehall and Saloon, but their relationship had soured. One of the girls employed there alleged that she had been robbed by one of Jim's friends. Al Updegraff, a barman hired by Peacock, urged her to press charges. Jim tried to talk her out of it and fired Updegraff. Peacock intervened and shots were exchanged. Updegraff then had Jim arrested. Jim then telegraphed Bat and asked for his help.

On April 16, 1881, Bat arrived in Dodge City on the 11:50 train. Stepping down from the car, he saw Peacock and Updegraff walking together in the crowded street. Stopping about twenty feet from them, he yelled: "I've come over a thousand miles to settle this. I know you are heeled—now fight!"

All three men drew their guns and began shooting. Jim Masterson and Charlie Ronan joined in. Windows were smashed and bullets lodged in surrounding buildings. One slug hit the ground, kicking dirt up into Bat's mouth. The ricocheting bullet hit fleeing bystander Jim Anderson. Updegraff was also wounded by a bullet that passed through his right lung.

Peacock and Bat ran out of bullets. While they were reloading, Mayor Alonzo B. Webster and Sheriff Fred Singer intervened carrying shotguns. Bat was arrested and paid a small fine. Jim sold his interest in the Lady Gay and the two brothers took the evening train out of town.

DENVER GAMBLER

Bat Masterson moved to Denver, though he frequently returned to Dodge City to dabble in politics there. He backed Luke Short during the Dodge City War in 1883 and was a member of the so-called "peace commission."

On November 1, 1884, he published the single-edition newspaper *Vox Populi* there. Legally, Kansas had been dry since 1880 and in March 1886, Bat became a special deputy sheriff to close the saloons in Dodge City and file arrest warrants against their owners. They soon opened again. That year, Bat also eloped with actress Nellie Spencer, after beating her actor husband with a pistol.

Meanwhile Bat made his living in Denver as a professional gambler. In 1890, he became manager of Ed Chaise's Palace Saloon and Gambling House. The Palace then opened a variety theater and, the following year, Bat married Emma Walters, an actress there.

In 1892, he joined the Denver gambling firm of Watrous, Banninger and Company, and oversaw their operations in Creede, Colorado. He was also a lawman there— city marshal or deputy sheriff according to differing accounts. Overrun with gunmen, card-sharps, conmen, and prostitutes, it was one of the last boom towns on the frontier. Its Boot Hill was called "Shotgun Graveyard."

He returned to Denver full-time in 1894. By then it was the capital of the West.

FRONTIER DAYS ARE GONE

In 1897, Bat Masterson traveled to Carson City, Nevada, where he lost a great deal of money backing the heavyweight champion "Gentleman Jim" Corbett against Bob Fitzsimmons.

Back in Denver, Masterson formed the Colorado Athletic Association with Otto Floto, the celebrated sports editor of the *Denver Post*. Bat was official referee. But then Floto wanted total control, Masterson pulled out to form the rival Olympic Athletic Club, where he was elected president. However,

prize fighting was then illegal in Colorado. Floto had access to the funds to bribe the police and drove Masterson out of business.

The days of the frontier were over and opportunities for the professional gambler in Denver were limited, so Bat turned to drink and, in 1902, he was asked to leave.

NEW YORK CITY

On his way east, Bat and two other men named Joseph C. Sullivan and Leopold Frank, played cards with George H. Snow, an elder in the Mormon church. Snow lost $16,000 and, when they arrived in New York, he reported the card-sharps to the police.

Bat Masterson was arrested and charged with grand larceny and carrying a concealed weapon. Sullivan and Frank were found to be carrying marked cards. Bat was bailed by theatrical manager John Considine, whose clients later included Charlie Chaplin. The charges were dropped when Snow admitted he could not be certain that Masterson was in on the scam. But a month later, Bat was again arrested for carrying a concealed weapon.

Considine, who had known Masterson out West, put him in touch with the editor of the *New York Morning Telegram*, William E. Lewis, who offered him a job as a sports writer. He wrote a thrice-weekly column for the newspaper for eighteen years. The job put him in touch with heavyweight champions Jack Johnson, Jess Willard, and Jack Dempsey. He also got to know writers Damon Runyon and Louella Parsons, later a legendary Hollywood columnist.

WHITE HOUSE GUNFIGHTER

He met Theodore Roosevelt and was a regular guest at the White House. Roosevelt offered to make Masterson U.S. marshal for Oklahoma Territory in 1905, but Bat declined because he knew he would be a target for every young hustler who wanted to make a reputation for himself as a quick-draw gunfighter. Instead, he became deputy U.S. marshal for the South District of New York at a then record salary of $2,000 a year. Meanwhile William Lewis's brother Alfred wrote fictionalized accounts of Bat's exploits in the West, further inflating his fame.

Bat wrote his own accounts for the magazine *Human Life* which were collected in the book *Famous Gunfighters of the Western Frontier*. Short of money, he had to pawn his six shooter—famed as "the gun that tamed the West." His transformation into an Eastern citizen was complete when he shaved off his mustache, then seen as a symbol of the old West, and he died of a heart attack at his desk in 1921.

By 1898, Denver had developed into a city and the days of the frontier were well and truly gone.

NO THANKS, MR. PRESIDENT

When Theodore Roosevelt was re-elected in 1904, he offered to make Bat Masterson the U.S. marshal for the Oklahoma Territory with twenty-two deputies under him and a salary of twice what he would receive as a deputy in New York. Masterson declined, saying:

It wouldn't do. The man of my peculiar reputation couldn't hold such a place without trouble. If I were to go out to the Indian Territory as Marshal, I can see what would happen. I'd have some drunken boy to kill once a year. Some kid who was born after I took my guns off would get drunk and look me over, and the longer he looked the less he'd be able to see where my reputation came from. In the end he'd crawl around to a gun play and I'd have to send him over the jump. Almost any other man could hold office and never see a moment's trouble. But I couldn't. My record would prove a never-failing bait to the dime-novel reading youngsters, locoed to distinguish themselves and make a fire-eating reputation, and I'd have to bump 'em off. So, Mr. President, with all thanks to you, I believe I won't take the place. I've got finally out of that zone of fire and I hope never to go back to it.

Theodore Roosevelt, 26th President of the United States from 1901 to 1909.

CHAPTER 12

THE DALTON BROTHERS
BREAKING BAD

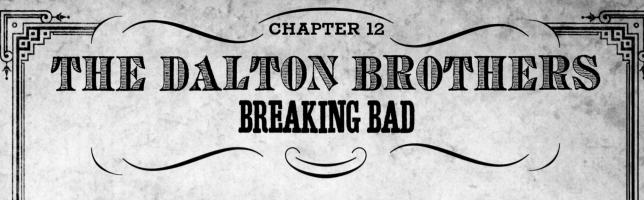

"FOR THE DALTONS, KILLING WAS IN THE LINE OF DUTY."

Although the Daltons became one of the most notorious gangs of outlaws in the Old West, they started their careers as lawmen. Indeed only four of the fifteen children of Mexican-American War veteran James Lewis Dalton and his god-fearing wife Adeline Lee Younger went bad, though two died in infancy and three were girls.

However, their mother was the half sister of Henry Younger, father of the outlaw Younger brothers, and the children were brought up in Cass, Bates, and Clay Counties in western Missouri, an area plagued by outlaws before, during, and after the Civil War. Around 1882, the family moved to Coffeyville, Kansas, and afterward to the Indian Territory, near present-day Vinita, Oklahoma, which was similarly lawless.

STARTING OUT GOOD

Born in 1859, the oldest brother Frank Dalton became a deputy U.S. marshal in the Indian Territory under Judge Isaac Parker, the famous "Hanging Judge of Fort Smith." His brother Gratton, "Grat," two years younger than Frank, rode with him in the posse. Frank was killed in a shoot-out with whiskey smugglers in 1887.

Grat replaced Frank as deputy U.S. marshal while Bob Dalton (born 1869), also became a detective for the Osage Indian Agency. But largely they spent their time shaking down newcomers. Bob became a killer at the age of nineteen. Although he had several sweethearts at the time, he did not like other men courting his cousin Minnie. Her boyfriend turned up dead with a bullet in his neck. He had been, Bob said, "resisting arrest." Grat had also shot his first man, suspected horse-thief Charles Montgomery, at a similarly young age.

Born in 1871, the youngest brother Emmett also pinned on a badge. The boys took bribes, smuggled whiskey, and were involved with horse stealing. Things came to a head when they shot down a Native American boy on the accusation that he was a wanted man. For the Daltons killing was in the line of duty.

THE DALTON GANG

The three Dalton brothers took refuge in the Ozarks. Then they headed on to New Mexico, where Emmett was shot in the arm when they tried to hold up a gambling joint near Santa Rita.

Frank Dalton (1859 – 87).

Emmett went home to recuperate while Grat and Bob went to California, where Bill Dalton (born 1866) had settled in Tulare County with his wife and two children. He had already begun a political career there, taking the side of the little man against the Southern Pacific Railroad.

On February 6, 1891, a Southern Pacific train was held up and robbed at Alila, California. Detectives suspected what they were soon calling the "Dalton Gang." Its leader, they decided, was Bob whose reward posters described him as:

> *About twenty three … ; height 6ft 1½ inches; well built and straight; light complexion, but florid and healthy looking; boyish beard and mustache; light hair and eyes; weight 180 to 190 lbs.; large, bony, long-fingered hands, showing no acquaintance with work; large nose and ears; white teeth; long sun-burned neck, square features … Is a good poker and card player; drinks whisky in moderation, but does not chew tobacco; smokes brown paper cigarettes occasionally.*

The four Dalton brothers were indicted on March 17, 1891, charged with train robbery and assault with intent to murder the express

car messenger. While Bob and Emmett escaped back to Indian Territory, Grat and Bill were tried separately. Bill was acquitted, but Grat was convicted and sentenced to twenty years in San Quentin. At his trial, eyewitnesses were shown a photograph of Bob and identified him as one of the robbers.

THE TRAIN ROBBING DALTONS

Meanwhile in the Indian Territory, Bob and Emmett formed a gang that would rival the fame of the James-Younger Gang. Other members included George "Bittercreek" Newcomb, Charley Pierce, and Blackface Charlie Bryant—so called due to a powder burn on his cheek. Others drifted in and out of the gang. Bob was clearly the leader and he laid down the rules. No "grangers"— homesteaders—were to be molested and no one was to be killed unless absolutely necessary.

The gang robbed a train near Wharton on May 9, 1891, and another at Red Rock on June 1. Charlie Bryant fell ill and the gang left him at the Red Rock Hotel in Hennessey, before calling a doctor. But Marshal Ed Short also came to his bedside and arrested him. On a train out of town, Short took pity on the sick man and loosened his handcuffs. Bryant then grabbed a six-shooter. In a face-to-face duel, he and the marshal shot each other dead. Bryant had always boasted: "I want to get killed in one hell-firin' minute of action." He got his wish.

The gang's next target was a Missouri, Kansas & Texas Railroad train at Adair. They robbed the depot first. Then when the train pulled in, they threatened to dynamite the express car unless the messenger opened it. When he did, they were confronted with railroad detectives and the Indian police. In the gun fight that followed, 200 shots were fired. None of the Dalton gang was hit. Three guards were wounded, and a town doctor was killed by a stray bullet. The robbers fled and disappeared.

Afterward, the Daltons said they would give up train robbing. They decided to rob banks instead.

Bill Dalton (1866 – 95).

COFFEYVILLE BANK ROBBERY

Grat busted out of San Quentin and he and Bill joined the others in the Indian Territory. Bob had decided that they should make one big hit, then retire. The heist would take place in their old hometown, Coffeyville, because it had two banks. No one had ever robbed two banks at the same time before. Bill thought this was crazy and refused to go along with it.

The plan was simple. They would ride into town as the banks opened, so there would be no time for anyone to make a withdrawal. Bob and Emmett would rob the First National Bank of Coffeyville as it was the largest and the most heavily guarded. Grat would hit the C.M. Condon & Co. Bank with gang members Bill Powers and Dick Broadwell. The escape routes were scouted and they reckoned that the whole thing should take fifteen minutes, maximum.

They bought new clothes and carried new Winchesters. It was important not to look like saddle tramps for such a historic raid. But as this was home territory, they decided to wear false beards.

As they rode into town on October 5, 1892, no one seemed to recognize them. But once they had dismounted, tied up their horses and made their way toward the banks, someone yelled: "There go the Daltons!"

The townspeople of Coffeyville had been warned they were coming by Deputy U.S. Marshal Chris Madsen who was known as one of the "Three Guardsmen of Oklahoma" along with lawmen Bill Tilghman and Heck Thomas. Word got out that the banks were being robbed. Residents prepared for a gun battle. When the gang exited the banks the good people of Coffeyville were armed and ready for them.

BULLETS START TO FLY

In the First National Bank, Bob and Emmett ordered everyone to get their hands up. They threw grain sacks on the floor and ordered the teller to fill them up. He protested that the vault was not open yet and they netted just $5,000.

C.M. Condon & Co. Bank, Coffeyville, Kansas. Scene of the Dalton bank robbery in 1892.

Shooting had already started outside and the Daltons tried to leave, using customers and staff as human shields. But the gunfire was so heavy they were forced back inside. The Dalton brothers then rushed for the back door. Store clerk Lucius Baldwin was waiting outside with a rifle. Bob shot him down. As they rushed down the alley into the street, Bob and Emmett killed Charles Brown and George Cubine. Cashier Tom Ayres got a bullet wound in the head.

The Daltons made it back to their horses unscathed and were about to make their getaway when they heard gunfire from the Condon Bank and realized that they would have to go and help Grat.

A DALTON TURKEY SHOOT

An intelligent employee of the Condon Bank had delayed Grat by convincing him (falsely) that the safe was on a time lock, and could not be opened for another 10 minutes. Grat had believed it and settled down to wait. At the front of the bank, Broadwell and Powers were soon engaged in a firefight and Grat decided it was time to get out of there. He asked where the back door was and was told there wasn't one. Again he believed what he was told.

He forced the tellers to carry $4,000 in silver dollars, weighing nearly 240 pounds, out of the bank and grabbed $1,000 in greenbacks. The three outlaws then ran for their horses. Powers was shot down as he tried to mount up. Broadwell was wounded. Dodging from one bit of cover to another, he managed to mount his horse and make his escape, but half a mile outside town he bled to death.

Grat Dalton was hit at least twice. But he kept shooting and staggered into what later became known as "Death Alley." A bullet from his Winchester downed Marshal Charlie Connelly. Bob and Emmett Dalton raced to Grat's rescue, but also found themselves pinned down in the alleyway. For the townsmen, it became a turkey shoot.

Bob appeared in the middle of the alley, apparently checking out a nearby roof. A sniper hit him squarely in the chest, knocking him over. John J. Kloehr, proprietor of the local livery stable, moved in and shot him again. Grat was now wandering blindly around. Kloehr fired again, hitting him in the throat and breaking his neck.

THE ROAR OF A SHOTGUN

Emmett could have gotten away. Although he was wounded in the arm and thigh, he was still clutching a sack of money. He swung his leg over his horse but, instead of riding off, he turned and rode toward Bob. He stretched out his hand to his wounded brother, but Bob was too weak to take it.

Then there was the roar of a shotgun wielded by barber Carey Seaman. Emmett was knocked from his mount. He surrendered. The battle was over. Grat and Bob Dalton, Dick Broadwell and Bill Powers were all killed. Emmett Dalton received 23 gunshot wounds but survived. Four citizens—including the marshal—were dead, along with a number of horses.

Powers' body was collected from out of town and the four dead outlaws were photographed. Their clothes were torn into strips by souvenir hunters and all but $22 of the stolen money was returned to the banks.

Emmett Dalton was carried to the Farmer's Hotel where he was nursed back to health by his sweetheart and his mother. He was later found guilty of murder and sentenced to life in Kansas State Prison. Released for good behavior after fourteen-and-a-half years, he married his childhood sweetheart and had a successful career as a building contractor and real estate agent. Moving to California in 1920, he wrote movie scenarios. He died in 1937 in Hollywood, at age sixty-six.

THE DOOLIN DALTON GANG

Bill Dalton appeared at Emmett's bedside after the shoot-out at Coffeyville. Three of his brothers were now dead and a fourth faced life imprisonment. Eager to strike back at the authorities, Bill joined Bill Doolin, becoming second in command in an outfit they called the "Oklahombres." They pulled a series of bank robberies.

On September 1, 1893, Doolin, Dalton, Newcomb, Tulsa Jack Blake, Red Buck Weightman, and Dan Clifton bellied up to the bar of the Ransom and Murray Saloon in Ingalls. Meanwhile an ailing Arkansas Tom Jones was recovering in bed upstairs at the City Hotel. The authorities had been tipped off and lawmen were closing in.

As the outlaws started a poker game, Newcomb stepped outside, where he was shot by posse member Dick Speed. Though wounded, Newcomb managed to mount his horse and gallop out of town. Then a furious gun battle broke out.

A boy named Dell Simmons was killed and bystander N.A. Walker was hit in the chest. From his upstairs window, Arkansas Tom shot Speed and lawman Tom Houston.

During a brief lull in the firing, there was a call for the outlaws to surrender.

"Go to hell!" was Doolin's reply.

GUNS BLAZING

Closing in, the lawmen poured volley after volley into the saloon. The owners were wounded: Ransom in the leg, Murray in the arm and side.

Doolin made a dash to the nearby livery stable. He gave covering fire as Dalton and Red Buck followed, with Clifton and Blake bringing up the rear.

Doolin and Clifton galloped out of the back door, while Dalton, Red Buck, and Blake raced out of the front, guns blazing. Dalton's horse was hit in the jaw. He spurred it on, but after twenty yards it was brought down when a rifle slug broke its leg. Dalton chased after his two comrades on foot, only to discover that they had been stopped by a wire fence.

Under gunfire, Dalton ran back to his horse and retrieved a pair of wire cutters. He was cutting through the fence when lawman Lafe Shadley rode up. Dalton turned and fired at Shadley, putting three slugs into him so close together that the wounds could be covered with the palm of your hand.

As the lawman lay dying, Dalton finished off cutting the fence. Seeing Dalton's predicament, Doolin rode back and pulled him up behind. As they galloped away, they stopped at the top of the hill to loose off one final volley at anyone who might be chasing them. They only succeeded in hitting Dr. Briggs' fourteen-year-old son in the shoulder.

DESPERADO BILL DALTON

Bill Dalton turned out to be just as much of a desperado as his brothers. On April 1, 1894, he and Bittercreek Newcomb entered a store in Sacred Heart owned by former lawman W.H. Carr, who was serving seventeen-year-old Lee Hardwick. Carr recognized Dalton and pulled a gun. Newcomb drew too. They fired simultaneously. Carr hit Newcomb in the shoulder; Newcomb hit Carr in the wrist, knocking the gun from his hand.

As Carr stooped to retrieve the gun, Hardwick grabbed a shotgun. Dalton loosed off four shots wildly. Carr came up firing and Newcomb shot him in the stomach. Nevertheless the old lawman kept on firing as the two outlaws turned and fled.

George "Bittercreek" Newcomb (1866 – 1895).

The Dalton gang following the 1892 Coffeyville,
Kansas raid. Left to right: Bill Powers, Bob
Dalton, Grat Dalton, and Dick Broadwell.

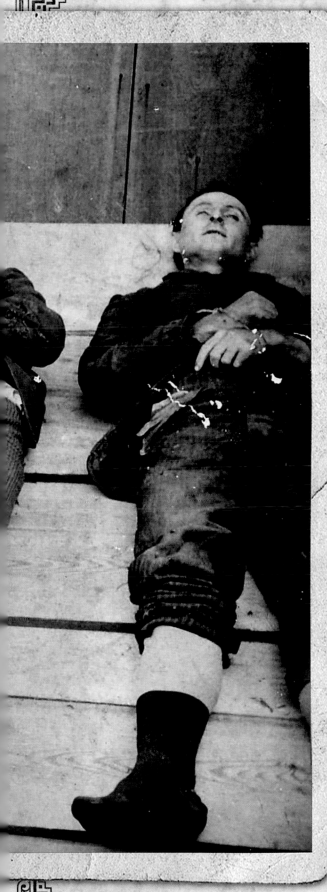

SHOOTING A MAN OF GOD

After a train robbery outside Dover on April 3, 1895, the Doolin Gang was ambushed by a posse. Tulsa Jack Blake was fatally wounded and Red Buck Weightman's horse was killed, but he climbed up behind Newcomb and they made their escape. At a nearby farm owned by an elderly parson, Red Buck stole a fresh horse and gunned down the preacher when he protested. Shooting a man of God was too much for Doolin and Dalton, and they decided to expel Weightman. Given his share of the loot, he was told to leave the gang.

On September 25, 1895, a posse surrounded Dalton's wife's house near Ardmore. He was playing with his young child, Grace, on the porch. After being told to surrender, Dalton made a grab for his Winchester a few feet away. Deputy Marshal Loss Hart fired. The bullet entered Dalton's back and came out just above his heart. He was dead within minutes.

TWENTY-ONE HOLES

The Three Guardsmen—Chris Madsen, Heck Thomas, and Bill Tilghman—continued to pursue the Doolin Gang. Tilghman caught Doolin in a bathhouse at Eureka Springs and took him to the jail at Gutherie, where the whole town turned out to cheer. But soon Doolin broke out.

He hid out at the ranch of writer Eugene Manlove Rhodes in New Mexico. In August 1896, he decided to go and fetch his wife and child, who were living with his father-in-law, a minister, just outside Lawson. But Heck Thomas was staking out the place. As he approached on the night of August 25, Thomas ordered him to stop. Doolin whipped up his Winchester. There were lawmen along both sides of the road. A bullet from one of them knocked the rifle from his hands. Doolin drew his revolver and managed to squeeze off a couple of shots, before Thomas hit him with a bullet from his rifle. Posse member Bill Dunn finished Doolin off with a shotgun. There were twenty-one holes in his body.

SMITH & WESSON

Horace Smith and Daniel B. Wesson founded the Smith & Wesson company in Norwich, Connecticut, in 1852 to develop the Volcanic Rifle which had a lever action mechanism and used Rocket Ball ammunition. This was a development of the Minié ball, a cone-shaped bullet with a cavity in the base, whose edges were forced outwards by the exploding charge, sealing the bullet against the sides of the barrel. The Rocket Ball took this principle one step further, hollowing out almost the entire length of the bullet and packing it with powder. This had the added advantage of doing away with the paper cartridge.

Smith & Wesson went on to develop the rim-fire cartridge, where the ball, powder, and fulminate were packed together in a copper case. All they needed was a weapon that could use it. In 1855, they obtained exclusive rights to produce bored-through cylinder pistols patented by Rollin White. Their first effort was a .22 caliber.

1

2

3

4

5

6

By the early years of the Civil War, the caliber had increased to .32. In the 1860s, center-fire ammunition was developed. A percussion cap or primer was placed in the middle of the cartridge base, which was struck by a pin on the hammer face. Fresh primer could be inserted in the base and the cartridge reloaded with ball and powder. This was a tremendous advance for the frontiersmen far from fresh supplies.

Between 1869 and 1880, Smith & Wesson produced a series of revolvers that rivaled Remington's and Colt's. The big advantage of their design was a catch that, when released, allowed the barrel to drop forward, so all the spent cartridge cases could be extracted in one go. This made reloading quicker. On the other hand, with Remington and Colt's revolvers, cartridges were ejected one at a time using a rod stashed under the barrel.

1. Smith & Wesson Model 3 Russian Revolver, 1875.
2. Smith & Wesson Volcanic Lever Action Pistol, 1857.
3. Smith & Wesson New Model No. 3 Revolver, 1887.
4. Smith & Wesson Model No. 3 Second Model, 1872.
5. Smith & Wesson .44 Double Action First Model Revolver, 1881.
6. Smith & Wesson New Model No. 3 Target Revolver with Shoulder Stock.
7. Smith & Wesson .44 Double Action First Model Revolver, 1881.
8. Smith & Wesson .38 Single Action Second Model Revolver, 1880.
9. Smith & Wesson .38 Safety Fifth Model Revolver, 1887.
10. Smith & Wesson .38 Double Action Fourth Model Revolver, 1898.

It was early in the morning
When he rode into the town
He came riding from the south side
Slowly lookin' all around
He's an outlaw loose and running
Came the whisper from each lip
And he's here to do some business
With the big iron on his hip

Lyrics from Big Iron *by Marty Robbins (1959)*

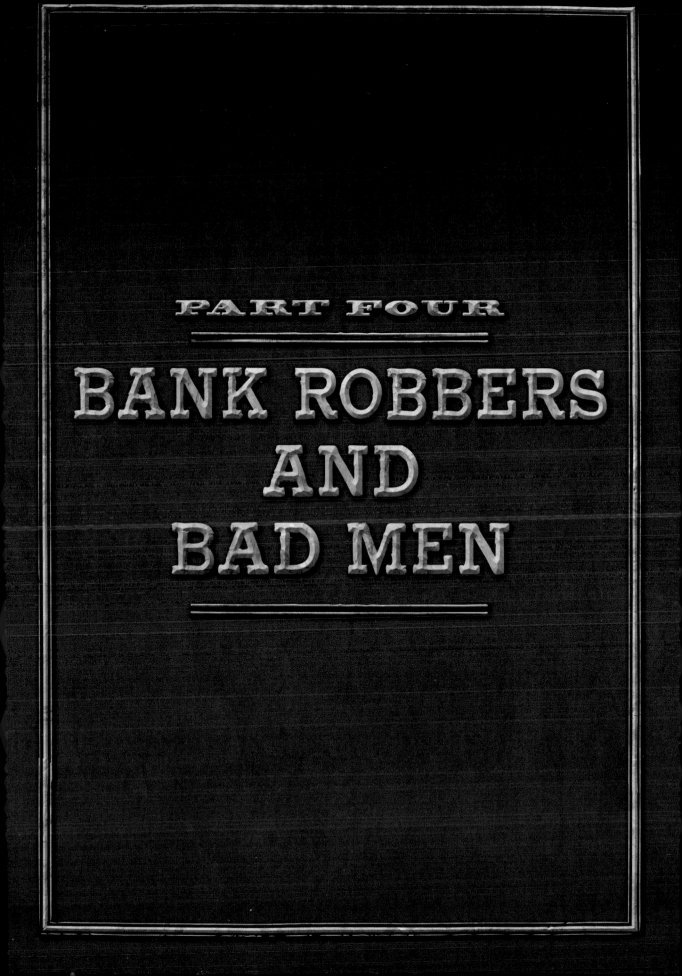

PART FOUR

BANK ROBBERS
AND
BAD MEN

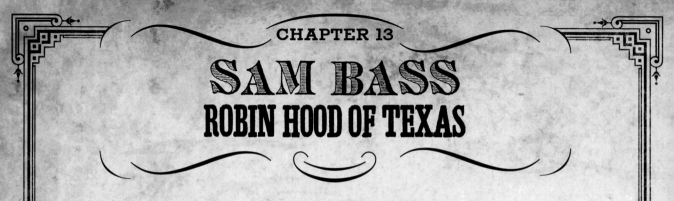

CHAPTER 13

SAM BASS
ROBIN HOOD OF TEXAS

"IF A MAN KNOWS ANYTHING, HE OUGHT TO DIE WITH IT IN HIM."

Sam Bass (1851 – 78)

Sam Bass did not start out as a bad man. An orphan, he drifted into crime after several legitimate businesses had failed and soon became the model of a gentleman highwayman, until he was cut down by the Texas Rangers.

Born in Mitchell, Indiana in 1851, Sam lost his mother at the age of ten and his father at thirteen. His uncle, David Sheeks, then became guardian of the seven children. At eighteen, Bass left for St. Louis, then drifted down river to work in a sawmill in Rosedale, Mississippi for a year.

In 1870, he moved to Denton, Texas, where he worked as a farmhand for Sheriff Thomas J. Egan, better known as "Dad Egan." Around that time, Bass was described as being around five feet eight, weighing about 140 pounds, with black hair, dark eyes, and a sallow complexion. He walked with a stoop, seldom looked anyone in the eyes, and rarely spoke. When he did, his voice had a sharp, nasal twang.

THE DENTON MARE

Bass, Sheriff Egan's brother Armstrong, and Henry Underwood, a veteran of the Union Army who had killed a man, acquired a racehorse which became known as the "Denton Mare." She was not the fastest horse in Texas, but she won regularly enough for Bass to leave Egan.

The following year, he won a string of ponies from a Native American in Sill, Oklahoma. When the owner refused to hand them over, he seized them at night and headed to San Antonio where he sold the mare and teamed up with twenty-six-year-old Joel Collins, who already had indictments for theft on his record, as well as assault with intent to kill.

RUSTLING CATTLE AND STEALING HORSES

Collins had a plan. He would organize a cattle drive. Without informing the owners, he loaded twenty-seven hundred beeves on a train and shipped them to Sidney, Nebraska, then drove them to Deadwood where gold had been found. There they sold the cattle and paid off the hands.

Figuring the Texans who Collins had defrauded would not find them in the Dakotas, they bought some wagons and went into the freight business. This proved strenuous and the winter was cold, so they bought a saloon and bawdy house, which soon ran into trouble. They began stealing horses. Then, with a small gang, they robbed a stagecoach, killing the driver, John Slaughter.

ROBBING THE UNION PACIFIC

One of their number, a Texan named Jack Davis, said that a lot of gold was being shipped by the Union Pacific Railroad to the east. At ten o'clock on the night of September 19, 1877, the bandits boarded the train when it stopped for water at Big Spring, Nebraska. Forty minutes later, it was on its way again—minus three thousand brand new $20 gold pieces. Minted in San Francisco, these were the only gold coins made in the West that year and would be easily identified. Soon roving posses were combing the countryside, hoping for a reward.

Realizing the danger, Bass and Davis bought a team of horses and a wagon, hid their loot in it, and sought the protection of a detachment of cavalry, pretending that they were poor farmers looking for a new spread. Meanwhile Collins and Pennsylvanian Bill Heffridge reached Buffalo Station, a watering stop on the Kansas Pacific Railroad, where Sheriff Fred Bardsley asked to search their packhorse. Although Bardsley had ten cavalrymen with him, Collins went for his six-shooter. The two outlaws were shot to pieces, though Heffridge had not even gone for his gun.

Jim Berry made it home to Missouri, but the local bank became suspicious of the gold coins he was making so free with. A posse ambushed him. He was shot in the leg and died of gangrene. The sixth member of the gang, Canadian Tom Nixon, headed for Chicago and may have escaped to Canada.

nothing like the $60,000 they had taken in Nebraska. Altogether they were worth about $2,000. After each foray, they would hide in the rough country outside Denton, only riding into town occasionally to drink, play poker, and live it up a little.

Despite his flourishing criminal career, Bass was amused that he could ride around the area—and even into Dallas—without being recognized. And as it was only the big corporations and the railroads that were suffering, he found that there was a great deal of sympathy for outlaws.

TRACKED DOWN BY TEXAS RANGERS

Even the Texas Rangers had taken very little interest until the shoot-out at Mesquite. But as the Frontier Battalion who handled the assignment only operated in west Texas, its commander Major John B. Jones decided to recruit a special detachment for the job. Junius "June" Peak, a former deputy sheriff and city marshal, was authorized to recruit seventeen men.

ROBBING TRAINS IN TEXAS

While Davis headed off to New Orleans then, it is thought, Central America, Bass returned to Denton, where he proceeded to spend his way through his stash of gold. When the stash dwindled, he formed a new gang with Sebe Barnes and Samuel J. Pipes and began robbing trains in Texas.

In the spring of 1878, they hit four trains in the Dallas area. During one robbery on April 10, at Mesquite, Texas, they encountered unexpected opposition and Barnes was badly wounded. The hauls from these hold-ups were

Sam Bass, standing on the left, photographed in Dallas, 1876. Standing next to him is John E. Gardner. Seated are Joel Collins (right), and Joel's brother Joe Collins.

Although most of the men had little background in law enforcement, they quickly got on the trail of the Mesquite outlaws. Two were quickly captured. Then Captain Peak's men and a posse led by Sam's old boss, Sheriff Egan, ran into the Bass gang at Salt Creek in Wise County. In the ensuing gunfight, Arkansas Johnson was killed and the gang's horses were captured. But they escaped on foot and, as seasoned horse thieves, they were soon mounted again and rode back to their hideout near Denton.

The gang remained popular. People provided the outlaws with horses and food. And they were given information about the activities of the Rangers and other lawmen. Some were so forthcoming that they were charged with harboring criminals. Among them were Henderson Murphy and his son Jim, who was also suspected of being one of the Bass gang, though this could not be proven.

However, while he was on trial at Tyler, Jim Murphy asked to talk to Major Jones and he confessed that he had ridden with Bass, while his cousin, Frank Jackson, was a regular member of the gang.

DOUBLE-CROSS AND BETRAYAL

After Jim Murphy left Tyler a free man, he sought out Bass. This took him ten days. When he did catch up with them, Bass and Barnes pulled their guns on him, suspecting him of being a spy. But Frank Jackson stood up for his cousin and Murphy promised to go in first on the next robbery.

Nevertheless, they kept a suspicious eye on him. When he wanted to go and see his father, he was told that he would be gunned down if he rode off.

For a month, Murphy had no opportunity to contact Major Jones. Then, during a night carousing at Denton, Murphy managed to get a note to Sheriff Jennings Everhard, saying the gang planned to ride into Mexico, robbing the bank at Round Rock on the way. The following day, Murphy also managed to send a letter at Georgetown to Major Jones.

Stopping at Waco, the gang left their horses in the livery stables and took rooms at the Longhorn Hotel, where Sam tossed his last double eagle gold coin on the bar. The following morning they rode on toward Round Rock.

LIEUTENANT REYNOLDS AND COMPANY E

Major Jones sent Corporal Vernon Wilson to San Saba with orders for Lieutenant N.O. Reynolds of Company E Texas Rangers. He was to take a detachment to Round Rock. Three other Rangers were dispatched from Austin, while Jones himself, who was at Tyler observing the trial of two of Bass's captured men, loaded up his rig and also headed for Round Rock.

Things began to go wrong. Wilson's mount had been standing in a stable for months and was too weak for such a long ride. After sixty-five miles, Wilson gave up with the mare, left her at Lampasas, and took the stage the next morning. After twenty-four hours without rest or food, he reached San Saba.

Lieutenant Reynolds was ill, but he picked a detachment of eight men and sent them to Round Rock on their best horses. Reynolds accompanied them in the back of a buckboard, cushioned with saddle blankets, driven by Corporal Wilson. They traveled all night, covering sixty-five miles. Crossing the San Gabriel River, they stopped for thirty minutes for breakfast. They still had forty-five miles to go. Despite the hundred-degree temperature and acute stomach pains, Lieutenant Reynolds pushed on.

SAM BASS REACHES ROUND ROCK

Bass and his men had arrived at Round Rock the previous day. They camped near the cemetery. Sam took his time to scout the town and take a look over the bank. He did not know that Major Jones and the Rangers from Austin were already there.

The Rangers kept out of sight while Major Jones spoke to three local deputy sheriffs—Morris Moore, Ellis Grimes, and Al Highsmith—who promised to do nothing unless the Rangers asked them to.

On the morning of July 19, 1878, the outlaws rode into town to scout likely escape routes. Murphy dropped back, saying he would buy corn for the horses. Bass wanted some tobacco, so he, Barnes, and Jackson tied up their horses at the back of Kopperel's general store, next to the bank, and went in. Although the deputies had promised Major Jones that they would not interfere, Morris Moore and Ellis Grimes walked up to the store.

Barnes was talking to the store clerk Simon Jude, when Grimes grabbed the outlaw's left arm and asked: "You packin' a gun?"

Barnes drew instantly. So did Bass and Jackson. All three gunned down Grimes. Morris Moore drew his gun and fired a shot. Bass was wounded in the hand, but Moore took a fatal shot through the chest. Then the three gunmen ran out of the back of the store, leapt into the saddle, and made off.

LETHAL FUSILLADE

The side street took them past Round Rock's only barber's shop, where Ranger Dick Ware was getting a shave. He ran out, covered in lather. He raised his .45 six-shooter with both hands and began shooting. The two other Rangers from Austin, Chris Connor and George Harrell, came around the corner and opened fire. And further down the street Major Jones opened up with a .41. Local citizens also joined in.

Barnes was shot and killed. Bass was hit to the right of his spine. The bullet tore through his body and exited to the right of his navel. It almost knocked him off his horse, but he clung on to the horn of the saddle. Then some two-hundred yards further on he fell to the ground.

Seeing this, Jackson stopped and turned. Despite the fusillade, he went back, pulled Bass up onto his horse and rode steadily out of Round Rock. The Rangers could not pursue

them as they had left their mounts at their camp outside town and Lieutenant Reynold's detachment did not arrive until ten minutes after the shooting was over. By then it was dusk so they gave up the pursuit until the next day.

Murphy was still in town and the citizenry were all for jailing him, but Major Jones intervened. Murphy then identified Barnes's body as that of one of the outlaws. Asked how he could be so sure, he said that the man already had three bullet holes in his right leg and one in his left. The corpse was examined and he was shown to be right.

THE DEATH OF SAM BASS

The following morning, Lieutenant Reynolds' detachment rode out after the outlaws. They found the gang's camp near the cemetery. Jackson had left Bass propped up under a pine oak, his wounds bound with strips of his shirt.

Holding up his injured right hand, Sam said: "Don't shoot. I'm Bass. I'm dying, get me to a doctor."

Bass was carried back into town on a rig. Dr. Edward Cochran did what he could for him, but his kidney had been destroyed. Shot on a Friday, he clung to life until Sunday, still talking with Major Jones. His last words were: "The world is bobbing around."

Sam Bass was buried in Round Rock, alongside Sebe Barnes. Frank Jackson rode into New Mexico and nothing further was heard of him, though it was rumored that he rode with Billy the Kid during the Lincoln County Wars. Safe from prosecution, thanks to Major Jones, Jim Murphy returned to Denton where he was shunned and scorned. Within a year, he had committed suicide with poison. Bass went on to become the stuff of legend with the popular cowboy song "The Ballad of Sam Bass."

TEXAS RANGERS

In 1823, Stephen F. Austin persuaded the Mexican government to allow him to employ ten men to protect families that had recently settled in Texas. They were to "range" over large areas, looking for possibly hostile Native Americans. The Rangers were formally constituted in 1835 with twenty-five men.

Under the Republic, they expanded rapidly and, during the Mexican-American War (1846 – 48), several companies crossed the Rio Grande to fight in the U.S. Army under Zachary Taylor. After the war, they were largely disbanded. But in 1857, a hundred-strong Ranger force under John Salmon "Rip" Ford fought the Comanche and other tribes who preyed on settlers.

When Texas seceded in 1861, the Texas Rangers fought for the Confederacy as the Eighth Texas Cavalry. During Reconstruction, they were disbanded and replaced by the hated Texas State Police. But with the election of Governor Richard Coke in 1874, the Texas Rangers were reconstituted as two units— the Frontier Battalion and Special Forces, comprising twenty to thirty men each. They signed on for three to six months, supplied their own horse and equipment, elected their own officers, and received $1.25 a day to "range and guard the frontier."

As well as fighting Indians, Major John B. Jones, commander of the Frontier Battalion, took on Sam Bass and his gang.

Major John B. Jones (seated center) with
the Texas Rangers Frontier Battalion.

JUNIUS W. PEAK

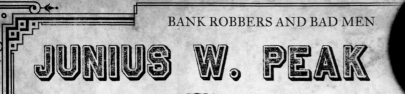

Born in Warsaw, Kentucky in 1845, Junius "June" Peak moved to Dallas in 1855, where his family built the first brick house in the county. At age sixteen, Peak left home and enlisted at Fort Arbuckle in the First Choctaw and Chickasaw Mounted Rifles, First Indian Brigade, raised for the Confederacy. Wounded at the battle of Chickamauga, he underwent a lengthy recovery in Atlanta. Then he became a scout in the Eighth Texas Cavalry and was back in Texas, when the Civil War ended.

Peak returned to Dallas and became deputy sheriff and a member of the Ku Klux Klan. In 1872, he was hired by New Mexico cattlemen to put an end to cattle rustling in the territory. Successful at stopping the rustling, he was elected city marshal of Dallas in 1874 and held the post for four years. In April 1878, Governor Richard Coke commissioned Peak as second lieutenant in Company B of the Frontier Battalion and charged him with raising a special Ranger detachment to track down outlaw Sam Bass and his gang. The following month, Peak was made Captain. With the aid of local posses he and his men harassed Bass, driving him from North Texas toward his ultimate capture and death in Round Rock.

On April 15, 1880, Peak left the Rangers and took a job building and equipping supply stations for construction gangs with the Mexican Central Railroad Company. His wife accompanied him to Mexico. They returned to Texas in 1884 and raised horses and cattle at their Live Oak Ranch in Shackelford County. In 1899, to further their two children's education, they returned to Dallas, where Peak went to work in real estate, serving as superintendent of White Rock Lake from 1919 to 1924. On April 20, 1934, he died at his home in Dallas, at age 89.

CHAPTER 14

BUTCH CASSIDY
THE HOLE-IN-THE-WALL GANG

"THOSE FELLOWS COULDN'T SHOOT … NO USE OF US SHOOTING BACK AT THEM."

Butch Cassidy (1866 – 1908?)

Butch Cassidy is another of the Western gunfighters whose reputation has become part of frontier myth.

His original name was Robert Leroy Parker. Born in Beaver, Utah in 1866, he was the eldest of the thirteen children of Maximillian Parker and Ann Campbell Gillies, Mormon converts from Britain who had pulled handcarts over the Great Plains in 1856. His father rose to become an elder in the Church of Jesus Christ of Latter-Day Saints, but none of his respectability rubbed off on his son.

The boy grew up on a farm near Circleville, Utah, where cowhand Mike Cassidy taught him to ride, shoot, rope, brand, and rustle horses and cattle. Under suspicion by the authorities, they fled Utah in 1884.

THE INVINCIBLE THREE

What happened to Mike Cassidy is not known, but Parker raced horses and found a job with a mining company in Telluride, Colorado. There he teamed up with Matt Warner. They joined Bill and Tom McCarty in the McCarty gang that robbed the San Miguel Valley Bank on June 24, 1889. Afterward, Warner and the McCartys went north toward Oregon where they dubbed themselves the "Invincible Three." Despite this hubris, they were captured and jailed. When they were released, Matt Warner and Tom McCarty went straight. Bill continued his career as an outlaw. He and his nineteen-year-old son Fred tried to rob a bank in Delta, Colorado.

When the townspeople shot Bill off his horse, Fred went back to rescue him—and was shot down too.

Meanwhile Parker drifted into Wyoming. Wanted by the law, he started calling himself George Cassidy, taking the last name of his old mentor. In Rock Springs, Wyoming, he worked in a butcher's store and became "Butch" Cassidy.

Butch Cassidy's mugshot from the Wyoming Territorial Prison, Laramie in 1894.

THE WILD BUNCH EMERGES

At the time, the war between the cattlemen and the homesteaders was beginning in Johnson County, Wyoming. Cassidy took refuge with the outlaws and dispossessed homesteaders behind a ridge that could only be entered through an easily defended defile known as the Hole-in-the-Wall. They became known as the Hole-in-the-Wall Gang. They survived by rustling, dispatching cattle to buyers in Utah and Colorado, and selling small quantities of beef locally.

In 1892, Butch Cassidy's rustling career came to an abrupt end when he was arrested for stealing a horse worth $5. A tough sheriff cracked him over the head with a pistol. His defense was that he had bought the animal from a rustler. Nevertheless the judge sent him to Wyoming Penitentiary.

The governor released him on January 19, 1896, on the promise that he would leave Wyoming, never to return.

On August 13, 1896, Cassidy, Elzy Lay, Harvey "Kid Curry" Logan, and Bob Meeks walked into a bank in Montpelier, Idaho, put on masks and escaped with approximately $7,000. They hid out in Robbers Roost in a remote corner of south-east Utah. There they were joined by Ben Kilpatrick, Harry Tracy, William "News" Carver, Laura Bullion, and George "Flatnose" Curry and formed the Wild Bunch. Soon after, they were joined by Harry Longabaugh from Pennsylvania, who became known as "The Sundance Kid."

NOTORIOUS LEADER

In April 1897, Butch Cassidy and Elzy Lay rode into the coal-mining town of Castle Gate, Utah. Wearing bib overalls and riding swayback mares, the two heavily whiskered men spitting gobs of tobacco juice appeared to be itinerant workers. They gambled a little and drank, returning day after day until they attracted no attention.

On April 21, they returned in time for the noon train that was bringing the miners' wages. These were carried to the paymaster's office on the second floor of the company store, some seventy-five yards from the depot. Arousing no suspicions, Butch and Elzy hung around at the bottom of the stairs. As the

WOMEN OF THE WILD BUNCH

The Wild Bunch, for an outlaw gang, were notable for having women among their number. Most notable was Laura Bullion, a former prostitute in San Antonio who became the girlfriend of Bill Carver. When he was killed, the story was that Sundance and Ben Kilpatrick—alias The Tall Texan—rolled dice for her. Ben won. She was convicted of robbery and sentenced to five years in prison for the hold-up of a Great Northern train in 1901.

Josie and Ann Bassett were both romantically involved with Butch Cassidy, but he sent them away, along with Elzy Lay's girlfriend Maude Davis, when they were planning the robbery at Castle Gate, Utah.

Annie Rogers followed Kid Curry throughout his career. Then there was Etta Place, who became the common-law wife of Sundance, though it is thought that he shared her with Butch Cassidy. She was the only woman who went with them to South America.

Laura Bullion (1876 – 1961).

THE SUNDANCE KID

Harry Alonzo Longabaugh was born in Pennsylvania in 1867. By 1884, his family had moved to Cortez, Colorado, where Harry worked as a horse wrangler. He then became a drifter under the names Harry Alonzo and Kid Chicago. However, he was arrested in Miles City, Montana, for grand larceny in 1887 and was jailed in Sundance for eighteen months. Released on February 4, 1889, he rode away as The Sundance Kid.

There are conflicting reports whether he was in on the robbery of the San Miguel Valley Bank with Cassidy and the McCarty Gang. However, Pinkerton's circulated a description saying he was six feet tall, slim, and walked with downcast eyes. He combed his hair in a pompadour style. Bow-legged, he walked with his feet wide apart and carried his arms straight at his side, with his fingers together and thumbs sticking out.

With two accomplices, he robbed the Great Northern Railroad in Malta, Montana, on November 29, 1892. The three were arrested, but Sundance escaped. He escaped again on October 31, 1897, from Deadwood jail, after a bungled bank robbery.

On July 14, 1898, he held up the Southern Pacific coming into Humboldt, Nevada, with Kid Curry. Throughout 1899 and 1900, he and other members of the Wild Bunch pulled off a series of lucrative robberies.

After hitting the National Bank in Winnemucca, Nevada, on September 19, 1900, the gang split up. Sundance went to California, but returned to join Cassidy in Fort Worth in November.

After robbing a Great Northern train near Wagner, Montana, Sundance met Etta Place, possibly a prostitute from San Antonio. She had dark hair and stood five feet five. They may have married. He took her to meet his parents in Pennsylvania, during a tour of the East Coast.

In 1901 they took a ship to Buenos Aires, Argentina. He was reportedly shot to death alongside Cassidy at San Vicente, Bolivia, on November 8, 1908. However, some accounts say that he survived and returned to the United States.

The Sundance Kid and Etta Place before they headed to South America in 1901.

paymaster came by, a pistol was shoved in his face and he was relieved of $8,000 in cash.

A customer in the store named Frank Caffey tried to interfere, but was dissuaded by a six-shooter pointed at his belly. As the robbers made off, an unarmed citizen yelled: "Bring that money back."

The sheriff could not be summoned as the telegraph wires had been cut. An impromptu posse set off after them, but Butch and Elzy did not even bother to return fire.

"Those fellows couldn't shoot," said Cassidy afterward. "No use of us shooting back at them."

This daring raid established Cassidy's reputation as leader of the gang. It was achieved without violence and with the minimum of effort. Cassidy sought to make non-violence the trademark of the gang. On June 24, he led a lightning raid on a bank in Belle Fouche, South Dakota, thundering out of town with $30,000.

ROBBING THE OVERLAND FLYER

At 1:00 a.m. on June 2, 1899, a trestle bridge on the Union Pacific Railroad near Wilcox, Wyoming, about six miles west of Old Rock Creek Station, was barricaded, forcing the *Overland Flyer* to a standstill. Masked men boarded the train.

The train was divided and the trestle was dynamited, isolating the express car which was then surrounded. The attendant, E.C. Woodcock, was ordered by the gang to open the door. When he refused, the door was blown off. Perhaps suffering from the concussion received in the explosion, Woodcock was then unable to remember the combination to the safe. So the safe was blown up and robbed of $30,000, though some of the bank notes were scorched by the explosion or stained by the juice of the raspberries also being carried in the car.

Even though the robbers were masked, the newspapers quickly identified them as the Hole-in-the-Wall gang, alias the Wild Bunch. Posses combed the countryside. One,

led by Converse County Sheriff Joe Hazen, stumbled across them camped out near Teapot Creek. In the ensuing gunfight, Sheriff Hazen was killed. The robbers escaped by swimming the river.

Two of the outlaws were thought to have robbed the general store and post office in Big Piney soon after. They took $200, skogy boots, spurs, overalls, blue flannel shirts, camel's hair underwear, brown gauntlet gloves, pocket knives, and a Meanea bridle, with chain and bit.

The description of the thieves was given:

> One is about five feet nine or ten inches in height; about 26 years old, light complexion, inclined to be florid; light hair and eyes; Weight about 160 pounds; had a nickel-plated revolver with bone or pearl handle. Another of the men is about five feet six inches tall; dark complexion; dark or black mustache; dark eyes.

MR. E.H. HARRIMAN, WOODCOCK, AND JOE LEFORS

On August 29, 1900, train robbers using the same *modus operandi* robbed a Union Pacific train near Tipton, Wyoming. As luck would have it, Woodcock was again the express car attendant. This time he opened the door and the thieves made off with $50,000 in gold.

However, Mr. E.H. Harriman who now owned the Union Pacific was getting tired of having his trains robbed, so employed special agents, whose number included Joe LeFors, and extended the telephone lines from Cheyenne.

Trains were now well-protected, but there were still banks to rob. On September 19, 1900, the First National Bank in Winnemucca, Nevada, was robbed. This has been attributed to the Wild Bunch. However, the bank robbers were identified as men who had been camping in the area for at least ten days, which would not have given Cassidy time to get from Tipton on horseback.

The gang hit a train again on July 3, 1901, relieving the Great Northern's *Coastal Flyer* of $50,000 near Malta, Montana. Afterward they hid out on an island in the Missouri River. Then they split up.

Ben Kilpatrick and Laura Bullion were arrested in St. Louis on November 5. He got fifteen years; she five. When Kilpatrick was released in 1912, he tried to rob the *Sunset Flyer* between Dryden and Sanderson, Texas, but was hit on the head by the guard and died.

SOJOURN TO SOUTH AMERICA

With their picture circulating, the remaining gang members decided to move to South America. Cassidy made one last attempt to gain amnesty as there were no murder charges outstanding against him. In 1896, he had approached Governor Heber Wells of Utah, which had just achieved statehood. Heber advised him to make his peace with Union Pacific boss Harriman. This had been sunk by the Tipton hold-up. A second attempt was thwarted by a storm.

By the end of 1901, Cassidy, Sundance, and Etta Place were in Argentina, living on a ranch in the Cholila Valley. However, they seem to have continued robbing banks and mines.

In December 1907, they sold the ranch and disappeared from the Cholila Valley. The following year they were reported to be working in a tin mine. Following other mine robberies, they were cornered in San Vicente by the Bolivian cavalry and killed during a shoot-out. According to legend, as soldiers stormed their hideout and they were down to their last two bullets, Cassidy put a bullet in Sundance's head, then put the last bullet in his own. Accounts date their deaths anywhere from 1908 to 1911.

LIFE AFTER DEATH

However, there were continued sightings of Cassidy. A machinist in Spokane, Washington, named William T. Phillips, claimed to be Butch Cassidy and wrote his life story *Bandit Invincible: The Story of Butch Cassidy* in 1934. He died in 1937.

Cassidy's sister, Lula Parker Betenson, told an interviewer in 1970 that her brother had visited her in 1925. She said he had been living in the north-west under an assumed name and had died in 1937, but she denied that William Phillips was her brother.

The final shoot-out scene from the 1969 film *Butch Cassidy and the Sundance Kid*, starring Paul Newman and Robert Redford.

THE FORT WORTH FIVE, 1900

The Wild Bunch were so pleased with their exploits that they posed for a portrait at the studio of photographer John Swartz, 705½ Main Street, Fort Worth. It showed (left to right): Standing: Bill Carver (alias News Carver) and Harvey Logan (alias Kid Curry). Seated: Harry A. Longabaugh (alias The Sundance Kid), Ben Kilpatrick (alias The Tall Texan), and Robert Leroy Parker (alias Butch Cassidy).

Legend has it that the picture was taken after the bank raid at Winnemucca, Nevada, and Cassidy sent it to the president of the bank, George S. Nixon, with a "thank you" note. In fact, Swartz was so proud of the picture that he displayed a copy as publicity for his studio. An agent from the Wells Fargo office a block away at 817 Main recognized the sitters and sent a copy to Pinkerton's.

CHAPTER 15

KID CURRY
THE WILDEST OF THE WILD BUNCH

"HE IS THE ONLY CRIMINAL I KNOW OF WHO DOES NOT HAVE ONE SINGLE GOOD POINT."

William Pinkerton about Kid Curry

Harvey Alexander Logan, better known as "Kid Curry," was the wildest and perhaps least known of the Wild Bunch.

Born in Tama County, Iowa, in 1867, he was the third of six children. When his father died, his mother moved the family to Dodson, Missouri, where she died in 1876. The children were brought up by their aunt and uncle. But Harvey soon headed for Texas with his younger brothers Hank, John, and Lonnie, and their cousin Bob Lee. Breaking horses on the Cross L Ranch near Big Spring, he befriended George "Flat Nose" Curry, whose name he took. His brothers soon adopted the same last name.

At the age of sixteen, he got involved in a saloon brawl at the end of a cattle drive in Pueblo, Colorado. To evade the law, they moved on to Wyoming where the four brothers began rustling. They started their own ranch near Landusky, Montana, in 1888 with a stolen herd of cows.

During the Johnson County War, they hired their guns to the Red Sash Gang, but when its leader Nate Champion was killed, they returned to their ranch.

KILLING PIKE LANDUSKY

Harvey Logan possessed a fearful rage, particularly when drunk. In October 1894, after a confrontation with neighbor James

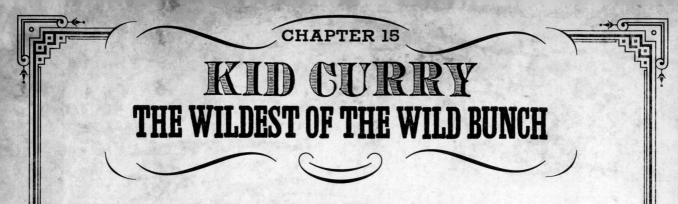

Della Moore (also known as Annie Rogers) and Harvey Logan, 1901.

Ross, he was charged with assault with a deadly weapon.

He had a running dispute with Powell "Pike" Landusky, the fifty-five-year-old miner who had founded the town. One of Landusky's stepdaughters had an illegitimate child, though the father appears to have been Lonnie. On Christmas Eve 1894, Harvey, Lonnie, and fellow rustler Jim Thornhill had been drinking heavily when they bumped into Landusky.

A fistfight broke out in which the younger men got the better of Landusky. Harvey pulled a gun and shot Landusky in the head. Fearing that they would not get a fair trial for the killing, the three men fled on a stolen buckboard and escaped.

Eventually reaching New Mexico, for a while, Kid Curry and his brothers rode with the Black Jack Ketchum Gang.

FALLING OUT WITH BLACK JACK

Returning to Montana, Harvey heard that a friend of Landusky's, rancher James Winters, was trying to get the reward on his head increased. With John and Lonnie, he rode to Winters' ranch. But Winters knew he was coming and opened fire. John fell from his saddle, mortally wounded. The other two returned fire but were driven off.

Returning to New Mexico, they fell out with Ketchum over the takings from a train robbery. The two brothers lay low for a while, working on a ranch near Sand Gulch, Colorado. Then Harvey started his own gang with Lonnie, Walt Putnam, Tom O'Day, and his old friend, George Curry. In April, 1897, Harvey was involved in the killing of Deputy Sheriff William Deane of Powder River, Wyoming, when he and his gang were rustling horses.

In June, they robbed a bank in Belle Fourche, South Dakota. O'Day was captured after his horse was spooked and ran off. A posse under Sheriff John Dunn of Carbon County caught up with them at their camp near Lavina on Montana's Musselshell River.

The sheriff called for them to surrender. In the inevitable shoot-out, Harvey's horse took a bullet through the neck. It went on to hit his right wrist. He dropped his gun, but managed to mount the injured beast, but it dropped dead after a mile. Harvey was captured along with George Curry and Walt Putnam.

Taken to Deadwood, they overpowered their guards and escaped from jail. They then headed back to Montana, robbing two post offices on the way.

RIDING WITH THE WILD BUNCH

On July 14, 1898, Kid Curry, George Curry, and the Sundance Kid robbed a Southern Pacific train shortly after it pulled away from the depot in Humboldt, Nevada. They got away with a disappointing $450.

Kid Curry was with the Wild Bunch when they robbed the Union Pacific *Overland Flyer* near Wilcox, Wyoming. After the murder of Sheriff Hazen, he hid out in Brown's Hole, one of the gang's hideouts on the borders of Wyoming, Colorado, and Utah.

Kid Curry went with Butch Cassidy and other members of the Wild Bunch to rob a train near Folsom, New Mexico. At the shoot-out at Turkey Creek, Sam Ketchum and Elzy Lay were wounded. Ketchum died of his wounds. Lay escaped, but was later caught and jailed.

Cassidy and Kid Curry escaped too. Curry hid out in Fannie Porter's brothel in San Antonio, where he met Della Moore, alias Annie Rogers. The law was closing in. On February 28, 1900, Lonnie was visiting his aunt in Dodson, Missouri, when a posse turned up. Lonnie was killed in a hail of gunfire.

In March, Harvey and fellow Wild Bunch member "News" Carver were spotted in St. John's, Arizona, passing money thought to have come from the Wilcox robbery. Deputies Andrew Gibbons and Frank LeSeuer who went after the pair were shot dead.

KEEP ON RUNNING

On the run, Curry and Carver headed for Alma, New Mexico, where Butch Cassidy and Elzy Lay were working on the WS Ranch. They were cornered in Triangle Canyon, south of San Simon, Arizona, by lawmen George Scarborough and Walter Birchfield. Harvey shot his way out, mortally wounding Scarborough. Then "Flat Nose" Curry was killed by Sheriff Jessie M. Tyler. Kid Curry took revenge.

A few weeks later, Kid Curry got into an argument with the Norman brothers. When the smoke cleared, both brothers were mortally wounded. Then on March 27, 1901, he fell out with local man Oliver Thornton in Painted Rock, Texas. Thornton suffered fatal gunshot wounds and Kid Curry hurriedly left town.

Back with the Wild Bunch, Kid Curry was at the train robbery at Tipton, Wyoming. Then he headed for Fort Worth, Texas, where he met up with them again for the famous photograph, which soon found its way onto hundreds of wanted posters. Soon after that, News Carver was ambushed and killed at Sonora, Texas.

After the final robbery of the *Coastal Flyer* near Malta, Montana, Kid Curry killed Jim Winters who had slain his brother five years earlier.

PLAYING FOR HIGH-STAKES

Figuring that there was no hiding place west of the Mississippi, Kid Curry headed for Knoxville, Tennessee. He had been there an hour when he was involved in a dispute over a high-stakes pool game. When his opponent pulled a gun, Kid Curry smashed him across the face with the barrel of his .45, knocking him to the floor.

When the police turned up, Kid Curry shot three of them, then ran out of the back door, but fell thirty feet into a culvert. As he was scrambling to get out, a patrolman shot him in the shoulder. He fled into the darkness. Outside town, he stopped and bandaged his

GEORGE "FLAT NOSE" CURRY

Born on Prince Edward Island, Canada, around 1864, Curry moved with his family to Nebraska when still a child. Some authorities believe that he was uncle to the Logan boys.

At the age of fifteen, he drifted West and began rustling. Along the way, he was kicked in the face by a horse, giving him his nickname. Later he joined Logan's gang and went into bank-robbing. Both men were captured in 1897, after holding up the Butte County Bank at Belle Fourche, South Dakota. However, in Deadwood jail, they overpowered the guards and escaped.

He and Kid Curry rode with the Wild Bunch. After participating in more robberies of post offices and trains, Curry was rustling cattle in Moab County, Utah when Sheriffs Jessie M. Tyler and William Preece finally caught up with him on April 17, 1900. After a six-mile running gunfight, Curry was eventually hit in the head by a long-range rifle shot. As he took cover behind some rocks, the posse surrounded him. When he offered no further resistance, the lawmen crept forward and found him dead.

Kid Curry then killed both Tyler and his deputy, Sam Jenkins, in a gunfight in retribution. George Curry is buried in Chadron, Nebraska.

THOMAS "BLACK JACK" KETCHUM

Thomas Edward Ketchum was born in 1863 in San Saba County, Texas. His older brother, Green Berry Ketchum Jr., became a wealthy cattleman and horse breeder, while middle brother Sam and young Tom worked as cowboys in West Texas and New Mexico.

In 1892, Sam, Tom, and others stopped a train on the Santa Fe Railroad at gunpoint and stole $20,000. With a posse on their tail, they hightailed it into Arizona. Then in December 1895, he shot and killed John N. "Jap" Powers, a neighbor in Tom Green County, Texas. Fleeing to New Mexico, he let Mrs. Powers take the rap. She went to jail.

The Ketchum brothers worked on ranches, stealing supplies before they moved on. In June 1896, they robbed a store in Liberty, New Mexico. The owners caught up with them at the Pecos River, but a shoot-out left most of the posse dead.

Heading west to Arizona, the brothers rode with the Hole-in-the-Wall Gang and members shifted between the two outfits. They began robbing trains by decoupling the mail and express cars before ransacking them.

On July 2, 1899, Ketchum got involved in a saloon fight in Cape Verde, Arizona, killing two miners. Now he was eligible for the death penalty.

After another train robbery, the gang were jumped by a posse near Turkey Creek, New Mexico. In the ensuing shoot-out, Sheriff Farr was killed and his deputy Henry Love was wounded.

A series of robberies ended with Ketchum single-handedly holding up a Colorado & Southern Train near Fulsome, Arizona. The conductor blasted him with a shotgun. He escaped but was found the next day, propped against a tree.

His arm was amputated. Convicted of train robbery, he was sentenced to death. An appeal to the U.S. Supreme Court upheld the verdict. Interviewed in jail, he told journalists that he "expected to go straight to hell after his death."

Striding up the steps to the gallows, he told his executioners: "I'll be in hell before you start breakfast, boys." Then "Hurry up, boys, get this over with." The inexperienced hangman was told to "Let her rip."

The hangman puts the noose around Black Jack Ketchum's neck, April 26, 1901, Clayton, New Mexico.

shoulder with his shirt. Twenty miles on, a pack of hounds caught up with him and he was captured.

Meanwhile, Annie Rogers was arrested for passing banknotes from the Montana robbery in Nashville, while Ben Kilpatrick and Laura Bullion were also arrested in Knoxville. Kilpatrick and Bullion both served time. Annie was released in June 1902 after being acquitted.

Logan was convicted for numerous crimes. Awaiting transfer to an escape-proof prison in Colorado, he broke out of Knoxville jail. Attaching wire to a broom, he fashioned a small noose and lassoed a guard who walked too close to the bars. Tying him with strips of cloth, he took his keys and pistols. Using the guard as a human shield, he found the sheriff's horse, forced the guard to saddle her, then rode out of town.

"ARE YOU HIT?"

Kid Curry planned to join Butch and Sundance in South America. Unable to make the necessary arrangements, he returned to Colorado where he tried to form a new gang. On June 7, 1904, he held up a train outside Parachute, Colorado, but only got away with a few dollars.

The posse cornered Kid Curry and his two accomplices in a small canyon near Glenwood Springs. In an exchange of fire, he was hit and crawled behind a rock for cover.

"Are you hit?" asked one of the outlaws.

"Yes, and I am going to end it here," came the reply.

There was a shot. The two accomplices escaped and, when the posse closed in, they found a body of a man with a hole in his head and a .45 in his hand. It was not clear whether he had been killed in the gunfight or had committed suicide.

The lawmen did not know who he was and the body was dropped in a grave in Glenwood Springs. Later he was disinterred and identified, though rumors persisted that Kid Curry had escaped to join Butch and Sundance in South America, where he was shot down beside them.

PINKERTON'S ASSESSMENT

During his lifetime, Kid Curry was wanted on warrants for fifteen murders, but it was generally said that he had killed more than twice that number, although some historians put the actual number at nine. William Pinkerton, head of Pinkerton's Detective Agency, called Logan the most vicious outlaw in America.

"He has not one single redeeming feature," Pinkerton wrote. "He is the only criminal I know of who does not have one single good point."

One of Pinkerton's most famous detectives, Charles Angelo Siringo was assigned to track down the Wild Bunch after the Wilcox train robbery.

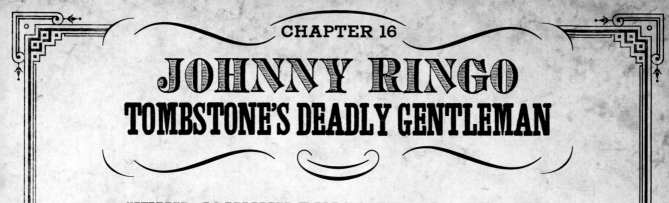

CHAPTER 16

JOHNNY RINGO
TOMBSTONE'S DEADLY GENTLEMAN

"WHY, JOHNNY RINGO, YOU LOOK LIKE SOMEBODY JUST WALKED OVER YOUR GRAVE."

Doc Holliday, in the movie Tombstone *(1993)*

Johnny Ringo was in Tombstone when Wyatt Earp and Doc Holliday were there in the 1880s. However, he was not, as he is sometimes billed, "Tombstone's deadliest gunfighter." Another myth has also grown up around him that he quoted Shakespeare at length. This is pretty unlikely, to say the least. He was definitely, however, a very bad man.

Born in Greens Fork, Indiana, on May 3, 1850, John Peters Ringo was the oldest child of Martin and Mary Ringo. In 1856, to escape the increasing vigilante activity in Indiana, the family moved to Missouri where he became a cousin of the Youngers through the marriage of his aunt to their uncle. It is thought that Johnny learned about guns from the local gunsmith, who was the father of Captain John Sheets, killed in the James-Younger Gang robbery in Gallatin in 1869.

TROUBLED YOUNG MAN

Ringo went to school in Gallatin, but he only had an elementary school education. After two Confederate nightriders were lynched on the Ringo farm in 1862, Martin Ringo decided to sell up and move west. On the way, after surviving an Indian attack in Wyoming, his father accidentally shot his own brains out when the trigger of his rifle was caught in his boot strap. This left fourteen-year-old Johnny to bury his father and shoulder responsibility for his family's safety and welfare. Johnny took his family responsibility very seriously. He was already a crack shot.

The family stayed on Uncle Coleman Younger's ranch near San Jose for about a year before moving into town. Johnny was said to be a tall, handsome man with auburn hair, dark somber eyes, easy manners, and showing the marks of refinement. But he was troubled and began drinking heavily.

During the wheat harvest of 1870, Ringo earned enough money to return to Missouri to visit with family members there. Word reached him that his younger brother had contracted tuberculosis and there were concerns over the family's finances, but he did not return home. Instead, he traveled to Texas to find work as a cowboy.

MASON COUNTY WAR

Johnny fell in with a group of ranchers in Llano County. Among them was Moses Baird, who befriended him. In neighboring Mason County, there was growing tension between German immigrants and local ranchers. Johnny was already known for gunplay. A judge in Burnet fined him $75 for firing a revolver in the town square on Christmas Day 1874. The Mason County War kicked off the following year.

Another of Ringo's friends was ex-Texas Ranger Scott Cooley. He was the adopted son of local rancher Tim Williamson, who was killed by a German farmer. Ringo became part of the Scott Cooley faction and, when Moses Baird was killed in an ambush in Mason County, Ringo and Bill Williams went to visit James Cheyney, who had led Baird into the trap, and shot him down as he washed his face at a water trough.

More killings followed. Three months later, Ringo was arrested in neighboring Burnet County and charged with threatening another man's life. There was an uproar and, four months later, he was set free by his rancher friends and headed to Mason County.

Hunted down again in October 1876, by a combined force of Texas Rangers and local lawmen from Llano County, Ringo was taken to Austin. In jail, he met John Wesley Hardin.

HEADING FOR TOMBSTONE

When the charges against him were eventually dismissed, Ringo ran for constable of Llano County. He won the election, stayed on in the job for almost a year, then pulled up stakes for New Mexico, where it seems he murdered two brothers in a saloon altercation. On the run from murder indictments, he fled into Arizona, where he wounded Louis Safford on December 14, 1879. Back in Austin, Texas, he was jailed briefly by Ben Thompson in May 1881. Then he headed for Tombstone.

The only known photograph of Johnny Ringo. Probably taken circa 1880.

His reputation as a gunslinger preceded him. As Texans arrived in Tombstone to cash in on the mining bonanza, tales spread about his past. But, by then, the drink was getting the better of him.

Johnny fell in with the Clantons, rustling cattle. The sheriff of Cochise County John Behan looked the other way when the Clantons rustled Mexican beef, but when Wyatt Earp came to Tombstone, things changed. After Old Man Clanton and half the gang were murdered in Guadalupe Canyon by angry Mexican ranchers, Ringo became head of the rustlers. His chief lieutenant was Curly Bill Brocius.

NO WITNESSES

When the Gunfight at the O.K. Corral happened in October 1881, Johnny Ringo was back in California visiting his sisters. No one is exactly sure when he returned, but on November 26, 1881, Ringo and his friend Dave Estes held up a poker game in a saloon in Galeyville, Arizona, stealing $500 and a horse. Ringo was arrested shortly after, but at the hearing no witnesses showed up.

On December 28, 1881, Virgil Earp was shot and crippled for life by unknown assailants. Wyatt Earp accused Ringo of being one of the men responsible. In response,

Curly Bill Brocius at the Bird Cage Theater in Tombstone.

STATEMENT FILED NOVEMBER 13, 1882, COCHISE COUNTY, ARIZONA

Turkey or Morse's Hill Creek, 14th July, 1882
Statement for the Information of the Coroner
and Sheriff of Cochise Co. A.T.

There was found by the undersigned John Yoast the body of a man in a clump of Oak trees about 20 yards north from the road leading to Morse's mill and about a quarter of a mile west of the house of B.F. Smith. The undersigned viewed the body and found it in a sitting posture, facing west, the head inclined to the right. There was a bullet hole in the right temple, the bullet coming out on the top of the head on the left side. There is apparently a part of the scalp gone including a small portion of the forehead and part of the hair, this looks as if cut out by a knife. These are the only marks of violence visible on the body. Several of the undersigned identify the body as that of John Ringo, well known in Tombstone. He was dressed in light hat, blue shirt, vest, pants and drawers, on his feet were a pair of hose and undershirt torn up so as to protect his feet. He had evidently traveled but a short distance in this foot gear. His revolver he grasped in his right hand, his rifle rested against the tree close to him. He had on two cartridge belts, the belt for the revolver cartridges being buckled on upside down. The undernoted property were found with him and on his person.

1 Colt's revolver Cal: 45 No. 222, containing 5 cartridges
1 Winchester rifle octagon barrel Cal: 45 Model 1876 No. 21896, containing a cartridge in the breech and 10 in the magazine

1 Cartridge belt containing 9 rifle cartridges
1 Cartridge belt containing 2 revolver cartridges
1 Silver watch of American Watch Co. No. 9339 with Silver Chain attached
Two Dollars & Sixty cents ($2.60) in money
6 pistol cartridges in his pocket
5 shirt studs
1 small pocket knife
1 Tobacco pipe
1 Comb
1 Block matches
1 small piece tobacco

There is also a portion of a letter from Messrs. Hereford & I. Zabriskie, Attorneys at Law, Tucson to the deceased John Ringo.

The above property is left in the possession of Frederick Ward, teamster between Morse Mill and Tombstone.

The body of the deceased was buried close to where it was found. When found deceased had been dead about 24 hours.

Thomas White; James Morgan; John Blake; Robert Boller; John W. Bradfield; Frank McKinney; B. F. Smith; W. J. Darnal; W. W. Smith; J. C. McGrager; A. E. Lewis; John Yoast; A. S. Neighbours; Fred Ward.

Statement by citizens in regard the death of John Ringo
Filed Nov. 13/82
W. H. Seamans, Clk.
By Louis A. Souc, Deputy.

Johnny challenged Wyatt and Doc Holliday. Ringo and Holliday faced each other in Allen Street on January 17, 1882. They each laid their hand on their gun. Wyatt Earp stood by, ready to intervene. But Acting Police Chief James Flynn stepped in, arresting both Ringo and Holliday. They were both fined $30 for carrying weapons.

RETURNING TO CALIFORNIA

In March 1882, Morgan Earp was shot and killed while playing pool. Ringo denied playing a part, but the following month, he returned to California.

When Ringo went back to Tombstone in May, Wyatt, and his posse were still on the hunt for Morgan's killers. So Ringo headed into Mexico, where he apparently lived under an assumed name for a couple of months. Returning to Arizona in July 1882, Ringo, Billy Claiborne, and Buckskin Frank Leslie went on a drinking spree all over southeastern Arizona. At Antelope Springs, they split up. Ringo headed down the trail to Sulphur Springs for another day of drinking. Totally drunk, he staggered out to his horse and said he was going to Galeyville.

On July 14, 1882, teamster John Yoast found the body of Johnny Ringo under an oak tree in Morse's Canyon. It was estimated that he had been dead for just one day. His boots were missing and his Winchester was leaning against a tree. He had a Colt .45 in his hand and he had been shot in the head.

The verdict was suicide, but there have been numerous other theories about how he met his end.

STATEMENT BY SHERIFF WILLIAM M. BREAKENRIDGE

As I was coming back from Sulphur Springs Valley, shortly after Sheriff Behan returned from his unsuccessful trip after the Earp crowd, I met John Ringo in the South Pass of the Dragoon Mountains. It was shortly after noon. Ringo was very drunk, reeling in the saddle, and said he was going to Galeyville. It was in the summer and a very hot day. He offered me a drink … of whiskey … I tasted it and it was too hot to drink. It burned my lips. Knowing he would have to ride all night [to] reach Galeyville, I tried to get him to go back with me to the Goodrich Ranch and wait until after sundown, but he was drunk and stubborn and went on his way. I think this was the last time he was seen alive …

On the opposite side of the creek from Smith's house was a bunch of five black jack oaks growing up in a semicircle from one root, and in the center of them was a large flat rock which made a comfortable seat. Ringo was found sitting there with a bullet hole in his head.

His watch was still running, and his revolver was caught in his watch chain with only one shot discharged from it …

His boots were gone and he had taken off his undershirt and torn it in two, and wrapped it around his feet, and when he was found the shirt was worn through, showing that he had walked for some distance …

When Ringo awoke, he must have been crazed for water and started out afoot. He was within sound of running water when he became crazed with thirst and killed himself.

[Mrs. Smith, whose house was just across the creek, reputedly heard the shot about two o'clock in the afternoon … the day after I met Ringo.]

William "Billy" Breakenridge was assistant marshal in Tombstone, Arizona, during the Gunfight at the O.K. Corral.

DERRINGER

Born in Easton, Pennsylvania in 1786, Henry Deringer was the son of a colonial gunsmith who made Kentucky rifles. After serving his apprenticeship at the gun-maker's in Richmond, Virginia, he set up his own armaments plant in Philadelphia, supplying guns to the U.S. government. He specialized in long-barreled, percussion-cap pistols designed to fit in the belt.

In 1825, he began making single-shot weapons. At the request of customers, he began cutting down the barrel without reducing the caliber, making the pistol easy to use and accurate at short range. His famous pocket pistol was less than six inches long and was bored in calibers from .36 to .45—.41 being the most popular. Colt, Remington, and others produced their own version.

John Wilkes Booth used a Deringer pocket pistol to assassinate Abraham Lincoln. In his hurry to file his story, a reporter spelled the name with two Rs. The name stuck and the small pistol is now known as a derringer.

1. William W. Marston Three Barrel .22 Derringer, 1863.
2. Sharps Breechloading Four Shot Pepperbox Pistol, 1860.
3. Remington Zig Zag Derringer, 1861.
4. Remington Double Derringer, 1866.
5. Remington Double Derringer (open), 1870.
6. Remington Double Derringer, 1870.
7. Moore's Patent Firearms Co. No. 1 Derringer, 1880.
8. Marlin No. 32 Standard Pocket Revolver, 1875.
9. James Reid "My Friend" Knuckle Duster Revolver, 1861.
10. Frank Wesson Small Frame Single Shot Pistol, 1862.
11. E. Allen and Co. Vest Pocket Derringer, 1870.
12. Connecticut Arms Hammond Bulldog, 1865.
13. Colt Open Top Pocket Model Revolver, 1871.
14. Brown Manufacturing Co. Southern Derringer, 1869.

And I did it all for the money and fame,
And noble was nothing but feeling no shame,
And nothing was sacred except staying alive,
And all that I learned from a Colt .45.

Lyrics from The Last Gunfighter Ballad
by Guy Clarke (1976)

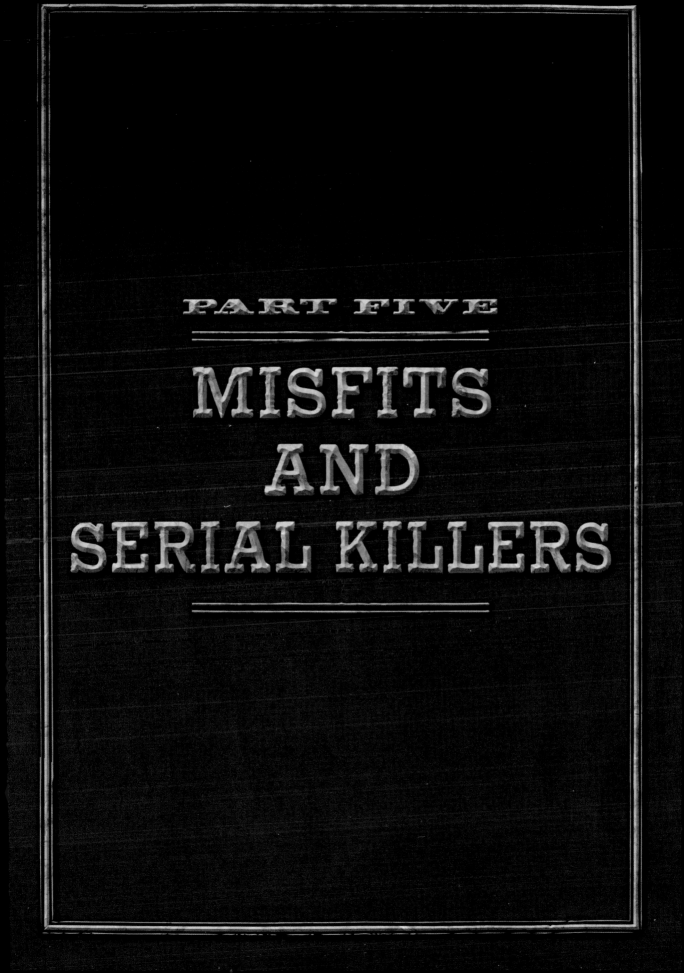

PART FIVE

MISFITS AND SERIAL KILLERS

CHAPTER 17

BOONE HELM
THE KENTUCKY CANNIBAL

"MANY'S THE POOR DEVIL I'VE KILLED ... THAT I'VE BEEN OBLIGED TO FEED ON ..."

Boone Helm (1828 – 64)

Canada was not immune to the gunmen of the Old West who frequently strayed across the border. One of the worst was Boone Helm, alias the Kentucky Cannibal.

Born in Kentucky in 1828, Helm moved with his parents to a new settlement in Missouri when he was young. He enjoyed the rough pursuits of border life. A favorite trick was to hurl his Bowie knife into the ground, then retrieve it from horseback at full gallop. He was also known for his great physical strength and rowdyism, liking nothing more than displaying his prowess at fighting.

Helm drank a lot. Once, while the circuit court was in session, the sheriff tried to arrest him. Helm resisted the officer, then rode his horse up the stairs into the courtroom to berate the astonished judge with profanities.

At the age of twenty, he married. But neither a wife, nor the baby daughter that came along the following year, persuaded him to give up his wild ways. His wife sought a divorce that was readily granted.

KILLING LITTLEBURY SHOOT

Helm decided to move on to Texas or California. Littlebury Shoot, a neighbor and friend, promised to accompany him, though he probably only said this to pacify Helm when he was drunk. When Shoot changed his mind, Helm stuck his Bowie knife between his ribs, killing him instantly.

Boone fled west. Shoot's brother and a few friends set off after him. Tracking him for some distance they captured him by surprise at an Indian reservation and returned him to Monroe County for trial. He was convicted of murder, but there were doubts about his sanity and he was sent to a lunatic asylum. The staff there found him harmless and allowed him daily walks in the surrounding countryside. It

Boone Helm in about 1850.

was easy for him to give his minder the slip and he headed to California.

There, he killed several people and escaped arrest by fleeing to Dalles, Oregon Territory in 1858.

HOSTILE INDIANS

Fearing extradition back to California, Helm set off for Camp Floyd, Utah, some sixty miles south-west of Salt Lake City, with several companions. To one of them, he boasted: "Many's the poor devil I've killed, at one time or another—and the time has been that I've been obliged to feed on some of 'em."

He suggested to another colleague named Groves that they organize a party of Snake Indians and steal two-thousand horses from the Walla Walla tribe. This was enough for Groves. He rode back to Dalles and, from there, warned the Walla Wallas. Meanwhile Helm and five companions headed on to Camp Floyd. Five-hundred miles of their route would take them through a wilderness of mountains, unmarked by trails and filled with hostile Indians.

HELM ESCAPES ALONE

Helm and several companions left Grande Ronde River for Camp Floyd in late October 1858. The mountains were already covered with snow. A contemporary description of the conditions read:

Cold weather had set in for a season whose only changes for the next six months would be a steady increase of severities. The thermometer, seldom above zero, often marked a temperature thirty or forty degrees below zero in the mountains. The passes were snowed up to the depths of twenty and thirty feet. Wild game, however abundant in summer, had retreated to the forests and fastnesses for food and shelter. Snow-storms and sharp winds were blinding and incessant. Deep ravines, lofty mountains, beetling crags, and dismal canyons, alternated with impenetrable pine forests, inaccessible lava beds, and impassable

torrents, encumbered every inch of the way. Death on the scaffold or escape through this terrible labyrinth gave the alternative small advantage of the penalty. Small as it was, Helm and his companions took the risk and plunged into the mountain wilderness. He alone escaped.

In April 1859, a traveler named John W. Powell met Helm at the Snake River. He accompanied him to Salt Lake City. During the journey, Helm told him the horrifying tale of what had happened in the mountains.

Soon after they reached Salt Lake City, Helm fled, having murdered two citizens in cold blood.

NO DRUNKEN DESPERADO

Helm traveled north, murdering along the way. He stole a herd of horses in Washington Territory, which he sold on Vancouver Island. Arriving eventually at Florence, Oregon, in the spring of 1862, he came up against a miner known as Dutch Fred. He was a gambler and pugilist but, unlike Helm, was no drunken desperado.

Seeking to provoke a fight, Fred's enemies plied Helm with drink. Once suitably drunk, Helm approached Fred at the faro table. Issuing foul-mouthed curses, Helm flourished his revolver and challenged Dutch Fred to a duel. Fred sprang up, pulled his knife, and advanced on Helm. But bystanders intervened. Both were disarmed. Their weapons were lodged with the saloon-keeper for safekeeping and Fred returned quietly to his game.

Helm apologized and left, but a few hours later he returned. Fred was still there. Helm asked for his pistol back, promising the saloon-keeper that he would leave immediately and make no trouble. But as soon as he got the gun, he fired at Fred who was still seated. Fred got up. He was unarmed. Helm shot him through the heart and he fell dead.

Helm then turned to the stupefied crowd and said: "Maybe some more of you want some of this." No one volunteered.

"I ATE HIM UP"

Helm was captured on Frazer River in the fall of 1862. A newspaper in British Columbia reported:

The man, Boone Helm, to whom we referred some weeks since, has at last been taken. He was brought into this city last night strongly ironed. The first clue of the detectives was the report that two men had been seen trudging up the Frazer river on foot, with their blankets and a scanty supply of provisions on their backs. The description of one corresponded with the description given by the American officers of Boone Helm. Helm's conduct on the road is conclusive evidence that he was aware he was being pursued. He passed around the more populous settlements, or through them in the night time. When overtaken, he was so exhausted by fatigue and hunger that it would have been impossible for him to have continued many hours longer. He made no resistance to the arrest—in fact, he was too weak to do so—and acknowledged without equivocation or attempt at evasion that he was Boone Helm. Upon being asked what had become of his companion, he replied with the utmost sang froid:—

"Why, do you suppose that I'm a—fool enough to starve to death when I can help it? I ate him up, of course."

The man who accompanied him has not been seen or heard of since, and from what we have been told of this case-hardened villain's antecedents, we are inclined to believe he told the truth. It is said this is not the first time he has been guilty of cannibalism.

BOUGHT WITNESSES

The British Columbia authorities returned Helm to the United States, where he was to be held in the penitentiary in Portland, Oregon, until proper provision could be made in Florence.

Three of Helm's brothers had followed him to the Pacific coast. All eventually met violent deaths. At the time of Boone Helm's trial, one of the brothers, known only as "Old Tex," was mining in the diggings at Boise, Idaho. He turned up with a heavy purse and bought the silence of witnesses. Once Boone was free, his brother said to him:

Now, Boone, if you want to work and make an honest living, go down to Boise with me. I have plenty of mining ground, and you can do well for yourself—but if you must fight, and nothing else will do you, I will give you an outfit to go to Texas, where you can join the Confederate armies, and do something for your country.

After mining with Old Tex for a short while, Boone said that he would go to Texas. Good to his word, his brother furnished him with clothing, a horse, and a well-filled purse. But instead of heading south, Helm set out on new adventures.

CANADIAN KILLINGS

Only later was it discovered that he had killed more men in British Columbia. A letter published in the *Colonist* newspaper on April 4, 1864, said that Helm had made his way to Cariboo. In July 1862, Helm was reported to have been at Antler Creek, some ten miles from Barkerville over the heights of Prosperpine Mountain.

A miner named W.T. Collinson told of what happened that spring some thirty-one years later.

Tommy Harvey, alias "Irish Tommy," and myself left Antler Creek with Sokolosky and two Frenchmen for Quesnelle Forks. This was on or about the 18th of July, 1862. We journeyed together until we arrived at Keithley Creek, where the three aforementioned gentlemen, carrying on a mule and two horses about $32,000 in coarse gold, stopped for dinner. Harvey and I continued on three miles ... where we cooked our repast a la mode Cariboo.

Others reported that Helm had befriended Sokolosky and the two Frenchmen in Antler Creek. Either way, in an exchange of gunfire the three gold-laden miners were shot dead. Helm and a friend buried most of the gold, then turned back to Quesnelle Forks quickly to establish an alibi before returning to retrieve their stash later.

"THROW UP YOUR HANDS!"

Collinson's story continued:

We stayed at the Forks next day and saw the murdered men brought in. They had made a brave fight, every man's pistol (good six shooters) was empty, and each man had a bullet through his head. Boone Helm and his chum killed these three men, took and hid the dust, and if no stranger has found it, it is there yet. For Boone left the country, I have proof of that ...

After leaving the Forks, I ... journeyed on down, stopping at Beaver Lake, Deep Creek, and Williams Lake. I met Boone Helm and his chum at Little Bloody Run ... a few miles above Cook & Kimble's Ferry.

The first thing I heard was, "Throw up your hands!" and looking up, I saw the muzzle of a double-barreled shot-gun about four feet from my head. It took his partner about five minutes to cut my pack-straps, after taking my six-shooter and purse. The latter contained three Mexican dollars and three British shillings. One of my old shirts contained a good wad ... a small bag containing bullets attracted their attention and saved my dust, which being tied in the old shirt pocket ... was not seen. They emptied my pistol, gave it back to me and told me to "git" and not look back. As my road was downhill, I lost no time.

ROBBED AND MURDERED

Methodist minister Arthur Browning arrived in Quesnelle Forks the day after the murders and saw the bodies of the murdered men brought in. He described what he saw:

The trail leading down the mountain to the Forks of Quesnelle was a mile long and as I came near ... I saw on the trail ... a procession of men carrying three stretchers. I found on meeting them that they were carrying three dead men. They were found on the trail coming from Cariboo, robbed and murdered for ... each of them [had been] carrying bags of gold ... Who was the murderer, or who were the murderers? Everybody said in whispers it was Boone Helm, a gambler and cutthroat who had escaped the San Francisco Vigilance Committee ...

Pursuit down the trail was determined on, and $700 raised to pay the cost of pursuers. Boone, I imagine, got wind of all this, and escaped across the line.

It seems that Helm did not go across the line immediately. The *Colonist* reported that he turned up in Victoria, British Columbia, on October 13, 1862, where Helm was arrested "upon a charge of drinking at saloons and leaving without settling his score ... Sergeant Blake, who made the arrest, said that he understood the accused had killed a man at Salmon River (Florence) and fled to British Columbia."

When Helm was brought before the police magistrate three days later, the chief of police swore that he was known as a bad character and the proprietor of the Adelphi Saloon testified that Helm had bought drinks there and when asked to pay replied: "Don't you know that I'm a desperate character?"

WORKING ON A CHAIN GANG

The magistrate ordered Helm to find security and to be of good behavior for the term of six months. He defaulted and spent a month in a chain gang building and repairing the streets of Victoria.

The *Colonist* reported that authorities held Boone Helm:

[in] safe-keeping for some three or four weeks, in the expectation that a charge would be preferred against him by our cousins on the other side, and a request made for his surrender, but as nothing transpired, he was released and three days afterwards the demand came.

HENRY PLUMMER (1832 – 1864)

Born in Addison, Maine, Plummer headed west to the goldfields of California when he was nineteen. Elected marshal of Nevada City, he killed the husband of a woman he was having an affair with, pleading self-defense. Sentenced to ten years, he was pardoned within a year.

Back in Nevada City, Plummer shot a man who attacked him with a Bowie knife during a brawl in a bawdy house. Fearing that because of his previous conviction he would not get a fair trial, he fled to Washington Territory where he killed Patrick Ford in a shoot-out after being ejected from a dancehall. He fled to Montana where a gold-strike had been made at Bannack. The miners' association there elected him sheriff.

To prevent the immediate lynching of suspects, he established the first jail in the territory and was nominated as a deputy U.S. marshal. In the fall of 1863, there was a rash of crime. A Vigilante Committee was set up that went after the miners' sheriff who opposed lynching. Plummer and two deputies were themselves then lynched on January 10, 1864. Those responsible depicted Plummer as a seducer, murderer, and robber chief. No evidence has been found to support this.

By then, Helm had disappeared and it was not until the spring of 1863 that he was arrested again, this time at Fort Yale in the Fraser Canyon. According to the *Colonist*:

> ... *a notorious character named Boon* [*sic*] *Helm, who it is said to have committed a murder somewhere on the Salmon River, has been arrested by the British Authorities at Fort Yale on the Fraser River, and handed over in due form to the custody of a Mr.*

> *Brandian, a special officer sent across for the purpose by the U.S. Authorities.*

Helm was transported from Victoria to Port Townsend where, according to one report he "dug out of Townsend jail and once more made his way to the hills." Others said he was taken back to Florence where he was acquitted. Either way he was next heard of in Montana where he was said to be an accomplice of crooked Sheriff Henry Plummer.

LET'S BE FRIENDS

In Virginia City, Montana, Boone Helm was drinking in Dempsey's Saloon when William Rumsey, a stagecoach driver who had just stood up to a band of robbers, came in. Helm invited him and other persons present to drink with him. Rumsey drank with the company two or three times. Helm called for more drinks.

"I've had enough," said Rumsey.

"Take another, take another," said Helm. "It's good to keep the cold out."

"Not another drop," replied Rumsey, "I know my gauge on the liquor question, and never go beyond it."

"You *shall* drink again," said Helm, with an oath, casting a malicious glance at Rumsey.

"I *won't* drink again," was the immediate reply, "and no man can make me."

"No man can refuse to drink with me and live," replied Helm, seizing his revolver as if to draw it.

Rumsey was too quick for him. Before the desperado could draw his pistol, Rumsey had his leveled at his head. Addressing him in a calm, steady tone, he said: "Don't draw your pistol, or I'll shoot you, sure."

The men gazed sternly at each other for a minute or more. Helm finally loosed his grip on his pistol, and said: "You're the first man that ever looked me down. Let's be friends."

I AM NOT AFRAID TO DIE!

On December 23, 1863, the Vigilance Committee of Alder Gulch was set up. Its aim was to suppress the activities of "road agents" thought to be responsible for up to a hundred murders in the area. The Montana vigilantes blamed the lawlessness on Sheriff Henry Plummer, who was said to be the leader of a gang of road agents.

After Plummer and his deputies had been hanged in Bannack, the vigilantes moved on to Virginia City where the committee arrested six suspected road agents, one of whom was Helm. Three vigilantes closed in on him as he stood in the street talking.

"If I'd had a chance," Helm said, "or if I had guessed what you all were up to, you'd never have taken me."

When he was brought before the secret vigilante court, he solemnly declared that he had never killed a man in all his life. They made him kiss the Bible and swear to this, which he did with perfect calmness. His judges were not impressed. Then to one of their number whom he knew, he confessed to a murder or two in Missouri and in California and admitted that he had been in prison once or twice, but denied being a road agent, accusing others who had been arrested along with him. They cursed him. Reconciled to his fate, Helm asked for a glass of whiskey, saying: "I have looked at death in all forms, and I am not afraid to die."

LYNCHING BOONE HELM

Six-thousand men assembled in Virginia City to see the lynchings which were to take place in a half-finished log building. The ropes were passed over the ridgepole. As the front of the building was open, spectators could get a full view of the victims as they stood on the boxes ready for the drop.

Helm looked around at the other four who were about to be hanged and told fellow prisoner Jack Gallagher to "stop making such a fuss. There's no use being afraid to die."

Helm had a sore finger and delays in the procedure seemed to irritate him.

"For God's sake," said he, "if you're going to hang me, I want you to do it and get through with it. If not, I want you to tie up my finger for me."

Feeling the cold, he said: "Give me that overcoat of yours, Jack" as Gallagher was stripped for the noose.

"You won't need it now," Gallagher replied. George "Clubfoot" Lane was also impatient and jumped off his box killing himself.

"There's one gone to hell," said Helm.

Jack Gallagher was next. As he struggled, Helm watched him calmly.

"Kick away, old fellow," said Helm. "My turn next. I'll be in hell with you in a minute!"

Although Helm had not gone to Texas to fight for the Confederacy, he was a Confederate to the end.

"Every man for his principles!" he shouted. "Hurrah for Jeff Davis! Let her rip!" And he sprang off the box, utterly hard and reckless to the last.

JACK GALLAGHER (18?? – 64)

Also known as "Three-Fingered Jack," Gallagher was born at Ogdensburg, New York. Moving west when he grew up, he was in Kansas in 1859 before making his way to Colorado, where he killed a man in Denver in 1863. He then fled to Montana, where he became a deputy under Sheriff Henry Plummer, and worked in Virginia City where he was thought to have been involved in the murder of fellow deputy John Dillingham in June 1863. Later he seriously wounded a man named Jack Temple in a gunfight at a Virginia City saloon. With another outlaw named Bill Hunter, he was said to have robbed a Mormon who was on his way to Salt Lake City. On the evening of January 13, 1864, Gallagher and others were drinking and playing faro in a local saloon while the committee was voting on his arrest and execution. When he discovered this, Gallagher remarked: "While we are here betting, those vigilante sons of bitches are passing sentence on us." The next morning, he found out how very right his prediction was, when he was hanged along with George "Club-Foot" Lane, Frank Parish, Boone Helm, and Haze Lyons.

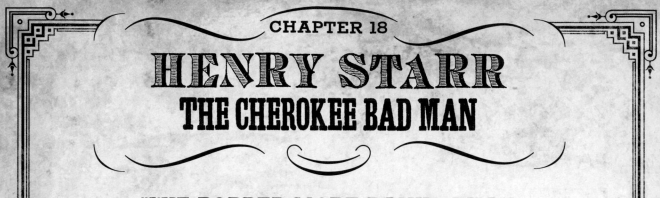

CHAPTER 18

HENRY STARR
THE CHEROKEE BAD MAN

"I'VE ROBBED MORE BANKS THAN ANY MAN IN AMERICA."

Henry Starr (1873 – 1921)

Born at Fort Gibson in the Indian Territory on December 2, 1873, Henry Starr was the son of George Hop Starr, who was half Cherokee. His mother, Mary, was one-quarter Indian. Although Henry was more than half white, in the ethos of the times, he felt more Indian than European and held a grudge against the white man. Indeed, he was brought up in the clan of his grandfather, Cherokee outlaw Tom Starr, who terrorized the Indian Territory before the Civil War. His uncle Sam Starr was another outlaw who became famous as husband of "bandit queen" Belle Starr.

Henry Starr eschewed liquor, tobacco, tea, and coffee. He lived on roots, berries, nuts, and game, making him perfectly at home in the wilderness and elusive when wanted. The influence of patriarch Tom developed in him a Native American's agility and endurance. He was known as "The Bearcat" for his cunning and courage, and his grandfather also taught him expertise with guns.

In 1886, Henry's father died, leaving his mother to bring up three children. She married a man named C.N. Walker. Henry hated him, thinking him inferior because he had no Indian blood in his veins. Within months, Starr left home and, at the age of sixteen, started working on a ranch near Nowata, Indian Territory. Five feet nine, he had a strong athletic build and straight black hair. A skilled horseman with an uncanny dexterity with a lasso, he soon became proficient as a cowboy.

PEDDLING WHISKEY AND STEALING HORSES

In June 1891, he was fined for "introducing liquor into the Indian Territory," though he later protested his innocence. In December, he was arrested for stealing a horse. Again he denied the charges:

While working for the Roberts boys, two strange horses drifted into a pocket formed by two farms and a pasture joining them. As there was no water in this pocket, it was plain that they were runaways. The boys said for the first one who rode that way to let them

Henry Starr.

into the gate to water, as no doubt someone would be on the hunt for them. I let them in and, not noticing that one of them bore saddle marks, I rode him several times. I also informed other ranchers that he was a stray. In something like a month, Charles Eaton, his owner, came after him, and seemed pleased to find him in such good condition, even offering to pay me for my trouble. This was in October, '91, and in December, the same year, while I was in Nowata, a vicious-looking fellow, who said he was a deputy United States marshal, read a writ charging me with the larceny of Eaton's horse ... The warrant had been sworn out by Charles Eaton, the same fellow that had been so profuse in his thanks for the care I took of his horse, and that simply stunned me, nor do I know this day what made him prefer the charge, as he swore the truth later.

Deputy U.S. Marshal Floyd Wilson.

After being locked up in Fort Smith, Starr was released on a $2,000 bond furnished by his cousin Kale Starr and J.C. Harris, the tribal chief of the Cherokees. But he jumped bail and began his career as an outlaw.

STARR'S FIRST MURDER

Starr and accomplices Jesse Jackson and Ed Newcombe began to rob stores and railroad depots throughout the Indian Territory. They stole $1,700 from the Nowata Depot, in July 1892. That November, they hit Shufeldt's store at Lenapah, taking $300, and Carter's Store in Sequoyah, making off with $180. Deputy Marshals Henry C. Dickey and Floyd Wilson had a warrant for his arrest and were already on his tail.

On December 12, 1892, the two lawmen stopped by the X.U. Ranch owned by Arthur Dodge. He denied knowing Starr, but said he had seen him ride by occasionally. So the deputies scoured the surrounding countryside. The following day, they were having dinner back at the X.U. Ranch, when Dodge arrived home, saying that he had seen Starr while working that day.

Floyd Wilson mounted his horse and set off after Starr. Henry Dickey had to saddle a fresh mount and followed a little way behind. Wilson caught up with Starr near Wolf Creek. He was thirty yards away when Starr spotted him and ran.

"Hold up!" yelled Wilson. "I have a warrant for you."

The lawman dropped from his saddle, put his rifle to his shoulder, and fired a warning shot over Starr's head. Starr returned fire, hitting Wilson. The deputy tried to load a fresh cartridge, but the gun jammed. He threw down his rifle and reached for his revolver. Two more shots from Starr knocked him to the ground. Then Starr walked over to the defenseless officer and put a bullet through his heart, firing so close that the muzzle flash scorched his clothes.

By the time Dickey turned up, it was too late. Starr had made off on Wilson's horse.

A QUESTION OF KILLING

On the run from the law, Starr had two close calls with Deputy U.S. Marshals Rufus Cannon and Ike Rogers, an African-American.

The first occasion was when Starr had made an arrangement to meet his mother and sister at the home of J.O. Morrison, on the prairie nine miles north-west of Nowata, but his stepfather had told Deputies Cannon and Rogers that they could find Starr there. As they approached the house, Starr could not make up his mind what to do. He retold the story:

At that time I was paying attention to Mr. Morrison's daughter, May, and in her presence I would not run. Perish forever the thought! There were several ladies present, and they pleaded with me not to kill the officers.

"Ladies," I replied, "it is not a question of my killing them but of keeping them from killing me!"

I kept out of sight in the hall at the head of the stairs with my rifle drawn, and could have killed them as easy as shooting two rabbits had I so desired. Both knew I was in the house, for they had discovered my well known horse tied in the barn, but at the time each assured the other that I was not any place around. As they started off, I watched them from the window. Roger's hat blew off as he passed the window, and he looked up, but I had covered and he only pulled his hat over his eyes and went on without looking. They made no attempt at my arrest, and I could tell by their action that they did not want me very bad.

HENRY STARR'S FIRST OFFENSE

In his memoirs, *Thrilling Events: Life of Henry Starr* written while in the Colorado penitentiary, Henry Starr related his first brush with the law.

I got a job close by herding some fine steers to the Open A. One day I went to Nowata, and a man I had known for four or five years was on his way to the Delaware Indian payment a few miles distant and asked me to take his grip over to the payment grounds. He had come on horseback and I was in a buggy, and pleased to be of any slight service to him, so I put the grip in and started.

About two miles out, two deputy marshals overtook me and commanded with drawn guns that I get down from the buggy and allow them to search it. I readily complied, and to my surprise and consternation, the grip contained two pints of whiskey. I told them that I had no knowledge of the grip's contents, also that I did not drink.

"So," said one of them, "then you must have intended to sell it, and that makes the charge against you more serious."

It was a penitentiary offense at that time to sell liquor in the Indian Territory. I did not inform on the owner of the grip, for I was satisfied that it would not help me. I knew that those scheming officers were stuck to make fees out of my bad luck. A United States court (the first white man's court in the Indian Territory) covering whiskey and

misdemeanors had been established at Muskogee the year before, and they took me there. That night, I, an innocent man, felt the murder-breeding leg-irons and chains.

The man I was working for immediately signed my bond and took me back with them. They knew I was innocent, but advised me to plead guilty, pay a fine and have it over with, instead of fighting a long-drawn-out trial, with no witness to help me. When my case was called about two months later, I made a plea of "guilty." One of the deputy marshals, on being questioned by the judge, had manhood enough to say that he didn't think I was a whiskey peddler. He didn't believe that I knew anything about the whiskey being in the grip. The judge fined me $100, a stiff penalty for the offense of introducing. I paid the amount and returned to Nowata, sad at heart.

Though my friends all knew I was innocent, it did not remove the reflection from my character. I was lowered and cheapened in my own estimation. There was a tribal penitentiary at Tahlequah, the Cherokee capital. The convicts sent there by the council wore stripes, and as a child, the sight of them filled me with terror. My father and mother had brought me up to think it was an awful thing to be arrested. I felt doubly disgraced, being placed in jail and chained to a bed at the same time, and I was only a kid.

TWO-HUNDRED SHOTS

The next time Starr ran into Cannon and Rogers, he had Jackson and Newcombe with him. It was near Bartlesville, Indian Territory on January 20, 1893. The two deputies were at the head of a posse of more than fifteen Indian policemen. There was a running gun battle. A bullet blew Jackson's right arm off. He was hit again in the side and captured, but Newcombe and Starr managed to escape.

In his report to Marshal Yoes at Fort Smith, Rogers said that "about two-hundred shots were fired." He also noted that while it was possible that the man they had captured might possibly recover, "we are now on the trail of Starr and his confederate and will yet run them down. We are determined to rid society of this gang."

Meanwhile Starr teamed up with a man named Frank Cheney. Together they robbed the depot of the Missouri-Kansas-Texas Railroad of $180. Another $390 came from Haden's Store in Choteau, Indian Territory. Then in February 1893, they hit the general store and railroad depot at Inola, Indian Territory, making off with $200.

ROBBING THE BENTONVILLE BANK

Bank robbery became Starr's specialty. On March 28, 1893, with the law hot on their trail, he and Cheney entered the Caney Valley Bank in Caney, Kansas, with their revolvers drawn. Cheney took an old two-bushel sack into the vault and emerged with $4,900. Then they locked the bank's employees and customers in a back room and left. One Kansas newspaper called the heist "one of the boldest and most daring robberies known to border history." Soon after, they robbed a passenger train of $6,000 at Pryor Creek, Oklahoma.

Starr and Cheney then formed a gang with Bud Tyler, Hank Watt, Link Cumplin, Kid Wilson, and a villain known only as Happy Jack. Together they robbed the People's Bank in Bentonville, Arkansas. But Starr was already famous and alarm spread when they entered. They made off with $11,000 and

some silver. Outside, a young lady grabbed Starr. He was taken by surprise and dropped the silver. There was no time to recover it as they raced out of town, followed by a volley of bullets.

Afterward, they split the cash at Cheney's farm, then went their separate ways, never to reunite. By then, agents from Wells Fargo and numerous deputies were after them, and there was a $5,000 reward on Starr's head.

ARRESTED FOR ROBBERY AND MURDER

Aiming to flee to California, Starr and May Morrison went to Emporia, Kansas, on a covered wagon with Kid Wilson as bodyguard. From there, they took a train to Colorado Springs. They checked into the Spalding House on July 1, 1893, registering as Frank Jackson, Mary Jackson, and John Wilson. However, they were recognized by a merchant who had done business in Fort Smith. He told the desk clerk, who informed the police.

The local Chief of Police L.C. Dana was keen to arrest Starr without bloodshed. Two days later, Starr was eating alone in the restaurant. Dana and J.W. Gathright surprised him there and took him without a fight. Wilson was picked up later in the red light district. "Miss Jackson" was woken in her room and admitted to being Starr's wife of six months. In a search of their room, the lawmen found $1,460 in cash, a revolver under the pillow, and $500 in gold.

May was released and sent back to her parents in the Indian Territory. Starr and Wilson were returned to Fort Smith in manacles. There Starr was tried for thirteen counts of robbery and the murder of Floyd Wilson. Starr told the jury his version of the Floyd Wilson killing:

When Wilson called on me to surrender I called back, "You can't take me, Wilson; go away." "Throw away that gun and put up your hands or I'll kill you," he replied. He probably thought I was only a kid and was afraid of him. I didn't want to kill him. "All right," I told him. "I'll lower my gun

BELLE STARR

Born in Carthage, Missouri, Myra Belle Shirley was the daughter of a wealthy innkeeper. After her brother, a Confederate guerrilla, was killed by Union troops, her family moved to Scyene, Texas to escape the border war, following the burning of Carthage in 1863.

She married former guerrilla Jim Reed and had two children. Her husband turned to crime and was killed by a deputy sheriff in 1874. Four years later she moved to the Indian Territory—now Oklahoma—where she lived for a time with Bruce Younger, a relative of Cole Younger, perpetuating the myth that she had an affair with Cole and a daughter named Pearl by him.

In 1880, she married Sam Starr, Henry Starr's uncle. Three years later they were found guilty of horse theft and spent nine months in jail. Afterward Belle was indicted several times for rustling and armed robbery, but never tried. Her cabin was said to be used as a hideout by Jesse James and other outlaws.

"You can just say that I am a friend to any brave and gallant outlaw," Belle told the *Dallas Morning News*. She also showed the reporter her revolvers, saying: "Next to a fine horse I admire a fine pistol."

In December 1886, Sam Starr was killed in a gunfight and Belle was shot and killed in an ambush near her home in Younger's Bend two years later. It was never determined who murdered her, but suspects included her new common-law husband and her son with whom, it was said, she was having an incestuous relationship.

Belle Starr, sitting side saddle on her horse staring intently at the photographer in Fort Smith, Arkansas. She is wearing a single loop holster that has a pearl handle revolver in it, a riding crop in her right hand. The man on the horse is Deputy U.S. Marshal Benjamin Tyner Hughes.

and give you a chance to shoot first and you better make a clean job of it. If I kill you it will be in self-defense. Shoot!" Wilson took cool aim at me, fired, and the ball sang past my ear. Then I put a bullet through his heart, mounted my horse and rode away.

The jury did not believe Starr's story. He was convicted and sentenced to death. An appeal to the Supreme Court overturned that decision and a second trial was granted. Starr was convicted again. This decision was again overturned. At a third trial, he pleaded guilty to the robberies and manslaughter, and was sentenced to fifteen years in the federal prison at Columbus, Ohio.

DISARMING CHEROKEE BILL

While Starr was still at Fort Smith, Crawford Goldsby, alias Cherokee Bill, attempted to escape using a gun smuggled into him by a trustee. A guard was killed and the jailbreak ended in a stand-off. Starr stepped in, offering to persuade Cherokee Bill to surrender, provided he was not shot down afterward. On that understanding, Starr disarmed Bill and handed him over to the guards. This earned Starr a pardon from President Theodore Roosevelt which was granted in 1903.

Starr was then determined to go straight. He returned to Tulsa, where he worked in his mother's restaurant. There he took a second wife, named Ollie Griffin, and they had a son who they named Theodore Roosevelt Starr.

However, the authorities in Arkansas were still after him and sought his extradition. Starr fled to the Osage Hills, saying:

I preferred a quiet and unostentatious interment in a respectable cemetery rather than a life on the Arkansas convict farm.

THRILLING EVENTS

In the Osage Hills, Starr fell in with his old pals. They hit the bank in Tyro, Kansas on March 13, 1908. Then, with Kid Wilson, he stole $1,100 from the bank in Amity, Colorado. Starr hid out in Arizona and New Mexico, but a letter to a friend in Tulsa gave him away. He was arrested and extradited back to Colorado.

There Starr was sentenced to twenty-five years for armed robbery. In jail in Colorado, he became a trustee, studied law, and wrote his autobiography, *Thrilling Events: Life of Henry Starr.*

He was paroled in 1913 on the stipulation that he would never leave the state. Nevertheless he rode to Oklahoma and, over six months, he is thought to have pulled off fourteen bank robberies in the state. They were all daylight robberies, carried out quickly and efficiently, at two-week intervals. It was the worst streak of robberies the people of Oklahoma had ever suffered. As a result, the state legislature passed the "Bank Robber Bill," which appropriated $15,000 for the capture of bank robbers and placed a $1,000 bounty on Starr's head—payable "Dead or Alive."

While the authorities relentlessly tracked all of his old hideouts in the Osage Hills, Starr was living in Tulsa, at 1534 East Second Street, just two blocks from the Tulsa County sheriff and four blocks from the mayor. However, his luck was about to run out.

DOING A DOUBLE DALTON

On March 27, 1915, Starr led a gang of seven into the town of Stroud, Oklahoma. His plan was to rob two banks at the same time, the same double-raid as the Dalton Gang had tried in Coffeyville, Kansas in 1892. They hit the Stroud National Bank and the First National Bank. The haul was $5,815. However, as he fled, Starr was hit in the leg by a bullet fired by a seventeen-year-old boy. He was captured along with another outlaw named Lewis Estes.

Starr recovered from his wound and stood trial. On August 2, 1915, he entered a plea of guilty over the Stroud robbery and was sentenced to twenty-five years in the Oklahoma State Penitentiary at McAlester. Interviewed at McAlester, Starr said he had begun to see the error of his ways. He told a reporter from the *Oklahoma World:*

Movie poster for Henry Starr's silent western movie *A Debtor to the Law* (1919).

> *I'm forty-five years old now, and seventeen of my forty-five years have been spent "inside." Isn't that enough to tell any boy that there's nothing to the kind of life I have led?*

His seeming change of heart earned him another parole on March 15, 1919.

NEVER GONNA CHANGE

As part of his campaign to show that crime does not pay, Starr produced and starred in the silent movie *A Debtor to the Law*, portraying the senselessness of the bank robbery in Stroud. It was a huge success. He went on to produce other Westerns, but turned down an offer from Hollywood, fearing that, if he went to California, the authorities in Arkansas might again try and extradite him for the Bentonville heist.

He married his third wife, Hulda, and they set up home in Claremore, Oklahoma. But he could not give up his old ways for long.

On the morning of February 18, 1921, Henry Starr and three accomplices drove into Harrison, Arkansas, where they entered the People's State Bank and robbed it of $6,000. This time he was smartly dressed for the robbery and was wearing a suit. But during the heist, Starr was shot in the back by the former president of the bank, and his partners fled. It was the first bank robbery in the U.S. where the perpetrators escaped in an automobile.

Starr was left to face the music alone. He was carried to the jail where doctors removed the bullet. Knowing his time was up, he boasted to the doctors on February 21, 1921: "I've robbed more banks than any man in America."

The following morning, February 22, 1921, he died with his wife, Hulda, his mother, and his seventeen-year-old son by his side.

THE RECKONING

Starr died as he had lived, in a violent manner. But true to the code of the outlaw, he never revealed a single partner in any crime. He never shot anyone in the commission of a crime, only in shoot-outs with lawmen. He served his time in jail without complaint and had succeeded where others had failed—robbing two banks at once.

During his thirty-two years in crime, he seems to have lived up to his boast that he had robbed more banks than anyone else—and his claim that he had robbed more banks than both the James-Younger Gang and the Doolin-Dalton Gang put together. He started robbing banks on horseback in 1893 and ended up robbing his last in a car in 1921. He seems to have knocked over twenty-one banks, making off with a total of nearly $60,000.

AN OUTCAST IN HIS OWN LAND

In his autobiography, Starr explained about the bitterness he felt toward the white man while growing up in the Indian Territory of pre-state Oklahoma.

> *I had always looked upon the Indian as supreme, and the white renters as trash who moved from year to year in covered wagons with many dogs and tow-headed kids peeping out from behind every wagon-bow, and who, at the very best, made only a starving crop. The Indian landowner was looked up to by his white renters, and always treated with courtesy and respect. But the years have brought about a change; the white man holds power, and the same hypocritical renter has grown arrogant and insulting. The Indian, and especially the full-blood in Oklahoma, is an outcast in his own country, and it is with a feeling of sadness and apprehension that I think of his future. Broken treaties, misplaced confidence and insults have made him lose interest in life. I have more white blood than Indian, and with my knowledge of both races, I fervently wish that every drop in my veins was red.*

CHAPTER 19

CHEROKEE BILL
INDIAN NATION KILLER

"DAMN A MAN WHO WON'T FIGHT FOR HIS LIBERTY."

Cherokee Bill (1876 – 96)

Cherokee Bill was only part Indian. Originally named Crawford Goldsby, his mother had mixed white, African, and Native American ancestry. She was a "Cherokee Freedman"—that is, she had been a slave in the Cherokee Nation and was freed after the Emancipation Proclamation in 1863. His father was a Buffalo Soldier in the Tenth U.S. Cavalry who claimed to be of mixed ancestry with African, Sioux, Mexican, and white forebears.

Crawford was born in Fort Concho, Texas in 1876. By the time he was seven, his parents had separated and his mother had moved to Fort Gibson in the Indian Territory. He was largely brought up by an African-American woman named Amanda Foster, who he called Aunty. Then he was sent to an Indian School in Kansas for three years, and spent a further two years in an Industrial School for Indians in Carlisle, Pennsylvania. Despite his schooling, it seems he could barely read and write.

A MANIA FOR KILLING

His mother remarried and Crawford did not get along with his stepfather. Rebelling against authority, he took to drinking and hanging out with a bad crowd. At a dance at Fort Gibson, Goldsby got into a fistfight. Getting the worst of it, he pulled a gun and shot Jake Lewis. Thinking that he had killed him, Goldsby fled. He joined the Cook Gang and became one of the most feared men in the Indian Territory. According to the *Indian Chieftain*:

He took to "scouting" as the outlaws call it, and became the worst desperado that ever cursed the Cherokee country. His Winchester was his constant companion, and villages and towns trembled at the approach of the "Gorilla." He seemed to have a mania for killing men.

Early in his criminal career, Cherokee Bill also killed his brother-in-law. Accounts differ. This was either because his brother-in-law beat his sister or there was an argument over hogs or, as the *Indian Chieftain* says, "he thought his brother-in-law got more of the parental estate than was due him." Goldsby was also said to have killed railroad man Samuel Collins for throwing him off the train at Fort Gibson for not paying his fare.

RIDING WITH THE COOK GANG

Goldsby joined up with the Cook Gang—Jim and Bill Cook, who were also part Cherokee, Thurman "Skeeter" Baldwin, Jess Snyder, William Farris, Curtis Dayson, Elmer "Chicken" Lucas, Jim French, George Sanders, Lon Gordon, Henry Munson, and Sam "Verdigris Kid" McWilliams, who was shot down in Braggs, just nineteen years old. They were largely African-Americans with Native American blood.

In June, 1894, Crawford Goldsby was with the Cook brothers when they were confronted at Fourteen Mile Creek near Tahlequah, Oklahoma by Sheriff Rattling Gourd with a warrant for Jim Cook. In the inevitable shoot-out, Cherokee Bill shot and killed lawman

Sequoyah Houston. Jim Cook was also badly wounded. When witness Effie Crittenden was asked whether Goldsby had been involved, she said no, but "Cherokee Bill" had been. This apparently was the nickname given to him by Bill Cook.

Cherokee Bill and the Cook Gang then began to terrorize the Indian Territory. Starting out small, they were first accused of whiskey charges and horse theft, before advancing to robbing banks, stores, and stagecoaches. And they were ruthless—shooting anyone who got in their way.

ROBBING AND KILLING

On July 16, 1894, the gang allegedly robbed a man named William Drew and two days later, held up the San Francisco train at Red Fork. However, the express messenger had the foresight to hide a package containing $1,000 in a book he was carrying and the gang got away with very little. Chicken Lucas's share, the *Indian Chieftain* said, was just ninety cents.

Thirteen days later, the gang robbed the Lincoln County bank in Chandler, Oklahoma, taking just $500 and killing a man named J.B. Mitchell and wounding others in the process. During the robbery Lucas was shot and captured by authorities.

That summer, Bill boasted of killing Station Agent Dick Richards at Nowata, though he later denied it.

Hotly pursued, the Cook Gang was surrounded at the home of a friend some fourteen miles west of Sapulpa on August 2, 1894. During the volley of gunshots, one of the lawmen was shot and severely wounded. Two of the gang members, Lon Gordon and Henry Munson were killed, and Ad Berryhill was captured. The rest of the gang fled.

CRIME WAVE

Continuing with their violent lawlessness, the Cook Gang robbed the J.A. Parkinson & Company store in Okmulgee, on September 21, getting away with over $600. On October 11, they first robbed the depot of the Missouri Pacific Railroad in Claremore, Oklahoma and less than two hours later, robbed the railroad agent at Chouteau.

Nine days later, they wrecked the Kansas City and Pacific Express five miles south of Wagoner, Oklahoma, making off with the loot. Two days after that, they robbed the post office and Donaldson's store at Watova. Only one of the gang bothered to wear a mask.

On November 8, the gang rode into Lenapah. They were robbing the Shufeldt and Son General Store when an innocent passerby, named Ernest Melton, stuck his head in to see what was going on. Cherokee Bill raised his rifle and shot him in the head. Shortly afterward, a posse of U.S. marshals found the outlaw's hiding place, but Bill escaped.

Continuing to elude the posse, Cherokee Bill, now alone, robbed the train station at Nowata on December 31. There was now a $1,500 reward on his head.

Crawford Goldsby alias Cherokee Bill.

CAPTURED AGAIN

Cherokee Bill was captured on January 30, 1895. The *Ohio Democrat* of February 9, 1895, carried the story:

CHEROKEE BILL AT LAST TAKEN IN BY A COLORED MAN.

W.C. Smith, Deputy Marshal, has distinguished himself again in effecting the capture of Cherokee Bill, the companion of Bill Cook, in the Indian Territory during the last five months. Cherokee Bill's headquarters were known to be Nowata, IT. Smith made arrangements with Ike Rogers and Clint Scales, colored citizens living near there, to lay in wait for Bill. The outlaw stopped at Rogers' house and went to bed with Rogers without any fear of a trap. Wednesday morning after breakfast, Rogers stepped behind Bill, seized a club and struck him over the head knocking him down. Bill boasts that he had killed fifteen men and admits the killing of Station Agent Dick Richards at Nowata last summer. He also confessed to killing his brother-in-law at the same place some weeks ago.

Bill was taken to Fort Smith, Arkansas to be tried for the murder of Ernest Melton. On February 26, 1895, he was found guilty. Judge Isaac Parker described him as a "bloodthirsty mad dog who killed for the love of killing" and as "the most vicious" of all the outlaws in the Oklahoma Territory. On April 13, the seemingly unconcerned Crawford Goldsby was sentenced to death.

THE HIDDEN GUN

Bill's attorney J. Warren Reed delayed his hanging by a series of appeals. More than two-hundred prisoners were being held in the federal jail at Fort Smith at the time and hardly a day went by without an escape attempt. On July 10, 1896, the head jailer Captain J.D. Berry, former deputy sheriff of Franklin County, Arkansas, sensed trouble was brewing and ordered a search.

On Death Row, they found a full-loaded .45 revolver hidden in a bucket of lime. Another nine .45 cartridges were found in Cherokee Bill's cell. Sherman Vann, an African-American trustee serving ninety days for larceny, had brought the lime in, but denied knowing anything about the gun or ammunition. Henry Starr, who was in jail in Fort Smith at the time, was questioned.

There were rumors that Cherokee Bill was planning to kill someone in the jail. These even surfaced in the press. What the authorities did not know at the time was that Cherokee Bill had a second gun. This one was hidden behind a loose stone in the wall of his cell.

A RIOT ERUPTS

Inexplicably, Bill was allowed to roam Death Row freely during the day. On the night of July 26, 1896, turnkey Campbell Eoff and guard Lawrence Keating were performing the lockdown when Eoff found that the key stuck in the lock of the cell next to Cherokee Bill's. It had been stuffed with paper.

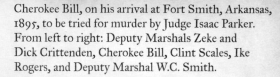

Cherokee Bill, on his arrival at Fort Smith, Arkansas, 1895, to be tried for murder by Judge Isaac Parker. From left to right: Deputy Marshals Zeke and Dick Crittenden, Cherokee Bill, Clint Scales, Ike Rogers, and Deputy Marshal W.C. Smith.

"There's something wrong here," he said.

As Keating approached to help, Cherokee Bill pushed open the door of his cell, shoved the revolver through the bars at Keating, and ordered him to hand over his pistol. Instead, Keating went for his gun. Bill shot and fatally wounded him.

Eoff, who was unarmed, fled. Bill fired twice, but missed because George Pearce, another prisoner in on the plot, emerged from his cell wielding a broken table leg and got in his line of fire.

Three night guards had just come on shift. They opened fire, driving Bill and Pearce back. There was pandemonium. Some of the cell doors were still unlocked and a full-scale riot erupted. As Bill returned fire, Death Row was filled with so much smoke, it was difficult to see.

Deputy Marshal Heck Bruner arrived with a shotgun. The prisoners retreated to their cells. When he loosed a blast, the buckshot ricocheted off the bars.

Fearing a mass breakout, local citizens armed themselves and Marshal Crump arrived to take control of the situation.

HENRY STARR'S DEAL

Bill kept firing at anything that moved and made a strange gobbling sound, halfway between the cry of a turkey cock and the bark of a coyote, made famous by Cherokee outlaw Ned Christie who had been gunned down in 1892.

Henry Starr, an old acquaintance of Bill's, was on Death Row at the same time, awaiting the outcome of his appeal over the murder of Floyd Wilson. He managed to attract the attention of a guard.

"If you will keep the men who are watching the corridor from shooting at me, I'll go to Cherokee Bill's cell and get his gun for you," he said.

Starr was released from his cell and made a deal with Marshal Crump. In his autobiography, Starr explained the deal:

I pledged myself to get Bill's gun if he would give me his word of honor that he [Marshall Crump] would not shoot him [Bill] when disarmed, which he did. I went at once to Bill's cell and told him that he could not possibly get out—that he might be able to kill a few more guards but that would avail nothing, and to take my advice and give his gun to me, which he did, loaded all around. I walked to the end of the corridor and handed the gun to the guards. It was that simple.

Once he was handcuffed, Cherokee Bill's cell was searched and little tobacco sacks filled with .38 cartridges were found. He expressed remorse at having shot Keating, claiming he had only done so in self-defense.

"Damn a man who won't fight for his liberty," he said.

More than a hundred shots had been exchanged during the attempted jailbreak.

A GOOD DAY TO DIE

For disarming Cherokee Bill, Henry Starr's death sentence was canceled. He was allowed to plead guilty to manslaughter and sentenced to fifteen years. The president pardoned him after five.

Cherokee Bill was found guilty of the murder of Officer Keating. Again Reed filed an appeal with the Supreme Court, while Parker was forced to grant another stay of execution. But then the Supreme Court affirmed the decision in the murder of Ernest Melton, and the hanging was set for March 17, 1896. As he stepped into the courtyard at Fort Smith and saw the gallows, Bill said: "This is as good a day to die as any."

Hundreds of spectators arrived for the spectacle. Reportedly, when he was asked if he had any last words, he said: "I came here to die, not to make a speech."

When Crawford "Cherokee Bill" Goldsby died at the end of a rope, he was just twenty years old. His mother then took his remains back to the Fort Gibson area where he is buried at the Cherokee National Cemetery.

HANGING CHEROKEE BILL

A fulsome account of Cherokee Bill's hanging was given in the *Fort Smith Elevator* in 1896:

[Cherokee Bill awakened] this morning at six, singing and whistling. He partook of a light breakfast about eight o'clock, which was sent to him by his mother from the hotel. At 9:20, Cherokee Bill's mother and the old negress who raised him were admitted to his cell, and shortly after Father Pius, his spiritual advisor, was also admitted. The usual noise and hubbub that is always heard within the big iron cage that surrounds the cells was noticeably lacking this morning.

Cherokee Bill's fellow prisoners, many of them under sentence of death, seemed to be impressed with the solemnity of the occasion, and an air of subdued quiet pervaded the jail. Many of the men who were already standing within the shadow of the gallows gathered in a group near the cell occupied by the condemned man and conversed in low tones. To his most intimate associates since his confinement, Cherokee distributed his small effects …

By 10:30, the corridor in front of Cherokee's cell was crowded with newspaper representatives, deputy marshals, and other privileged individuals, all taking note of every passing incident. Occasionally the condemned man would throw aside the curtain which concealed the interior of his cell and make his appearance at the grated door in order to give some instructions or to make some request of the officer who stood guard.

About eleven o'clock, Marshal Crump, after a short conversation with Cherokee, announced that the execution would be postponed until two o'clock, in order to give his sister an opportunity to see him before the death sentence was carried out. She was coming in on the east-bound Valley train, and would not arrive until one o'clock. The 2,000 or 3,000 sight-seers surrounding the big stone wall and within the enclosure dispersed.

It was a struggling mass of humanity that had gathered on and around the steps and walls and when the time came there was a scramble even among those who were provided with passes. There was a crush and a jam for a few minutes but order was at last restored in a measure and all awaited the moment when the door should open for the coming of the condemned man. On the inside there was a repetition of the scenes of the morning. Bill's mother had packed up several belongings of her son and was ready when called upon to take final leave. Her parting was an affectionate one but she strove as much as lay in her power to restrain her emotion.

Bill was affected by it, but following the example of his mother, gave little or no indication that he was other than perfectly composed.

"Well, I am ready to go now most anytime," said he, addressing the guards.

He was taken at his word, and the jail was cleared. The crowd outside had swelled to increased numbers, all the available buildings and sheds being occupied. A pathway was cleared through the crowd, and very shortly after the clock struck two the door opened and the doomed man was brought forth, a guard on either side. The march to the gallows was taken up, and at Col. Crump's suggestion, Cherokee's mother and the old colored Aunty walked alongside Bill. Father Pius came next, the newspaper men following and the crowd bringing up the rear.

"This is about as good a day to die as any," remarked Cherokee as he glanced around. Arriving at the south end of the jail, he looked around at the crowd and said, "It looks like a regiment of soldiers."

He continued to look around at the crowd, eyeing them curiously.

At the door of the enclosure there was a jam. Everybody crowded up and there was a stop for a few moments. It took several minutes for everyone holding tickets to gain admittance, and by this time the condemned man and guards had mounted the scaffold. Bill walked with a firm step and, taking up a position near the west wall of the gallows, waited for the end.

Turning slightly and seeing his mother standing near, he said, "Mother, you ought not to have come here." Her reply was: "I can go wherever you go."

Colonel Crump suggested to him that he take a seat until all was in readiness, but he replied, "No, I don't want to sit down."

The death warrant was then read, during which Bill gazed about as if a little impatient to have the thing over with. He was asked at its conclusion if he had anything to say, and replied, "No Sir, without he (meaning Father Pius) wants to say a prayer."

The priest here offered a short prayer, the condemned man listening attentively the meanwhile, and then as if knowing what was to come next, he walked forward till he stood upon the trap. Deputy George Lawson and others arranged the ropes, binding his arms and legs, and it was while this was being done that Bill spoke to different ones in the crowd below.

"Good-bye, all you chums down that way," said he, with a smile. Just then he caught sight of a young man in the act of taking a snap shot with a Kodak and pulling it sharply back. There was a creaking sound as the trap was sprung and the body shot downward. The fall was scarcely six feet, but the rope had been adjusted carefully by Lawson and the neck was broken. The muscles twisted once or twice, but that was all ... Twelve minutes from the time the trap was sprung, the ropes that bound his limbs were removed, also the handcuffs and shackles, and the body was lowered into a coffin, and borne away and the crowd dispersed. At Birnie's, the coffin was placed in a box and then taken to the Missouri Pacific depot and put aboard the train. His mother and sister took it back with them to Fort Gibson.

Many no doubt felt Cherokee Bill's hanging was well-deserved. He walked to the gallows on March 17, 1896, surrounded by a crowd of 3,000.

CHAPTER 20

HARRY TRACY
THE GREAT ESCAPER

"NO MAN CAN TAKE ME ALONE."

Harry Tracy (1875 – 1902)

During the two months that Harry Tracy was the most wanted man in the West, he robbed more than twenty homes, stores, and saloons, held the lumberjacks of a logging camp hostage, hijacked a large steam launch, and killed some seventeen men.

Despite this mayhem, some who met him characterized him as gentlemanly. He thrilled farmers' wives with exciting tales over tea, generally portraying himself as Robin Hood. Even so, according to the *Seattle Daily Times* of July 3, 1902:

In all the criminal lore of the country there is no record equal to that of Harry Tracy for cold-blooded nerve, desperation and thirst for crime. Jesse James, compared with Tracy, is a Sunday school teacher.

Little is known about the early life of Harry Tracy. It is thought that he was born around 1875 and his real name was Harry Severns. Some sources say that he came from rural Wisconsin and ran away from home at an early age to work in the stockyards in Chicago. Then he migrated to Colorado, where he labored in the goldfields before moving on to Billings, Montana, to learn the cowboy trade. Others say he came from Poughkeepsie, New York, and he earned such a reputation out East that Boston policemen refused to arrest him single-handed. When he moved West, Tracy was imprisoned in Utah for burglary, but escaped with twenty-seven-year-old rustler Dave Lant to find refuge in Brown's Hole, one of the hideouts of the Wild Bunch.

SHOOTING VALENTINE HOY

On March 1, 1898, Tracy was with Lant and Patrick Louis "Swede" Johnson, a blond-haired Missourian. Johnson had killed fifteen-year-old William Strong on the Red Creek Ranch of Valentine S. Hoy when the boy hadn't brought his horse from the corral fast enough. Hoy and a posse were now on their trail for murder as well as rustling.

Harry Tracy.

They caught up with the outlaws on a steep trail leading from Ladore Canyon. As Hoy walked toward their hideout, Tracy warned him to go back.

"We don't want you, Tracy," shouted Hoy. "It's Johnson we want. This is not your fight."

"Come any closer, Hoy, and I will kill you," threatened Tracy.

Hoy kept on walking and Tracy killed him with a single shot through the heart.

Taking their revenge, the posse lynched Jack Bennett, a friend of Tracy's who was bringing supplies. Other lawmen from Utah, Colorado, and Wyoming closed in. It was cold that spring and their pursuers found where the outlaws were hiding out, killed their horses for food and cooked their meat over a campfire.

One freezing morning, Sheriff William Preece of Vernal, Utah, caught up with them. As another posse moved in, Lant and Johnson surrendered. Tracy refused, cursing the other two. Eventually, it got so cold that he could no longer hold a rifle and he too was forced to crawl out and surrender.

TAKEN INTO CUSTODY

While Johnson was to be taken back to Wyoming for the killing of William Strong, Lant and Tracy were taken by Colorado Sheriff Charles Neimann to Hahn's Peak, Colorado for the Hoy killing. They took a little-known trail, fearing that the Wild Bunch were intending to free the pair. As it was, Lant and Tracy knocked out Neimann and escaped.

Neimann trailed Tracy and Lant to Steamboat Springs. Then he took the stage, figuring the two fugitives were spoilt for transport. When they hailed the stage six miles out of Steamboat, they found themselves covered by Neimann.

Taking him to jail in Aspen, Neimann said: "Welcome home, Tracy. Your breakfast is waiting."

Within a few months, Tracy had carved soap into the shape of a gun, wrapped in tin foil, and escaped.

FALSE FACE BANDITS

Tracy moved on to Portland, Oregon, where he impressed the dancehall girls with his sharp suits and good manners. In 1899, he met small-time gambler Dave Merrill and married his sister Rose. Soon after Tracy and his brother-in-law went on a spree of daring, daylight hold-ups of stores and banks, using full-face masks. They became known as the "False Face Bandits."

Merrill started bragging in saloons. Picked up by a Portland detective, he was promised easy treatment if he told the authorities where Tracy was. The police descended on Tracy's small white cottage near the Willamette River.

Seeing them coming, Tracy jumped out a rear window and made off through the trees, dodging a volley of fire. He reached the railroad where the train had to slow for a curve. He leapt on board, then forced the engineer to jump off. But as he opened the throttle, the conductor pulled the emergency brake. A bullet creased Tracy's scalp, knocking him unconscious, and he was arrested.

JAIL BREAK

Tracy was sentenced to twenty years in Oregon State Penitentiary, Salem; Merrill to thirteen. In May 1902, Tracy promised Harry Wright, who was soon to be released, $5,000 if he would get them guns.

Good to his word, when Wright got out, he stole a horse and buggy, sold them, and used the money to buy two shotguns and a rope ladder. They were flung over the wall of the penitentiary wrapped in tarpaulin.

On June 9, 1902, after roll call, Tracy leapt to where the shotguns were hidden and blasted prison guard Frank B. Ferrell in the throat, killing him. He then aimed at Officer Frank Girard. Lifer Frank Ingram knocked the shotgun away from its target. He was shot for his trouble.

While Merrill hooked the rope ladder over the wall, Tracy kept firing, killing another prison guard and wounding two more. Using the injured men as human shields, they made good their escape. Tracy then shot them, killing one while the other played dead.

MASSIVE MANHUNT

What followed was said to be the greatest manhunt in American criminal history. Over the next ten days or so, as Tracy and Merrill zigzagged their way north past Portland, they were followed by over 250 law officers and militiamen, and a contingent of bloodhounds from the Washington State Penitentiary at Walla Walla.

Hiding out in the brush all day, they made their way through Salem that night. On the outskirts, they held up a farmer, taking civilian clothing and horses. When they were tired, Tracy hijacked a buggy, telling the occupants politely: "We need it more than you do."

They tried to head north into Washington, but the roads and railroads were now guarded by heavily armed men. They were hiding out in the woods near Gervais when Company F of the Oregon National Guard were ordered in by the governor. That night, Tracy and Merrill crawled through their lines.

The following morning, they reached a farmhouse. Tracy introduced himself, assuring the farmer's wife, who made their breakfast, that ladies were always safe with him.

The governor offered a reward of $7,000 and, after the hunt had gone on for five days, the *New York World* reported that the order had been given to shoot to kill.

KEEP ON RUNNING

On June 14, 1902, they forced boat owner Charles Holtgrieve to row them over the Columbia River. On the other side, they stole money and a horse from a farmer named Peedy, promising when they had finished with the horse they would leave it with a note pinned to its saddle. The horse was returned the next day with a $5 bill.

Cornered by a posse near Vancouver, Washington, they blasted their way through the police lines. While a farmer's wife cooked them a meal north of Castle Rock on the Cowlitz River, Tracy was thrilled to see his picture in the paper. But the story told how Merrill had traded him for a lighter sentence.

Nothing was heard of the fugitives, until Tracy appeared alone at the headquarters of the Capital City Oyster Company on South Bay at 5:00 a.m. on July 2. As usual, he announced who he was and got them to make him something to eat.

Over breakfast, Tracy told the crew that he had killed Merrill. It seems they had a quarrel and, to resolve the matter, they decided to have a duel. But before Merrill had a chance to turn and fire, Tracy shot him in the back.

Afterward, he boarded the big gasoline launch owned by the company and, while training his .30-30 rifle on his son, ordered Captain A.J. Clark to take the launch around Puget Sound. He also told one of the crew to get him some clothes so he could disguise himself. Tracy also needed some shoes. The ones he had on had been taken from a cripple, with one sole several inches thicker than the other.

HARRY TRACY'S WINCHESTER

Setting off at 9:00 a.m., Tracy wanted to take a boat trip across Puget Sound to Seattle. Passing McNeil Island where there was a federal penitentiary, he asked to sail close to shore so he could shoot at any prison guards he saw. The crew dissuaded him. He also threatened to kill the captain of a tug that came close. Most of the time he kept his gun trained on the captain and crew, but the only time he fired was at a seal. While Tracy was taking aim the captain thought of seizing the opportunity to push him overboard, but Tracy was too quick for him.

When they reached Seattle at between five and six o'clock, he tied up the captain and crew, binding the captain's son by the elbows as his wrists were sore. Tracy said as he climbed over the side:

I'll send you a lot of money to make up for kidnapping you and the launch, for I'll have a lot of dough pretty soon now. And I won't forget you other fellows. You have acted pretty decent by me.

THE DUEL WITH DAVE MERRILL

Newspaper reporter W.N. Carter got the story on the duel between Harry Tracy and Dave Merrill from the crew of the launch on Puget Sound as told to them by Tracy himself:

"I shot him in the back because he intended to shoot me," Tracy said. "The day before the quarrel we found a newspaper which contained an account of our escape and the pursuit. That account gave Merrill equal credit with myself for the deeds which I alone committed, as the papers have done right along. The fact of the case is that he did not have the nerve of a rabbit. He always wanted to sneak through the country, keeping under cover, and preferred to go hungry rather than show himself for the purpose of getting food.

"That is not my style. No man can take me alone. And if I had a proper traveling companion, a man of nerve, I couldn't be taken by a regiment of deputies. If I am shot it will be from behind. And with another man to guard the opposite direction, a man of some nerve, who knew how to handle a gun, we could go wherever we wanted to and not be compelled to keep under cover a portion of the time as I am in traveling alone.

"But Merrill was n.g. He was never anything but an impediment to me, and I am glad he is out of the way. I never could trust him on guard except in places where there was no danger, anyway, and then he was so frightened that at times he would wake me up needlessly in the fear that we were being surrounded.

"So when I got the paper and saw that the reporters and the people thought he had some nerve, it made me hot. I thought at first I would shake him and travel alone, but before we decided to separate, I taunted him with his cowardice and he got huffy. Then we agreed to fight a duel. This was in the woods in Lewis County, not far from Chehalis.

"We agreed to start together from a line and walk ten steps each, in opposite directions, and then turn simultaneously and begin to fire. From his haggling in arranging the terms, I was convinced that he intended to turn before he had taken the ten steps, and I was determined not to let him get the drop on me. So when I had taken eight steps, I turned around and took a shot at him. I hit him in the back. The first shot did not finish him and I shot again. I then concealed the body in the brush and proceeded on my way.

"Merrill got what he deserved. He fell into the pit which he had dug for me. He intended to turn and shoot me in the back; then he would have sneaked out of the country through the big timber and would not have been heard of for months. I would not only have been dead, but would never have been found, because he would have been afraid to tell where my body was."

Dave Merrill, mug shot from Oregon State Penitentiary.

Captain Clark said that Tracy had been carrying his infamous .30-30 rifle with around two-hundred rounds of ammunition, but complained that he did not have a six-shooter.

"But I will soon fix that," Tracy said to a crewman. "I'm going to search for a policeman first, and get his gun before I do any real business here."

BATTLE OF BOTHELL

After the crew of the launch got free, they informed the authorities and a posse was formed. About 5:30 the following morning Tracy was seen on a railroad track, walking in the direction of Bothell, a suburb of Seattle.

Soon after 3:00 p.m. that afternoon, the posse were closing in on a cabin near the railroad track where they thought Tracy had sought refuge. Suddenly Tracy appeared behind a tree stump. A shot from his .30-30 Winchester grazed the face of newspaperman Karl Anderson. He tumbled into a ditch. The cold water revived him. He was just getting up when Tracy fired again, twice, hitting Deputy Sheriff Raymond, who fell dead on top of Anderson.

Newspaperman Louie B. Sefrit returned fire. Tracy hit him, wounding him, though not seriously. Anderson had escaped from the ditch and, in a flanking movement through the brush, linked up with Deputies L.J. Nelson and Brewer. They heard three shots fired in rapid succession. Then they saw Deputy Sheriff Jack Williams crawl out of the undergrowth near the cabin. He was bleeding profusely.

He had been shot three times under the heart. Quickly he lost consciousness and died. Like Raymond, he still had his gun in his hand. Tracy disappeared, leaving the rest of the posse to deal with the dead and the wounded.

AT MRS. VAN HORN'S HOUSE

About half a mile outside of Bothell, Tracy commandeered a horse and buggy, posing as a deputy. He also took farmer Louis Anderson hostage, who later said he was "treated with a great deal of courtesy." Together they dodged the numerous posses and the companies of national guardsmen who were scouring the forests.

King County Sheriff Edward Cudihee plotted Tracy's progress using reports from people who had been forced to feed the pair along the way. This led Cudihee and his posse to the house of Mrs. R.H. Van Horn in Woodland Park on the outskirts of Seattle.

Tracy said that he had picked her house "because of its cozy appearance." Mrs. Van Horn said that, during his stay, Tracy spoke "almost incessantly, giving the impression of a man possessed of some education, considerable intelligence and a great deal of courtesy."

As Tracy was eating, the posse surrounded the house, but made no move to close in until late that night when Tracy came out for a stroll with Anderson and a member of the Van Horn family. A deputy approached them.

"Have you seen Tracy?" he asked.

"No," came the reply.

Then the deputy caught a glint of moonlight reflecting off Tracy's Winchester.

"Drop that, Tracy!" he yelled as another deputy joined him.

Tracy fired twice, killing both of them. More bullets pushed back Sheriff Cudihee and other members of the posse who tried to cut him off, as Tracy, pushing Anderson in front of him, made his escape.

THE UNINVITED GUESTS

That night they slept in a graveyard. The following evening, they watched the Fourth of July fireworks from the outskirts of Seattle. Next morning they appeared at the ranch of August Fisher, where Tracy demanded breakfast and a change of clothing. He refused to take Mr. Fisher's Sunday suit, but did take his son's work shoes, apologizing to the boy for the theft.

These cursed man-hunters are after me all the time. And I have to throw them off the track. I'm not afraid of the men—I can stand them off all right—but I don't like the dogs a little bit.

When he left, he did not tie them up because they had a baby and someone had to look after it. But he made them promise that they would tell no one of his presence for forty-eight hours. They complied, fearing that Tracy was hiding nearby.

After holding up another household belonging to the Johnsons, Tracy and Anderson doubled back to Seattle by way of Port Madison. He skirted the city until he came to South Seattle, and then cut around the end of Lake Washington to Renton. At this point he made himself the uninvited guest of the Jerrolds family.

A MOTHER OF MY OWN

Walking up from Renton, they met Miss May Baker, Mrs. McKinney, and young Charles Jerrolds picking salmonberries. Tracy stopped to talk.

"I guess you have heard of me; I am Tracy," he said, smiling. Then added, "You needn't be afraid of me. I never harmed a woman in my life, and I don't intend to begin now."

Tracy tied Anderson to a clump of bushes behind their house. He handed Charles Jerrolds two watches, which he told him to sell in order to buy two .45-caliber single-action Colt revolvers and a box of cartridges. He threatened to kill everybody in the house if the boy betrayed him. No sooner had the boy gone than Tracy told Mrs. Jerrolds that this was mere bluff. He even shed a tear at this point, saying:

E.M. Johnson of Kent, his wife, and their son and daughter, victims in one of the most spectacular chapters in the career of Harry Tracy, outlaw killer, 1902.

I wouldn't hurt you, Mother, for anything. I have a mother of my own somewhere back East. I haven't done just right by her, but I reckon all the mothers are safe from me, no matter what happens.

Then he laughed and talked with the three women just as if they had been old acquaintances. At dinner time, he brought in the wood and volunteered to get the water from the spring by the railroad track. As he did so a special train, carrying the posse that was hunting him, came round the bend. Rifle in hand, he ducked into the bushes as it passed. When Tracy returned to the house he laughed about it:

I reckon there are some gentlemen in that train looking for me. I saw a reporter there. They are always in the lead. First you see a reporter, then a cloud of dust, and after a while the deputies. It's the interviewer I'm afraid of!

BACK DOOR DEPARTURE

Over dinner, he enthralled them with tales of his exploits. Despite what he had been told to do, Charles Jerrolds had gone straight to the sheriff's office and deputies began to surround the house. Everybody was alarmed except Tracy himself, who kept his eye out for a photographer.

"My trousers are too short and they're not nicely ironed," he said. "I like to be neatly dressed before ladies. I guess I'll go out and hold up a deputy for a pair."

Miss Baker, who had been visiting the Jerrolds, was worried that she might not get home before dark. Tracy said it was a pleasant moonlit night, and that he would be glad to accompany her if he might have the pleasure.

More deputies appeared. One knocked at the door and asked: "Is Tracy in here?" Mrs. Jerrolds said no. But Tracy decided it was time to go. He asked whether the women would like to form a protective cordon around him.

"Oh sure," smirked Miss Baker. "We would like to get killed for you—I don't think."

From the back door, Tracy waved them all a merry goodbye. As luck would have it,

Anderson had been found tied to a tree. One of the deputies gave a shout, the others crowded round and some more came running and, in the confusion, Tracy quietly slipped away.

He told more tales of his daring escapes to the men of a logging camp that he virtually took over. Although they could easily have overpowered him as he ate, he kept his audience spellbound.

CALLING OUT THE LAW

Tracy played hide-and-seek with the officers of King County for weeks, then suddenly broke away for the Cascades on horseback. Weeks later, he was spotted in eastern Washington near the "Hole-in-the-Wall" country. By then, though, the old Wild Bunch gang had been disbanded. Tracy was the last outlaw.

At one point he made a telephone call to a sheriff from a country store he was holding up for food, saying:

I just wanted you to know I was still around. You've done better than the other sheriffs. You've talked with the man you want, anyway. Good-bye; I'm afraid you won't see me again.

Eastern Washington was well-provided with telephones, and regular calls were made to local lawmen reporting his whereabouts. But it was harder to disappear in the eastern part of the state than it was in the big forests of the west. Lawmen including the redoubtable Sheriff Cudihee held the passes and trails and gradually closed in on Harry Tracy.

Repeated sightings were reported. When he stopped a hunter to ask for food, as always, Tracy introduced himself by name. At one point, a posse shot and wounded him, but he disappeared into a swamp, throwing off the bloodhounds. Later he told a woman who he met walking down a road that the pellets in his back hurt a great deal.

A settler's wife near Ellsworth who prepared Tracy a meal was told: "I respect all womanhood." Later he appeared with two horses and Indian trackers talked of preparing a silver bullet for the man who could not be killed.

NOWHERE TO HIDE

Ten miles south of Creston, Tracy met young rancher George Goldfinch and ordered him to take him to a nearby ranch which belonged to the Eddy brothers. Lou Eddy told of the incident:

> *He wanted me to trade horses with him, and asked me what kind of animals I had. When I told him a three-year-old colt and a fourteen-year-old mare, he didn't care to trade, but decided to wait at the ranch until his own horses were rested.*

For two days and nights the outlaw hung around, showing the Eddys the tricks of the trade. His shirt front was cut off at the top of the waistband of his trousers and he kept his revolver concealed there. Pacing out sixty yards, he hit a knot in a pine board no bigger than a nickel, dead center.

He slept in the haystack rather than the house, figuring that it was safer, though he kept one of the Eddy brothers with him. He took a bath and a shave, but his rifle was always near at hand and he did not take his shirt off while washing, fearing being taken unawares.

George Goldfinch was released, but Tracy warned him he would kill the Eddy brothers if he went to the authorities. However, in Creston, Goldfinch wired Sheriff Gardner of Davenport. While he was dictating the message, Goldfinch was overheard by Section Boss J.J. Morrison. He quickly put together a posse comprising Constable C.A. Straub, Dr. E.C. Lanter, attorney Maurice Smith, and Frank Lillengren. Armed to the teeth, on August 5, they set out for the Eddy ranch, arriving there around four in the afternoon.

Some way from the ranch, they saw one of the Eddy brothers mowing hay. While they were talking a strange man emerged from the barn.

"Is that Tracy?" Eddy was asked.

"It surely is," he replied.

Tracy came out to help his host unhitch a team. He had left his rifle in the barn, but was carrying his revolvers. As the posse approached, he turned to the other brother and said: "Who are those men?"

BROWN'S HOLE

Now known as Brown's Park, Brown's Hole is an isolated mountain valley along the Green River in Moffat County, Colorado and Daggett County, Utah. Before the arrival of European-Americans, it was occupied by various Native American tribes.

During the California Gold Rush, it became wintering ground for cattle. It then became a hideout for rustlers and outlaws. Alongside the Hole-in-the-Wall in Wyoming and Robbers Roost in south-east Utah, it became home to Butch Cassidy and his Wild Bunch gang in the closing years of the Old West.

"Hold up your hands!" shouted the officers.

Using the other Eddy brother as a shield, Tracy backed into the barn, grabbed his rifle, and came out firing.

The posse took cover and returned fire. Tracy hid behind a rock, but found he was shooting into the setting sun. As it grew dark, he made a dash for a wheat field. The officers shot at him as he ran. A bullet hit him in the leg and he fell, but he dragged himself seventy-five yards in the direction of a shed where he kept a horse saddled, ready for an emergency.

As he made his way through the field, it was easy to follow his progress in the moving grain and he was hit again.

Before Sheriff Gardner arrived, a single shot was heard. Tracy had apparently shot himself. The posse kept on firing, not knowing their quarry was dead.

Eventually, members of the posse plucked up the courage to approach the corpse. It was taken to Davenport, where his clothes, hair, and armory were divided as keepsakes. The body was then sealed in a zinc-lined coffin. It was returned to Oregon State Penitentiary in Salem. Along the way, relic hunters chipped off splinters from the pine box.

At Salem, the coffin was opened and acid was poured on the face to discourage body snatchers who might be tempted to steal the body for exhibition. He was buried in an unmarked grave with no priest, no hymns, no prayers. Each member of the posse that had caught him was awarded $1,500.

WINCHESTER

The Winchester repeating rifle was a development of the Henry rifle used in the Civil War, produced by B. Tyler Henry at the Volcanic Arms Company, set up by Smith & Wesson in 1855, and its successor the New Haven Arms Company. An estimated ten thousand of these sixteen-shot rifles were made. The .44 ammunition was loaded into a tube running along the bottom of the barrel, giving them a phenomenal rate of fire. Confederates complained: "Damn Yankee rifle—they load it on Sunday and fire it all week."

After the Civil War, Oliver Winchester redesigned the weapon and the first Winchester rifle was produced in 1866, by what had then become the Winchester Repeating Arms Company. The Model 1866's brass frame earned it the nickname "yellow boy." It retained the .44 Henry rim-fire ammunition. The rifle version had a magazine capacity of seventeen shots and a twenty-four-inch barrel. The carbine held thirteen cartridges and had a twenty-inch barrel.

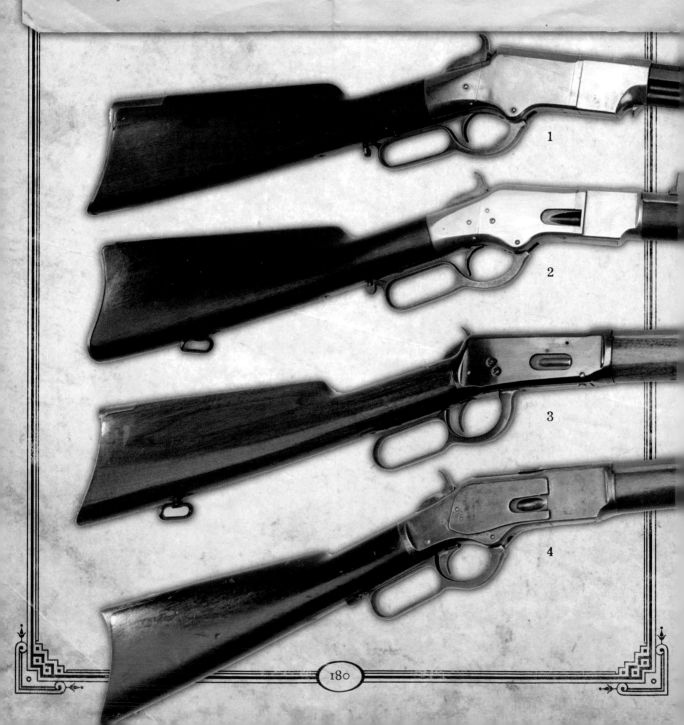

When center-fired ammunition took over, Winchester produced the Model 1873 which became known as "The Gun that Won the West" and was still in production in 1919. It was chambered for a .44-40-200 ammunition—that is, .44 caliber with 40 grains of powder and a bullet weighing 200 grains. As the case was longer, the magazine capacity for the rifle was reduced to fifteen and for the carbine to twelve.

This ammunition became so popular that Colt rechambered some of the single-action army revolvers to take it, calling the result "The Frontier Six-Shooter."

The original Winchester did not take the .45 Colt cartridge favored by the military. The .44-40 cartridge only produced a muzzle velocity of 1,300 feet per second and was not found to be up to the standard required for military use. However, as most shoot-outs occurred at distances of considerably less than four-hundred yards, this did not matter to gunmen.

A .45 version was produced in 1876—the Centennial Model—largely for hunting.

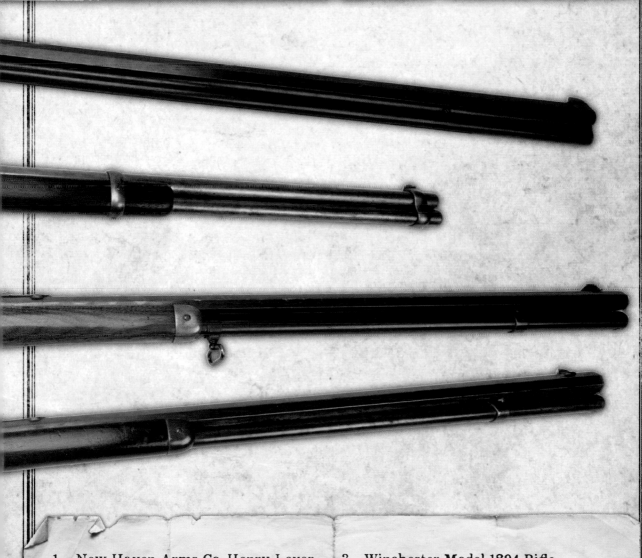

1. New Haven Arms Co. Henry Lever Action Rifle, 1855.
2. Winchester Model 1866 Third Model Lever Action Carbine.
3. Winchester Model 1894 Rifle.
4. Winchester Model 1873 Lever Action Rifle.

the story of a man who was too proud to run!

STANLEY KRAMER PRODUCTIONS presents

GARY COOPER in "HIGH NOON"

...NS presents GARY COOPER in "HIGH NOON"
...DGES · KATY JURADO · GRACE KELLY · OTTO KRUGER
...FRED ZINNEMANN · Screen Play by Carl Foreman · Music Composed
...tography Floyd Crosby, A.S.C. · RELEASED THRU UNITED ARTISTS

HIGH NOON AND THE U.S. PRESIDENTS

The 1952 western *High Noon* starring Gary Cooper, is said to be the film most requested for viewing by U.S. presidents. It has been cited as the favorite film of Presidents Dwight D. Eisenhower, Ronald Reagan, and Dill Clinton.

ALAN LADD · JEAN ARTHUR · VAN HEFLIN

GEORGE STEVENS' PRODUCTION OF

SHANE

Color by Technicolor

Co-starring
BRANDON DE WILDE
with JACK PALANCE
BEN JOHNSON
EDGAR BUCHANAN
Produced and Directed by
GEORGE STEVENS
Screenplay by
A. B. GUTHRIE, Jr.
Additional Dialogue by

SHANE AND THE SOUND OF GUNFIRE

Shane, the 1953 western starring Alan Ladd, was one of the first films to attempt to recreate the overwhelming sound of gunfire. It was also one of the first movies in which the actors were jerked backwards by hidden wires when they were shot from the front.

IF LOOKS COULD KILL

James B. Hawkins, a charter member of
Company D of the Texas Rangers, armed to
the teeth and ready for a fight.

FURTHER READING

This chronicle of the life and times of the gunfighters of the American West is designed to be an informative and entertaining introductory text. There are other more academic publications available should the reader wish to delve more deeply. Publications that were especially useful during the preparation of this book are listed below and contemporary newspaper articles are cited at the point where they appear within the text.

Adams, Ramon F. (1969) *Six Guns and Saddle-leather*. Norman, Oklahoma: University of Oklahoma.

Askins, Colonel Charles (2007) *The Gunfighters: True Tales of Outlaws, Lawmen, and Indians on the Texas Frontier*. Boulder, Colorado: Paladin Press.

Bartholomew, Ed Ellsworth (1958) *Western Gunfighters*. Houston: Frontier Press of Texas.

Boessenecker, John (1999) *Gold Dust and Gunsmoke: Tales of Gold Rush Outlaws, Gunfighters, Lawmen, and Vigilantes*. New York: John Wiley & Sons Inc.

Breihan, Carl William (1964) *Great Gunfighters of the West*. New York: Arrow Books.

Burrows, Jack (1987) *The Gunfighter Who Never Was*. Tucson, Arizona: The University of Arizona Press.

Burton, Arthur T. (1991) *Black, Red, and Deadly*. Austin, Texas: Eakin Press.

Cunningham, Eugene (1967) *Triggernometry: A Gallery of Gunfighters*. London: New English Library.

Cunningham, Eugene (1978) *Triggernometry: A Gallery of Gunfighters, Volume Two*. London: New English Library.

Custer, George Armstrong (1895) *My Life on the Plains*. New York: Sheldon & Co.

DeArment, Robert K. (2003) *Twelve Forgotten Gunfighters of the Old West*. Norman, Oklahoma: University of Oklahoma Press.

Garrett, Patrick Floyd, (Upson, Marshall Ashmun) (1957) *The Authentic Life of Billy, the Kid*. Norman, Oklahoma: University of Oklahoma Press.

Hardin, John Wesley (1961) *The Life of John Wesley Hardin*. Norman, Oklahoma: University of Oklahoma Press.

Horan, James D. (1976) *The Gunfighters*. New York: Crown Publishers Inc.

Horn, Tom, *Life of Tom Horn, Government Scout and Interpreter*. Norman, Oklahoma: University of Oklahoma.

Masterson, W.B. (Bat) (2009) *Famous Gunfighters of the Western Frontier*. Mineola, New York: Dover Publications Inc.

May, Robin (1984) *Gunfighters*. Greenwich, Connecticut: Bison Books.

McGrath, Roger D.(1984) *Gunfighters, Highwaymen, and Vigilantes*. Berkeley: University of California Press.

Metz, Leon Claire (2003) *The Encyclopedia of Lawmen, Outlaws, and Gunfighters*. New York: Facts on File.

Metz, Leon Claire (1976) *The Shooters*. El Paso, Texas: Mangan Books.

Miller, Nyle H., & Snell, Joseph W. (1967) *Great Gunfighters of the Kansas Cowtowns, 1867–1886*. Lincoln, Nebraska: University of Nebraska Press.

O'Neal, Bill (1979) *Encyclopedia of Western Gunfighters*. Norman: University of Oklahoma Press.

Parsons, Chuck & Brown, Norman Wayne (2013) *A Lawless Breed: John Wesley Hardin, Texas Reconstruction, and Violence in the Wild West*. Denton, Texas: University of North Texas Press.

Rosa, Joseph G. (1993) *Age of the Gunfighter*. London: Salamander Books.

Schoenberger, Dale T. (1971) *Gunfighters*. Caldwell, Idaho: Caxton Printers Ltd.

Sims, Judge Orland L.(1967) *Gun-toters I Have Known*. Austin, Texas: Encino Press.

Siringo, Charlie (1976) *A Texas Cowboy, Or Fifteen Years on the Hurricane Deck of a Spanish Pony: Taken from Real Life*. Lincoln, Nebraska: University of Nebraska Press.

Starr, Henry (1914) *Thrilling Events: Life of Henry Starr. Famous Cherokee Indian outlaw narrates his many adventures from boyhood to date*. Tulsa, Oklahoma: R.D. Gordon.

Trachtman, Paul (1974) *Gunfighters*. New York: Time-Life.

Walton, William M. (1884) *Life and Adventures of Ben Thompson, the Famous Texan*. Austin, Texas: Published by the author.

Younger, Cole (1903) *The Story of Cole Younger by Himself*. Chicago: The Henneberry Company.

He came a thousand miles — to k

JAMES STE

THE MAN Fro

DNALD CRISP · CATHY O'DONNELL · AE

THE MAN FROM LARAMIE

Starring James Stewart, *The Man from Laramie* (1955) was one of the first westerns to be filmed in CinemaScope to capture the vastness of the scenery.

INDEX

Page numbers in italic denote an illustration

"ARE YOU SATISFIED?"

The Hickok-Tutt shoot-out, Springfield, Missouri, 1865.

© 2016 Oxford Publishing Ventures Ltd

This edition published in 2016 by Chartwell Books,
an imprint of The Quarto Group,
142 West 36th Street, 4th Floor,
New York, NY 10018, USA
T (212) 779-4972 **F** (212) 779-6058 **www.QuartoKnows.com**

ISBN-13: 978-0-7858-3376-5

10 9 8 7 6 5 4 3

Printed in China

PICTURE CREDITS

Copyright holders, original photographers or image provenance are listed below. A work is in the public domain (PD) in its country of origin and other countries and areas where the copyright term is the author's life plus 70 years or less.

Cover: Front (main) J.B. "Wild Bill" Hickok/Gurney 1873; (background) Hickok gunfight with Davis Tutt/*Harper's New Monthly* 1867 / Colt Navy revolver/PD. Spine J.B. Hickok/PD. Back: Colt Army revolver/NRA Museums, NRAmuseums.com / Texas Rangers / © The Print Collector / Alamy Stock Photo.

Internal: 1 Interfoto/Alamy / 2 Granger, NYC/Alamy / 4 Gurney, New York 1873 / 6 *Hearst's Magazine* 1916 / 7 cartermuseum.org / 8 cartermuseum.org / 9 PD, Austin 1881 / 11 Andrew Burgess @ Matthew Brady, Mexico City 1864 / 12 Secretary of State, Topeka 1873 / 15 PD / 17 UTSA Libraries / 18 Philadelphia School of Dental Surgery 1872 / 20 lasvegasnmcchp.com / 21 PD 1879 / 22 Tombstone-1993-movie-free-download / 23 PD / 24 (top) tumblr.com; (bottom) legendsofamerica.com / 26 PD 1880 / 28 Conkling Studio, Dodge City 1883 / 30 PD, Dodge City 1880 / 33 PD / 34 PD, Abilene 1871 / 36 legendsofamerica. com / 38 PD / 41 PD / 42 El Paso mortuary 1895 / 43 (top) John Chester Buttre 1855; (bottom) Colts Patent Fire-Arms catalogue / 44/45 NRA Museums, NRAmuseums.com / 46 *The Long Riders* (1980) Pictorial Press Ltd / Alamy / 49 PD / 50 Matthew Brady 1866 / 53 Denver Art Museum / 55 loc.gov / 56 U.S. Army Corps of Engineers / 57 Missouri Valley Special Collections / 58 Robert B. Kice, Richmond, Missouri 1864 / 61 © Granger, NYC/Alamy / 62 Sumner Studios, Northfield 1876 / 64 (top) loc.gov; (bottom) Guerin, St. Louis 1898 / 65 legendsofamerica.com / 66 PD Fort Sumner, Texas 1880 / 68 © Andy Thomas, courtesy Studio of Andy Thomas / 70 PD/facial matching courtesy Lois Gibson / 71 PD Anton Chico, New Mexico 1880 / 72 PD engraving after Sarony, New York / 75 PD Las Vegas 1881 / 76 lastoftheplainsmen.freeforums.org / 77 Ben Wittick 1887 / 79 uwyo.edu / 81 wabilene.forumgratuit.org / 82/83 NRA Museums, NRAmuseums.com / 84 *High Noon* (1953) Zuma Press Inc/Alamy / 87 PD 1869 / 88 nebraskahistory.org / 89 *Harper's New Monthly* 1867 / 90 loc. gov 1865 / 94 Pan American Exposition, Buffalo, New York 1901 / 95 (top) © sharpstock / Alamy / 95 (bottom) CT State Library Archives / 97 PD Lamar, Missouri 1869 / 98 C.S. Fly 1881 / 99 (both) A.B. Mignon, Fort Worth 1876 / 100 C. S. Fly 1881/ 102 kshs.org/kansapedia / 104 PD 1879 / 105 © Joe Grandee, courtesy Joe Grandee Gallery / 106 Jack DeMaattos / 107 kshs.org/kansapedia / 108 Bisbee Mining and Historical Museum / 110 William Henry Jackson 1898 / 112 NARA / 113 PD / 114 usmarshalsmuseum.org / 115 kshs.org/kansapedia / 117 PD / 118 Cramers Art Rooms, Cherryvale 1892 / 120/121 NRA Museums, NRAmuseums.com / 122 *The Magnificent Seven* (1960) Pictorial Press Ltd / Alamy / 125 williamson-county-historical-commission.org / 128 © The Print Collector / Alamy Stock Photo / 130 © 616 Collection/Alamy / 131 kued.org / 132 loc.gov / 133 DeYoung, New York / 135 © AF archive/Alamy / 136 Schwartz, Fort Worth 1900 / 138 Pinkerton's National Detective Agency / 140 callofjuarez.wikia.com / 141 PD Clayton, New Mexico 1901 / 142 PD 1900 / 144 PD 1880 / 143 PD / 147 legendsofamerica.com / 148/149 NRA Museums, NRAmuseums.com / 150 rangers-on-the-bridge/University of Texas-San Antonio / 152 findagrave.com / 155 PD / 158 legendsofamerica.com / 159 odmp.org / 162 Roeder Bros 1886 / 164 Pan American / 167 nps.gov/fortsmithnhs / 168 E.D. Macfee, Wagoner, Indian Territory 1895 / 171 Fort Smith National Historic Site / 172 Museum of Northwest Colorado / 175 historylink.org / 177 Asahel Curtis, Seattle PI, 1902 / 180/181 NRA Museums, NRAmuseums.com / 182 cineclassico/Alamy / 183 SilverScreen/Alamy / 184 lastoftheplainsmen.freeforums.org / 186 Pictorial Press Ltd/Alamy / 191 Harper's New Monthly 1867.